WITHDRAWN

Routledge Author Guides
Tolstoy

# Routledge Author Guides

GENERAL EDITOR: B. C. SOUTHAM, MA B.LITT. (OXON)
*Formerly Department of English, Westfield College, University of London*

*Titles in the series*

Routledge Author Guides

# Tolstoy

*by*

## Ernest J. Simmons

*Sometime Professor of Russian Literature, Columbia University*

Routledge & Kegan Paul
London and Boston

*First published 1973*
*by Routledge & Kegan Paul Ltd,*
*Broadway House, 68–74 Carter Lane,*
*London EC4V 5EL and*
*9 Park Street,*
*Boston, Mass. 02108, U.S.A.*
*Printed in Great Britain by*
*Cox and Wyman Ltd,*
*London, Fakenham and Reading*

*ISBN 0 7100 7394 1 (c)*
*ISBN 0 7100 7395 X (p)*

*To Christopher and Robin*

# General Editor's Preface

Nowadays there is a growing awareness that the specialist areas have much to offer and much to learn from one another. The student of history, for example, is becoming increasingly aware of the value that literature can have in the understanding of the past; equally, the student of literature is turning more and more to the historians for illumination of his area of special interest, and of course philosophy, political science, sociology, and other disciplines have much to give him.

What we are trying to do in the *Routledge Author Guides* is to offer this illumination and communication by providing for non-specialist readers, whether students or the interested general public, a clear and systematic account of the life and times and works of the major writers and thinkers across a wide range of disciplines. Where the *Author Guides* may be seen to differ from other, apparently similar, series, is in its historical emphasis, which will be particularly evident in the treatment of the great literary writers, where we are trying to establish, in so far as this can be done, the social and historical context of the writer's life and times, and the cultural and intellectual tradition in which he stands, always remembering that critical and interpretative principles are implicit to any sound historical approach.

BCS

Sadly, Ernest Simmons died before the proofs of his book were passed for press and Marjorie Nicolson (William Peterfield Trent Professor Emeritus, Columbia University) was generous enough to read the page proofs on behalf of Ernest Simmons her close colleague and friend.

# Contents

# Preface

There has never been any doubt about Tolstoy's literary reputation as one of the world's greatest novelists. But in his own time and for some years after his death in 1910, he was also regarded as a major thinker and religious, social, and political reformer by multitudes of people in many countries. This reputation has almost vanished today, although most of the evils he struggled against in his didactic works are more dominant and of more anxious concern now than they were in the nineteenth century. There was a close connection between Tolstoy the literary artist and Tolstoy the thinker, and both appear to be a natural development of the kind of life he led. To demonstrate this fact in an effort to provide a total image of the man is the purpose of this book.

Whenever possible, Tolstoy is allowed to speak for himself on a variety of matters that deeply concerned him. For many of these quotations, and some biographical data, I have drawn upon my previous writings on Tolstoy. My own translations, as well as those by others, the sources of which are mentioned in the notes, I have rechecked against the Russian originals, and in some few cases I have made slight alterations in the renderings.

# Introduction

I

Count Leo Tolstoy was born three years after the Decembrist Revolt of 1825, an event that marked the beginning of the reign of Nicholas I, and he died seven years before the Soviet Revolution of 1917 which terminated the rule of Nicholas II.* In short, Tolstoy's long lifetime of eighty-two years spanned most of the reigns of four emperors (the other two are Alexander II and Alexander III), a momentous period during which Russia moved from feudalism to nascent capitalism, from a relatively isolated nation to a European world power, from a rigid autocracy to a feeble form of parliamentary government, and from an essentially imitative culture to a highly original one. The story of his life and literary and intellectual contributions are closely related to the historical, political, social, and cultural developments of these years.

Nicholas I ruthlessly crushed the Decembrist Revolt, executing its leaders and sending scores of its highborn conspirators to prison or Siberian exile. It had been an attempted revolutionary movement from above by noblemen, or members of the gentry, many of whom had campaigned with Alexander I in Western Europe after the failure of Napoleon's 1812 invasion of Russia. Abroad they were aroused by striking contrasts between life and government rule there and Russia's autocratic monarchy and widespread oppression of millions of enserfed peasants.

Perhaps the circumstances of Nicholas's accession to the throne contributed to his almost morbid fear of any form of popular opposition from within or revolutionary infiltration from beyond his borders. In

* In the text the common practice of Anglicizing certain Christian names, especially of Russian tsars, is observed. Otherwise, transliteration from the Russian is based, with a few minor exceptions, on the system regularly reproduced in a table, 'Transliteration,' in the weekly publication: *The Current Digest of the Soviet Press.*

any event, the fact helped to shape his absolutist conception of rule. Known as 'Nicholas the Stick,' he autocratically wielded it with brutality. He organized the Third Section which perfected a system of spying and tightened censorship. And he impressed upon his bureaucracy, the schools, the Church, and the press their patriotic duty to 'orthodoxy, autocracy, and national unity.' Though not insensitive to the plight of the peasants, who constituted about ninety per cent of the population, his efforts at reform were concentrated mostly on the feudal nobility.

Paradoxically the thirty years of Nicholas's repressive rule coincided with the beginnings of a remarkable intellectual and cultural awakening in Russia. Elements of it may be observed as early as the eighteenth century, particularly in the reigns of Peter I and Catherine II and later in that of Alexander I, but cultural developments during those years were markedly dependent on Western European influences. By the time Nicholas came to the throne the great Golden Age of Russian poetry, led by Pushkin, had begun to produce verse that was peculiarly native in form and content. Soon Gogol and Lermontov were contributing masterpieces, and before Nicholas died the playwright Ostrovsky and the novelists Turgenev, Dostoevsky, Tolstoy, and Goncharov, to mention only the most celebrated names, had started their literary careers. Moreover, original ballet, music, painting, and sculpture had made significant advances.

Equally important was the birth of an intellectual and critical spirit among the intelligentsia, a term that was not commonly used until the 1860s to designate what amounted to a new social class. At this time it consisted, though not entirely, of idealistic young nobles who crowded the universities where they studied and debated in a ferment of intellectual unrest, philosophical search, and literary activity. They were much influenced by German classical philosophy of Kant, Fichte, Hegel, and later Feuerbach, and by French socialists and English political scientists – St Simon, Fourier, Proudhon, Herbert Spencer, John Stuart Mill, and Robert Owen. Among them were names that soon became famous, such as the brilliant literary critic Belinsky and the political and social thinkers and revolutionists Herzen and Bakunin. Utopian socialism, economic democracy, industrial development, scientific education, and the emancipation of women were among the subjects of their discussions. Under the iron rule of Nicholas I they deplored – to paraphrase Herzen – the impoverishment of the peasantry, rapacious merchants, ignorant priests, and the army of corrupt and lazy government officials. Their collective feeling about the state of the country was perhaps correctly expressed by Pushkin who is reported to have said, after listening to Gogol read some pages of the manuscript of his great novel *Dead Souls*: 'What a sad, sad land is our Russia!'

By the middle of the 1840s, intelligentsia thinking on Russia's past, present, and future polarized among members of two dominating groups: the Westernizers, of whom Herzen and Belinsky were the principal mouthpieces, and the Slavophiles, led by the Aksakov brothers, Ivan and Konstantin, the poet Khomyakov, and the Kireyevsky brothers, Ivan and Peter. Though the Slavophiles hoped for certain reforms from Nicholas I, they saw Russia's present and future salvation in terms of a return to the way of life of the pre-Petrine past. They condemned Europe's materialism, capitalism, bourgeoisie, and its menacing proletarian growth, and stressed the virtues of the Orthodox Church and the peasant village commune, the *mir*, as institutions embodying the highest expression and communal spirit of the nation's ethos. The Westernizers saw nothing in Russia's past that was worth reviving and upheld the best in Western progress and culture as models for backward Russia to aspire to. Abroad, in forced self-exile, Herzen urged in philosophical writings the liberation of the serfs and political freedom. At home Belinsky gloried in the influence of the enlightened West on burgeoning Russian literature. He saw literature, which had already begun to adopt an attitude of social criticism, as the center of Russian intellectual activity and the principal instrument for conveying the need for reform.

Revolutionary uprisings in Western European countries in 1848–9 shocked Nicholas. He at once mobilized his armies and responded to the Communist Manifesto of Marx and Engels, which revolting Paris workers had published, with his own Manifesto which urged the people of Europe to submit to their rightful rulers. And he vowed that these destructive revolutionary forces would not be permitted in Russia. Not only did he provide financial support to hard-pressed monarchies, but he sent an army across the border to quell the Hungarian revolution. Though Russian Westernizers abroad, such as Herzen, Bakunin, and Turgenev, and their adherents in Russia were filled with excited anticipation of what this sweeping revolutionary movement might presage for their own country, Nicholas closed his borders to Europeans, introduced one security measure after another, intensified censorship, and regarded as a crime the slightest suggestion of criticism of the established order. Swept up in the surveillance dragnet were members of the Petrashevsky Circle, the young Dostoevsky among them. They were all sent to prison or exiled to Siberia at hard labor merely for reading about and discussing utopian socialism. Belinsky avoided a similar fate by death in 1848. Herzen and Bakunin remained in Europe to escape arrest and their followers among the intelligentsia in Russia were frightened into silence.

The fame that Nicholas I achieved as the 'gendarme of Europe' was dissipated in the Crimean War against Turkey and its allies, a disaster for Russia, which began in 1853. By the time of his death in 1855, shortly before the war's end, his regime with its imposing façade of monolithic power was revealed to be in a terrible state of political and moral weakness.

Tolstoy was twenty-seven when Nicholas died. His first literary period was nearly over, and it may be said that even this early in his career his unusual personality was already formed, and the future direction of his artistic, intellectual, moral, and spiritual development was plainly indicated in his writings, thinking, and activities. It was clear that he would be a leader and not a follower, for a powerful individualism was the driving force of his nature. His intense self-examination left him relatively unconcerned with important historical events and undercurrents of social and political thinking during the reign of Nicholas I. A nobleman born, he was passionately devoted to the idyllic rural life of his estate at Yasnaya Polyana. At first he took little interest in the established order, dropped out of the university, and avoided embarking on either of the two careers usually preferred by the nobility – the army or government service.

But Tolstoy's enormous intellectual curiosity, so often triggered by activities, observations of life, and his penchant for problem-solving in terms of his artistic, moral, and religious concerns, drove him into extensive reading of Western European and Russian literature in various fields. As a youth in the university he was somewhat contemptuous of its professors and their conventional notions of teaching and their outmoded understanding of such subjects as history. And he left in order to conduct his own education, to improve the condition of his serfs according to a plan he devised, and to regulate his daily behavior by an elaborate system of rules he wrote out. When he subsequently drifted into the army, first to fight the Caucasian hill tribes and then in the Crimean War, the experience served to prepare the way for his later condemnation of wars and those who perpetrated them, just as a remarkable statement in his diary of his views on religion at this time suggests the fundamental position he took on the subject twenty-five years later when it altered the remaining course of his life.

In short, from his youth Tolstoy was, so to speak, an 'intellectual loner,' a self-contained and conservative aristocrat, temperamentally unsuited to participating in organized efforts for social and political change. Though influenced by men and books, he was determined to reach his own conclusions independently. Aware of the abuses of the reign of Nicholas I, he scorned the remedies of Westernizers and Slavophiles. He detected in them, especially in the Westernizers, a degree of self-serving, insincerity, false democracy, theorizing for the sake of theory, and a lack of moral conviction. His own attitude towards the abuses tended to combine outspoken theory with forthright action such as debunking the Crimean War in his courageous sketch, *Sevastopol in May*, and his powerful theoretical attacks on education under Nicholas which he supported by his unique experience in teaching at his own village school. It is interesting that in his two trips abroad during these early years, partly to study school systems there, unlike the Westernizers he found as much to criticize as to praise in European culture.

## II

After the debacle of the Crimean War and Nicholas's death in 1855, his successor, Alexander II, who began as a mildly liberal ruler, immediately won admiration with some much-needed reforms and the announcement that he was seriously considering Russia's oldest and greatest problem – freeing the serfs. Herzen abroad and the radical intelligentsia at home, all of whom had been deeply disillusioned by the failure of the Western European revolutions of 1848–1849, were electrified by the news. The excited Herzen wrote the Emperor an open letter in which he pleaded with him to 'remove from Russia the shameful blotch of serfdom,' and he proposed the formula of emancipation with land and the preservation of the peasant communal organization, the *mir*, because, he wrote, 'we have nothing to borrow from bourgeois Europe.' (The Westernizers, in the face of their disappointment with revolutionary Europe, now turned to elements of Slavophile thinking.) Herzen emphasized this change of tactics in editorials in his magazine the *Bell*, published in London, and the radical intelligentsia cautiously took it up in their principal progressive organ, *Contemporary*, around which there now clustered the *raznochintsy*, intellectual commoners, of whom Chernyshevsky was the leader and Dobrolyubov their outstanding literary critic.

Preparations for emancipation dragged on for several years in the midst of fears among the landed gentry and violent upheavals on the part of impatient serfs. At this time Tolstoy was abroad and visited Herzen in London on a number of occasions. Though at first not disposed to like him, he later commented that Herzen was immeasurably higher than any of the political thinkers he had ever known. The admiration was mutual, although Herzen found Tolstoy stubborn in argument and felt that his head had not been picked over and swept clean. Tolstoy also talked with Proudhon at Brussels, shortly after the Emancipation Act on March 5, 1861. In welcoming the event, Tolstoy, who earlier had made a futile effort to free his own serfs, proudly told the great French socialist who opposed the ownership of property that Alexander II had not freed the serfs with empty hands but gave them property along with their liberty.

Back in Russia Tolstoy learned to his chagrin the irrelevance of his boast to Proudhon as well as the wisdom of the latter's socialist views on property. For he served as Arbiter of the Peace in his district during bitter quarrels between peasants and gentry caused mostly by restrictive measures, patently favoring the gentry, on the adjudication of land rights written into the Emancipation Act. Though he tried to be objective in his judgments, the gentry fiercely protested at his findings on behalf of peasants and he soon resigned the office. Another important reform aroused his ire – the establishment of Zemstvos in the countryside which were entrusted with jurisdiction over local affairs. As a democratic gesture a few peasants were often seated on these bodies, but control remained in the hands of the gentry. The operation of the Zemstvos added to Tolstoy's growing conviction of the stupidity of civil institutions. It seemed to him that justice and public welfare were sacrificed to a government order of things committed to the oppression of the weak and the iniquity of the strong. The accommodation of means to an end in the satisfactory handling of social problems was nearly always beyond him. These experiences entered into his future theorizing and writing on property and the peasants.

At best a half measure, the Emancipation Act intensified the radical movement in the 1860s. Demands for further reforms outstripped the government's intentions. Abroad the writings of Herzen and the fiery Bakunin increased dissatisfaction. In the *Contemporary* Chernyshevsky insinuated covert but meaningful passages in reviews and articles and kept in touch with groups that produced manifestos and leaflets urging preparations for insurrection. The brash literary critic Pisarev (Dobrolyubov died in 1861) was outspoken in demands for social change, and he and Chernyshevsky were attacked by both liberals and reactionaries as 'Nihilists,' a word popularized by Bazarov, the hero of Turgenev's *Fathers and Sons*, who called for the destruction of the old way of life. Student demonstrations and many small peasant clashes took place which to some extent were encouraged by an important new underground organization – Land and Freedom. The government grew alarmed when the movement spread to Poland where a rebellion to throw off the tsarist yoke, encouraged by Russian radicals, broke out in 1863. It was savagely put down: 128 ringleaders in various districts were executed and 18,672 participants were sentenced to hard labor in Siberia. This event, which turned much sympathetic Russian liberal opinion against the activities of the radicals, gave the government an excuse for taking 'patriotic measures.' Among them was suspension of *Contemporary*, the arrest of Chernyshevsky, who was sentenced to imprisonment for fourteen years and thereafter banishment to Siberia for life, and the arrest of Pisarev, who was given five years. Chernyshevsky wrote in prison his much celebrated novel *What Is to Be Done?* It is less a novel than an ode to the coming generations who, he said, would be the first to realize communism in Russia. The work became the inspiration of future Russian revolutionary youth, including Lenin.

During the political and social turmoil of the 1860s, Tolstoy appeared to be totally absorbed in happily married life (he married in 1862) and in the seven years it took him to write *War and Peace*. If his famous novel, centered in historical events of Russia's past, had anything to say to thousands of readers deeply disturbed by contemporary events, it was more or less by accident imbedded in the premises of his art – his insistence that emperors and so-called great leaders were not the real makers of history, and his belief that it was the common people, workers and peasants, who were the important factors in resolving the national crises of a country. Nor is there much in his correspondence or diary that reveals interest in the stirring events of this period or any concern over the dangerous efforts of radicals such as Chernyshevsky for whom he had no high regard. He does coldly refer to the tragic Polish revolt but only by way of mentioning that he ought to join the army again and help crush the uprising. Yet there are stray bits of evidence to suggest that his spiritual crisis a few years later had its roots in the 1860s. In 1865 he asserts in a notebook, apropos of peasant land-hunger, that Russia's national task is to endow the world with the idea of a social structure devoid of landed property. And he concludes that Russian revolution will not be against the tsar and despotism, but against landed property. The observation expressed more precisely the peasantry's real feeling in the 1860s than anything the radical intelligentsia had to say then.

As Alexander II's regime approached the 1870s its policy of combining reforms with despotic firmness against radicals had its successes. Rural and municipal self-government were expanded, and there were judicial, financial, military, educational and labor reforms. The program furthered the disintegration of feudalism and the ripening of capitalism in a few industrial centers.

At this time revolutionary activity centered more in Western Europe where emerging Marxism and the formation of the First Socialist International attracted disillusioned émigré Russian radicals, especially Bakunin and his young disciple Nechaev. It was generally recognized that backward Russia, which still lacked a class struggle in the European sense, was not yet ready for the development of Marxian proletarian socialism.

What did develop in the 1870s, however, was Populism or peasant socialism, an indigenous Russian movement that had a large and varied impact on the country and which in many respects contributed to the Marxian revolution that followed. Its initial inspiration, no doubt, went back to the Emancipation Act, the inchoate radical activity associated with it, and Herzen's famous appeal at that time, 'to the people,' which became the movement's rallying cry. Early leading theorists and activists were Herzen, who died in 1870, Bakunin, and Chernyshevsky and Pisarev before their imprisonment, and later Lavrov, Tkachev, and the literary critic and sociologist Mikhailovsky. Fundamentally, Populists shared the radical intelligentsia's disappointment over European parliamentary democracy in the revolutions of 1848–9, and like their leader Herzen, they concluded that Russia, which had not experienced this defeat, should seek its revolutionary destiny in the natural socialism of the peasant commune. Their program called for intellectuals 'to go to the people,' to the villages – and hordes of them did, mostly university students – to live the lives of the peasants, the only force in Russia, they believed, capable of overthrowing the power of tsar and gentry. And on the basis of the example of the *mir*, they hoped to establish throughout the land a new life of real freedom, equality, and economic democracy.

Populism expanded into something much larger than a political movement, for it expressed the yearning of a relatively small Europeanized intelligentsia to bridge the gulf between itself and the vast mass of underprivileged peasantry. It developed social and cultural aspects and became involved with Slavophile, religious, and nationalistic elements. Folklorists, painters, and composers discovered in peasants the embodiment of national ideals, of imagery, motifs, and melody. Among writers such as Nekrasov, Saltykov-Shchedrin, and Gleb Uspensky a literary vogue sprang up that celebrated the villages and their inhabitants in prose and verse. And Dostoevsky saw in the peasants 'God-fearing' folk who would one day bring a 'new word' that would solve Russia's tormenting problems.

Populism had an obvious and in some respects a seminal influence on Tolstoy. At the beginning of 1870 he returned to the matter of education with a pronounced emphasis not only on teaching peasant children, but also on training teachers especially for this purpose. He published two primers which contain legends, fables, and folktales, to which he later added more, some of them among his most enduring writings. The experience led him into theorizing about the language, artistic needs, and literary appreciation of peasants which eventually contributed important critical conceptions to his treatise *What Is Art?*

*Anna Karenina*, which was also written during this period, hardly belongs to the literature of Populism, but its scathing criticism of the gentry, aristocratic families of the city, and various governmental failings is in the spirit of the movement, as is his depiction of the 'conscience-striken' noble Levin, who 'goes to the people' in search of a philosophy of life compatible with the virtues of peasant existence.

Tolstoy's later controversial writings suggest that in some cases he transformed the political revolutionary idealism of Populist leaders into his own brand of spiritual revolution. Their denial that men of culture alone created progress, he staunchly supported. And he shared their belief that many so-called progressive aspects of capitalism and industrialization would have a dehumanizing effect on the Russian population. Moreover, he had a certain sympathy for Bakunin's anarchistic conviction that the State must go, though not through violence as Bakunin preached, and that a free federation of collectively functioning communes, organized from below, should be erected on its debris. Lavrov's idea that all States were inherently tyrannical, even revolutionary states, reappeared in Tolstoy's writings, for like the Populists he recognized the danger of transferring power from one set of oppressors to another. Further, many persecuted sectarians of the religious underground, who made common cause with the Populists, were known to Tolstoy, and later their thinking and activities clearly influenced him.

As it turned out, understandably enough, most peasants resented the young idealistic Populists who flocked to the villages. They were suspicious and puzzled by their language, manner, and altruism. The peasants were mostly uncommunicative, often drove them away, and sometimes turned them over to the police. Discouraged by their failure, many young Populists enlisted in the army in the war against Turkey in 1877. They hoped that Alexander II, who had declared the intention of liberating his Slavic brothers, the Bulgarians, from Turkish oppression, might also be inspired to liberate his own oppressed subjects in Russia. It was a war that Tolstoy scornfully condemned at the end of *Anna Karenina*, because, he said, peasant-soldiers, who did most of the dying, had no notion of what they were fighting for.

In the end some leaders among the Populists realized that they had underestimated the importance of immediate political objectives in attempting by a long-range program of persuasion and education to bring the peasantry to an acceptance of the need for revolutionary change in their own interests. Political freedom, they decided, must precede all other kinds of freedom. Populists revived the underground Land and Freedom organization of the 1860s, and one of its offshoots, The People's Will, a minority group, dedicated itself to political terrorism. A wave of demonstrations and strikes followed. The government's harsh response accelerated terrorist acts which culminated in the assassination of Alexander II in 1881. Tolstoy was profoundly affected by the event, but by that time he was well advanced on the path of his own revolution.

## III

Tolstoy's amazing letter in 1881 to Alexander III, who succeeded his assassinated father, was only the first of a number of direct appeals to sovereigns during his remaining years. He had won the right to public statement and the public expected it of him. For after his profound spiritual struggle in 1879–1880, Tolstoy began his extraordinary series of controversial writings which elaborated his religious, moral, social, and political beliefs. These works, along with his great novels earlier, had established him as perhaps the best known international figure in the second half of the nineteenth century. His letter pleaded with the Emperor to pardon the six revolutionists involved in the murder of his father. Tolstoy wrote that one cannot contend successfully with these revolutionists by a mixture of reform and repression, for their ideal is a sufficiency for all, equality, and freedom. Their ideal must be opposed by one that is superior but includes it – the ideal of love, forgiveness, and of returning good for evil. The results of the plea symbolized the hopes and failures of Tolstoy's immense future activity dedicated to the conviction that the kingdom of God on earth was attainable if only men would abide by the precepts of Christ. The revolutionists were executed and the saddened Tolstoy applied himself more assiduously to propagating his new philosophy of life.

It may be said with little exaggeration that during the next three decades, when all political, social, and economic factors in Russia were building up to a cataclysmic explosion, Tolstoy competed with revolutionaries for the minds of the Russian people. Unlike his previous standoffish attitude, he now assumed public positions on national issues, not only with his pen but also by direct action, as in his successful organization of famine relief in 1891 when he turned the eyes of the world on the government's bureaucratic deficiencies in handling starvation, or in his exposure of the government's cruel treatment of the religious sect, the Dukhobors, and the practical steps he took to resolve the matter. Like all authors of stature, Tolstoy was under police surveillance, but because of his international renown he was able to attack the government with a degree of immunity, although his followers were often rigorously persecuted. Revolutionaries were in a much more defenceless position. They recognized, once Marxism became their guiding light, that some of the ends Tolstoy sought were similar to their own, but his means were irreconcilable with theirs. For a time the revolutionaries considered him as one of them and made frequent use of his legal and illegal controversial writings for their own purposes. However, he was interested in the souls as well as in the minds of men. Though his larger, more universal moral and non-violent approach to mankind's ills won many disciples in Russia and elsewhere, it eventually ceased to attract revolutionaries committed to 'scientific socialism' while living under the persecution of a police State.

The People's Will had anticipated that Alexander II's assassination would result in popular upheaval and collapse of the monarchy. For the most part it provoked revulsion among the people, and Alexander III, who regarded himself as a special instrument of God to preserve the monarchy, abandoned intended liberal reforms of his predecessor and sponsored a series of repressive acts that fell heaviest upon the radical intelligentsia, their press, and the whole educational system. In this reactionary climate a kind of cultural despair gripped the country, intensified by the fact that Tolstoy appeared at this time to have forsaken *belles lettres,* and that Dostoevsky died in 1881 and Turgenev two years later. The young writers coming along avoided themes critical of the establishment.

During the 1880s and 1890s the pressure of military needs and foreign trade greatly stimulated the slow growth of capitalism in which the government's own entrepreneurial zeal played a considerable part. A sizeable industrial revolution, much aided by foreign investments, rapidly developed. Within a few years it began to transform the feudal economic and social aspects that remained in Russia. Hundreds of thousands of peasants, who had fared badly under the provisions of the Emancipation Act, deserted their villages for the cities to seek work in the new factories. And many of the landed gentry, whose economic power had been declining, also settled in the cities to engage in enterprises which often allied them with the swiftly growing class of the bourgeoisie. The 'landowners' monarchy,' it was said, was being transformed into a 'bourgeois monarchy.'

The most significant change brought about by this industrial revolution was the growth of a large and ultimately class-conscious proletariat. Men, women, and children worked as many as fifteen hours a day at extremely low wages, and often under wretched conditions. Frequently, they were victimized by long layoffs and lived in indescribable poverty in city slums. It was their cause that Tolstoy argued in his well-known book, *What Then Must We Do?* He viewed the city as a place where – in Oliver Goldsmith's words – wealth accumulates and men decay. Like the Populists, he saw this situation as one of the evil consequences of Western capitalistic influence, bringing in its train the vicious exploitation of the poor by the rich.

In *The Kingdom of God Is Within You* Tolstoy carries his destructive criticism still further, but this time largely in terms of applying and defending the tenets of his new faith. He attacks the whole structure of modern society and governments, whether absolute monarchies or constitutional democracies. With unsparing criticism he dwells on a variety of institutions and subjects, especially war, conscription, and violence, but including others such as the administration of justice, patriotism, political parties, religion, and the Church.

Nor did Tolstoy, in *What Is Art?*, spare the new culture in literature and the arts that seemed to be a response to the economic and social changes in Russian life at this time. The old realism gave way to foreign influences from the West, primarily French Symbolism and Impressionism. New Russian writers, such as Merezhkovsky, Hippius, Balmont, Bryusov, and Sologub, called themselves modernists, decadents, symbolists. For them life was filled with hidden meanings. Many acted the part of bohemians or sophisticated aesthetes, contemptuous of causes, convictions, and faiths, and they sought freedom for the individual from mundane and social demands. In his treatise Tolstoy excoriated the movement as a cult of unintelligibility, deplored their emphasis on the pornographical, and regarded their development in the arts and literature as the inevitable consequence of a civilization that had lost contact with everything that is moral, spiritual, and devoted to real love of mankind. When he turned once again to his own fictional art, he employed it, with few exceptions, to illuminate the convictions of his new faith, as in *Resurrection*.

More than once in his controversial writings during these years Tolstoy warned Russia of the certainty of bloody revolution if necessary social and political changes were not undertaken by the government. Before the end of the 1880s there existed in Russia the accepted class situation required for the application of Marxian doctrine – a bourgeoisie and a proletariat opposed to the government power structure. The initial volume of Marx's *Capital* had been published in Russian as early as 1872. And in 1882 the first notable Russian Marxist, Georgi Plekhanov, translated the *Communist Manifesto* for illegal circulation in his country. The next year he formed the first Russian Marxist organization. Former Populists, convinced by then of the futility of a peasant socialist revolution, were drawn to Marx's theory of achieving socialism through the bourgeoisie with the aid of the proletariat. Though forbidden by law, strikes by discontented workers, often organized by Marxist cadres, soon took place in various cities of Russia. Ameliorative legislation was of little use. And when Alexander III died in 1894 at a time of extensive industrial strife, the young Lenin was already a full-fledged and very active Marxist. Tolstoy, looking back over the dead Emperor's repressive rule, prophetically regretted the deplorable deeds of his reign.

## IV

Like his father, Nicholas II announced upon becoming Emperor that he would maintain the fundamental principles of autocracy firm and unshaken. It amounted to a declaration of war against his revolutionary opposition, with which he no doubt identified Tolstoy. The government increased its persecution of his disciples. Their attempts to live in conformity with Tolstoy's teaching, often in agricultural communes, brought them into conflict with the law for proselytizing Orthodox believing peasants, refusing to take oaths, rejecting conscription in the armed services, and distributing the master's forbidden writings. With every means in his power Tolstoy protested at the frequently cruel punishment of such followers. In fact, so immense was his reputation that he was deluged by requests for aid from victims of the government, especially harassed religious sectarians. His principal weapon for bringing pressure on the regime in such cases was a steady stream of lengthy letters, articles, and pamphlets abroad where they were widely published in translation.

So concerned was Tolstoy with the spectre of approaching revolutionary violence in Russia that he compromised with his conviction of the evils and futility of governments in order to write a letter to Nicholas II, in which, after reciting the violations of the natural rights of his subjects, he offered a program of reforms that would save his regime. His answer, perhaps, was the Church's excommunication of him in 1901, an act which the Tsar's government no doubt connived in as a means of turning the vast population of believers against him. The act provoked the opposite result – national and international indignation.

The spectre approached still closer, for by 1900 the economic boom brought about by flourishing industrial developments ended. A depression set in that lasted for three years. Thousands of workers lost their jobs while droves of hungry peasants kept pouring into the cities looking for work. Mammoth political demonstrations took place. The fearful Tolstoy wrote another appeal to Nicholas II to urge him to countermand a government order that troops shoot at demonstrators who refused to disperse. Autocracy, he told him, was an outmoded form of government, and he also protested against anti-semitic laws and the recent revival of legislation that permitted peasants to be flogged.

The gravity of the country's internal situation may well have been one of the factors in the outbreak of the Russo-Japanese War in 1904 – it could divert the masses from ideas of revolution. But it turned out to be a disastrous and unpopular struggle. With Tolstoy's well-known condemnation of all wars in mind, disciples and the foreign press insistently called for a public statement. He replied in an uncompromising article that received widespread publicity, in which he reaffirmed his views on the utter futility of wars in general and the present Russian involvement in particular, and he movingly described the terrible personal tragedies it was bringing to his countrymen and the Japanese people.

The government was confronted with successive defeats on land and sea in the Far East and a rising tide of bitter mass opposition at home much of which was promoted and directed by the two Marxist-based political parties, the Social Democrats, led by Plekhanov, Lenin, and Trotsky, and the Social Revolutionaries, who retained some Populist convictions such as the doctrine of terrorism. When on January 9, 1905, a large crowd appeared before the Winter Palace in St Petersburg to petition Nicholas II for reforms and were fired on by troops, who killed and wounded many people, the revolution began. Sporadic fighting broke out in the cities and uprisings in the villages. A general strike was declared by a newly formed revolutionary organization, the St Petersburg Soviet of Workers' Deputies. With the whole country paralyzed, a fearful government, threatened with destruction, was forced into concessions. On October 17 Nicholas II issued a Manifesto which promised freedom of speech, press, and conscience, freedom of assembly and association, a broad extension of the franchise, and the establishment of a legislative body. The move appeased the masses, the liberals, and even many organized radicals if not the hard-core ones among them.

Tolstoy viewed the violence and bloodshed of the revolution with dismay and adamantly refused repeated requests of the activists to lend his name publicly in support of their movement. He sought a moral revolution, he pointed out, and not a political one. Nor did he have any hope to offer those who acclaimed the concessions of the Emperor's Manifesto. He predicted that these promises would turn out to be illusory, that no government voluntarily surrenders its power, and that if the revolution had succeeded in supplanting the autocracy, its leaders would eventually revert to employing the very coercive powers they had set out to destroy. In fact, the concessions were soon forgotten or watered down. The first and second elected legislative assemblies, the Duma, which Tolstoy, like Lenin, regarded as a tsarist hoax, were quickly dissolved by Nicholas II. After the electoral laws had been rigged, the Third Duma, controlled by moderate parties and the Emperor's Prime Minister, soon quelled the remaining vestiges of revolutionary activity in the country, executed or imprisoned its leaders, or forced them to flee abroad. The first Russian Revolution was dead.

In a large measure the popularity in Russia of Tolstoy's non-violent programme for creating a kingdom of God on earth had dissolved in the violence and bloodshed of political revolutionary struggle. Many of his younger adherents deserted his cause to fight for the revolution. But faith in his panacea appears to have been somewhat restored in the course of the universal adoration accorded him on the occasion of his eightieth birthday in 1908. For after the disillusion and laceration caused by the failure of the 1905 Revolution, many found hope once again in the spiritual idealism embodied in Tolstoy's teaching.

# I

# Childhood, Boyhood, and Youth

## I

They agreed in the household that as a child Leo Tolstoy seemed to feel everything more intensely than others. His hair-trigger emotions, high spirits, and keen enjoyment of everything set him apart. His sister recalled that he was like a ray of light. He would dash into the room with a happy smile, as if he wished to tell everyone about a new discovery he had just made. If he were petted, tears of joy filled his eyes, and they nicknamed him 'cry-baby Leo.' He often expressed his uncommon sensibility in spontaneous outpourings of love and in eager efforts to win affection. In a sense, this acute sensibility defined the man and the literary artist.

Yasnaya Polyana, the family country estate where Leo Nikolayevich Tolstoy was born on August 28, 1828,* was an ideal playground for a boy. It is 130 miles south of Moscow and about 10 miles from the city of Tula. In front of the spacious manor house was an elaborate flower garden and beyond stretched a large park of ancient lime tree alleys, and clumps of hazel and birch. Extensive cultivated fields bounded the estate and beyond were the thick Zakaz woods cut by the Voronka River.

The Tolstoy line was an old one in Russia, belonging to the nobility, and through intermarriage of male and female branches was related to many of the most distinguished families. Some of its members had served in notable positions in the government, and in the eighteenth century Peter the Great conferred the title of Count on the family. Leo's paternal grandfather, the Governor of Kazan, had so depleted

* This date, as others in the book, is according to the Russian Julian Calendar which was twelve days behind the Gregorian Calendar in the nineteenth century, and thirteen days in the twentieth.

the family fortune that his son, Nikolai Ilyich Tolstoy, an army officer during Napoleon's invasion of Russia, found it expedient to reject his inheritance because it was so encumbered with debts. He took the usual way out, repairing his fortune by marrying, in 1822, a wealthy heiress, Marya Nikolayevna Volkonsky, only daughter of a celebrated relic of the age of Catherine II who later was to serve as prototype of Prince Bolkonsky in *War and Peace*. She was five years older than her husband and rather unattractive, but she brought him the rich estate of Yasnaya Polyana with its 800 serfs inherited upon her father's death in 1821.

Leo was the youngest of four sons – Nikolai, Sergei, and Dmitri. Then, shortly after giving birth to a daughter, Marya (Masha), his mother died in 1830. Though Leo was not quite two at the time and could hardly have remembered his mother, from the impressive things he learned about her from members of the family, old servants, and her letters, he revered her memory throughout his life. If genius is an accident of nature and has no ancestors or descendants, it is nevertheless subject, especially in childhood, to all the factors that influence ordinary mortals. The deep moral and spiritual image of his mother appears to have influenced the impressionable Leo, and the idealized memory of her that his vivid imagination evoked emerged years later in the brilliant characterization of Princess Marya in *War and Peace*.

So did the more real memory of his father in the creation of Nikolai Rostov in the same novel. Though this portrait is devoid of the spiritual, Nikolai Rostov, like Tolstoy's father, emerges in his maturity as a sensible, pragmatic man, kind but firm with his children and serfs, and zealous for the development of his estate, Bald Hills (Yasnaya Polyana). Tolstoy's father, having resigned from the army and become disillusioned with the reactionary regime of Nicholas I, eschewed further government service and settled down to the comfortable existence of a well-to-do landowner. Tolstoy wrote with admiration of his father's bright, happy demeanor, his kindness, and his dignified bearing before all, no matter what their social position. The son grew up with a still greater consciousness of his own worth and with the same unwillingness to humble himself, least of all to government officials.

Yasnaya Polyana was a palace of pleasure for the growing family of children. There little Leo was first introduced to the wonders of nature of which he became such an acute and sensitive observer. Endless games, many horses and dogs, hunting, swimming in the Voronka River, and various winter sports – all absorbed the children. Some thirty servants drawn from village serfs took care of their every need. They were on terms of intimacy and affection with the family, a position not unlike that of black servant-slaves in kindly Southern homes, although this was by no means the general rule on estates of Russian gentry or on those in the United States. Tolstoy preserved the happiest of memories of some of these house-serfs in his reminiscences of childhood, and charming images of them survive in his fiction. After his mother's death he was also surrounded at Yasnaya Polyana by the tender care of female relatives – a grandmother, aunts, and especially his beloved 'Auntie' Tatyana, a distant relative who played an important part in his rearing and was enshrined in the lovely portrayal of Sonya in *War and Peace*. 'I saw and felt how she enjoyed and I understood the joy of love,' he wrote of Auntie Tatyana in *Recollections*. 'That was the first thing. And the second thing was that she taught me the charm of an unhurried tranquil life.'[1]

Though Tolstoy's father did not particularly cultivate the society of neighboring estate owners, such visitors, along with relatives, were not infrequent at Yasnaya Polyana. Often a score or more people, family and guests, sat down to the main meal with a footman to serve behind each chair. On such occasions the host kept the company lively with his anecdotes and jokes.

Lessons did not interfere too much with the children's fun. At this early age, education, as was usual on landed estates, was provided by foreign tutors, largely as a device for beginning the study of languages early. Educationally they were often deficient in everything but their native tongue. In *Childhood* Tolstoy has left a memorable picture of his old German instructor at this time, a kindly man from Saxony whose reading, besides his German exercise book, seems to have been limited to a pamphlet on the manuring of cabbage patches, an odd volume on the history of the Seven Years' War, and a treatise on hydrostatics. But he did encourage in him, Tolstoy noted, virtuous precepts of tolerance and kindness to all the poor and unfortunate of life, among whom he included himself. From Auntie Tatyana he learned well the elements of French, the correct use of which had become a hallmark of social distinction among upper levels of Russian nobility. Yasnaya Polyana also contained a substantial library, built up by Grandfather Volkonsky, a cultural embellishment rather unusual among rural gentry. It may be assumed that little Leo pieced out the imperfections of his initial formal education by dipping into some of these books. For when he was about eight his father once asked him to read some Pushkin to the assembled company. Leo's selection of poems, which is on record, suggests a certain degree of artistic taste and understanding at this early age.

However, it was the rough-and-tumble child's world of Yasnaya Polyana that most occupied him, the 'wonderful period of innocent, joyful, poetic childhood'[2] as he mentioned in his *Recollections*. How impatiently the children waited for the hallowed period between Christmas and New Year when family, relatives, servants, and guests swarmed into the house, dressed in outlandish costumes (little Leo was got up as a majestic Turk with burnt-cork mustaches), prancing to the lively music, and excitedly opening gifts that the host distributed. But of all the games of childhood the one that Tolstoy recalled with most enjoyment and deep feeling was an invention of his older brother Nikolai. He had discovered, he told them, a remarkable secret which, when known, would make all men happy; there would be no more disease, no human misery, and no anger. All would love one another and become 'Ant Brothers.' (*Moravskiye bratya* – 'Moravian Brothers' – the religious sect about which young Nikolai had no doubt read or heard, was mistakenly transformed by the children into *Muraveinye bratya* – 'Ant Brothers' – which is phonetically somewhat similar.) The children adopted the idea with enthusiasm, and under chairs covered with shawls they cuddled together in the dark, waiting for the revelation which, Nikolai informed them, was written on a little green stick buried in a special place by the road in the Zakaz forest. Towards the end of his life Tolstoy wrote:

> The ideal of the Ant Brothers clinging lovingly to one another, only not under two armchairs curtained by shawls, but of all the people of the world under the wide dome of heaven, has remained unaltered for me. As I then believed that there was a little green stick whereon was written something which would destroy all evil in men and give them great blessings, so I now believe that such truth exists among people and will be revealed to them and will give them what it promises.[3]

## II

In the winter of 1837, when Tolstoy was not yet nine, the family moved to a large rented house in Moscow. The time had come to take the children's education more seriously, especially that of the two older sons who would soon be preparing for the university. This first venture into the great world outside Yasnaya Polyana was exciting and also disillusioning for the irrepressible Leo. He found it hard to get used to all these strange people who did not know him and did not seem to care about him.

In the following summer his father, on a business trip to Tula, fell dead in the street. And several months later Leo's grandmother also died. This first conscious experience with death of those close to him depressed and puzzled the boy. But he recognized later that his expression of grief over the loss was in imitation of that of the grown-ups, and it pleased him to hear them sadly exclaim that the Tolstoy children were now 'complete orphans.'

Saintlike Aunt Alexandra became the children's guardian, the property was placed in trust, and expenses had to be sharply cut. Results of the domestic changes impressed young Leo only when the family was obliged to move to much smaller Moscow living quarters and the Tolstoy children were given cheap presents at a Christmas party to which they were invited whereas their rich Gorchakov cousins received expensive gifts.

Despite altered circumstances, the new educational program continued. A bright young Frenchman, Prosper Saint-Thomas, had been employed to direct their studies, and occasionally teachers from Moscow University were obtained for tutoring in special subjects. Leo quickly fell afoul of the Frenchman's strict regimen and for the first time in his life he was threatened with a whipping. The experience made an ineffaceable impression on him, for seventy years later he told his Russian biographer:

> I now do not remember the reason for it, but I thought it was a most undeserved punishment for Saint-Thomas first to lock me up in a room, and then to threaten me with the rod. I experienced a terrible feeling of indignation, revolt, and aversion not only to Saint-Thomas, but towards that violence which he wished to exercise on me. This occasion was perhaps one reason for the horror and aversion for every kind of violence which I have felt throughout my whole life. [4]

Tolstoy never fitted easily into the mold of conventional education. If stimulated by a teacher or by curiosity, he was capable of amazing spurts of energy in the learning process and was aided in performance by uncommon assimilative powers and an excellent memory. Otherwise he shirked lessons and appears to have made little impression on his teachers from the age of nine to thirteen. The few extant schoolboy exercises reveal nothing more than the usual clichés of observation, mistakes in spelling, and a few examples of simplicity in expression.

Self-education appealed to him more. Sometimes it took the odd form of seeking answers to puzzling questions he concocted through the means of experimentation. For example, he wondered if the answer to achieving real happiness did not rest on the ability to learn to endure suffering, and he would hold out at arm's length a large, heavy dictionary until the operation became unbearable, or he would lash his bare back until the tears came. On another occasion he wondered whether it would not be possible to fly by sitting down on his heels, clasping his arms firmly about his knees, and jumping into space. (It may be remembered that in *War and Peace* Natasha Rostov, in enchanting circumstances, has exactly the same notion.) He tried it one day from the upstairs window of the study room and fortunately suffered only a slight concussion from a drop of some eighteen feet. Preoccupation with abstract problems, such as whether man existed somewhere else before he was born, surprised and amused his older brothers. In turn, they appealed to their fledgeling 'philosopher' to settle the familiar schoolboy conundrum: Did God exist? and Leo appears to have decided that He did not.

No doubt, the bid for originality and his exhibitionism, which included shaving his eyebrows so they would grow in thicker and shaving half his head for no apparent reason at all, had some compensatory connection with his harassed position as the baby-brother of the family. He had to struggle for acceptance as an equal and against the added disadvantage of an acute self-consciousness about his appearance: broad nose, thick lips, small grey eyes, and tufted hair. Although adults complimented him on his pleasant smile and clever face, when he looked at it in the mirror he had to confess to himself that he would have given anything in the world for a handsome face.

Young Leo competed with his brothers and their friends for the attention of the girls they met at parties. When he was asked, as an old man, about his early 'loves,' he said that the first and most intense was for pretty little Sonya Koloshin. In *Childhood* he tells how Nikolai (Leo) imagines a rapturous conversation with her one night in the dark of his bedroom. Unable to keep the secret, he wakes his brother to tell him of his love. And he rejoices to learn that he also loves her (Nikolai wanted all to love Sonya). But when the older brother describes in detail how he would like to kiss her body all over, Nikolai is outraged by this sensual touch and weeps bitterly over the defilement of his pure image. With this boyhood incident still green in his memory at the age of sixty-two, Tolstoy jotted down in his diary: 'I have been thinking of writing a novel of love – chaste love as with Sonya Koloshin – in which a transition to sensuality is impossible and which serves as the best protection against sensuality.'[5] Wisely, perhaps, he never attempted this work.

By the time he had reached thirteen Leo was regarded in the family as an original youngster but erratic and impulsive. When criticized for flights of bizarre behavior, his natural outgoing, affectionate nature turned shy; he grew introspective, shunned his playmates, and retreated to a heroic world of his own creation.

The family returned to Yasnaya Polyana from Moscow during the summer months, and when the two older brothers became involved in advanced studies, Leo, Dmitri, and Masha remained with Auntie Tatyana in the country. In August 1841 still another death struck the family – Aunt Alexandra died. The guardianship of the children was assumed by her younger sister Pelegeya Yushkov who lived in Kazan, and her immediate decision was that they should all move there.

## III

With its mixed Russian and Tartar population striving to assume metropolitan airs, Kazan was a far cry from Moscow. As the grandchildren of a former governor of the town, whose daughter was their sponsor the Tolstoy young people won immediate social acceptance. And the indulgent Yushkovs, with their large comfortable house, saw to it that their wards enjoyed the advantages of Kazan's high society.

The town boasted a respectable university which was able to attract distinguished foreign scholars to its staff. The oldest Tolstoy brother, Nikolai, transferred to its Philosophy Faculty from that of Moscow University, and two years later (1843), Sergei and Dmitri matriculated in the same division. Perhaps because of its reputed difficulty, the younger Leo contemplated a diplomatic career which required him to enter the Faculty of Oriental Languages. But he had to undergo extensive preparation which involved special teachers and courses in Arabic and Turko-Tartar in the local *Gymnasium*. Not until 1844 was he ready for his entrance examinations. He passed well all subjects in which he was interested but flunked history, geography, and statistics and was denied admission. His self-esteem deflated but still anxious to follow his brothers into the university with its special student privileges, striking uniform, and gay social life, he applied himself to the failed subjects, passed them on a re-examination, and entered Kazan University in the autumn of 1844.

Tolstoy was then going on seventeen and one deterrent to serious study was a growing awareness of the pleasures of social life. By now the three brothers (Nikolai had entered the army in 1844) had rented an apartment, and Aunt Pelegeya had insisted on each of them having a serving boy of his own. As eligible bachelors the brothers were in considerable demand in society. Like Sergei, Leo at this time was partial to people who were *comme il faut*, that is, who spoke excellent French, had clean nails, knew how to bow, dance, and converse with ease, and always wore an expression of indifference to everything. However, his appearance, behavior, and temperament ill-suited him to play the part. With his broad peasant face, big hands and feet, unruly hair, and his long, haughty silences alternating with bursts of conversation intended to be boldly original, he bewildered and even frightened the young ladies. Though he stared rudely at them and imagined scenes of delightful intimacies, the very offer of an introduction terrified him, and he cursed his shyness.

Looking back on the years of his youth and early manhood, Tolstoy described it, with a degree of exaggerated frankness, as one of 'coarse dissoluteness, employed in the service of ambition, vanity, and, above all, of lust.'[6] But the waywardness he slipped into during this youthful Kazan period seems to have been in imitation of older drinking, smoking, gambling, dandified comrades. If inordinate shyness kept him from Kazan's marriageable girls of quality, he sought the other way out as he describes '... when my brothers took me for the first time to a brothel and I accomplished this act, I then stood by the woman's bed and wept.'[7] And in his diary in 1847 he writes: 'It is six days since I entered the clinic ... I've had gonorrhoea, had it from that source whence it is customarily obtained.'[8]

Sex was both attractive and repulsive to Tolstoy, for young as he was he had already begun to develop a strong moral sense and transgressions of it caused him distress and much heart-searching. If we may regard certain meditations in Chapter XXIV of *Youth* as autobiographical, and some evidence supports this view, he attempted at this time to formulate an idealistic conception of love that would serve as a counterbalance to his guilty thoughts on the subject. It turns out to have three heads: beautiful love, self-denying love, and active love. His own ideal of love consisted of the best qualities of all three which, he believed, were fully realized in the person of an inaccessible beauty he had seen in a box at the theatre. Often he contemplated this beautiful vision in his thoughts, imagining her in various romantic situations, but when she vanished in the end she would leave him with the ecstatic feeling that real happiness was nearer to Him who was the source of all beauty and bliss, and tears of unsatisfied joy rose in his eyes.

A more serious obstacle than these extra-curricular activities to the pursuit of his studies was his stubborn unwillingness to accept the whole system of university education. He failed the mid-term examinations of his first year and was dropped. Not yet ready to admit defeat, he gave up his notion of a diplomatic career and transferred to the notoriously easy Faculty of Jurisprudence. Here he began the new term with a ruthless cross-examination of himself on the pros and cons of a university education. The future theorist on education found it dedicated to stuffing minds with stereotyped factual knowledge as an end in itself without any concern for ideas, first causes, or the relation of facts to life. The very textbooks, he decided, contributed to the conspiracy of dullness and futility in education, and at the age of eighteen the relentless future critic of history books in *War and Peace* damned history as 'nothing other than a collection of fables and useless trifles messed up with a mass of unnecessary dates and proper names.'[9]

One discerning professor, apparently aware of the young Tolstoy's questioning mind, set him the task of writing a comparison of Catherine the Great's *Nakaz*, a guide to her commission appointed to set up a new code of laws, with Montesquieu's *Esprit des lois* to which she was heavily indebted. At once the student took fire, did a considerable amount of research, and concluded his analysis with a sharp criticism of the Empress for attempting to justify her own conception of despotism by appealing to the republican ideas of Montesquieu.

This exercise in independent research appears to have been a factor in convincing Tolstoy to leave the university – its demands hindered the accomplishment of such tasks. Besides, he said, his essay on the *Nakaz* led him into reading many books in one direction, but the effort 'revealed to me limitless horizons. . . . I gave up the university precisely because I wished to occupy myself in this fashion. There I was obliged to work at and study things that did not interest me and were unnecessary.'[10]

No doubt another factor was a division of the Tolstoy property among the heirs at this time. Leo received as his share Yasnaya Polyana and several smaller holdings amounting to about 5,400 acres and 350 male serfs. He experienced a real or imaginary sense of responsibility for all these human beings now under his sole control. In April 1847, before his final examinations of his second year, he withdrew from Kazan University and set out for Yasnaya Polyana.

While still at Kazan, Tolstoy had spent his summer vacations at Yasnaya Polyana. There he followed his own intellectual interests in indiscriminate reading, especially in Rousseau's works which much excited him. Perhaps under the influence of his back-to-nature teaching, Tolstoy discarded his sophisticated *comme-il-faut* notions, roaming about the estate in slippers and bare legs, clothed only in a crude canvas robe which he had fashioned and sewn himself. And he filled his exercise books with fragmentary essays stimulated by his reading, one of which is entitled 'Some Philosophical Observations on a Discourse by J. J. Rousseau.' It touches on a theme relevant to his later mature thinking, namely, that the backward science of history should be studied for its own sake and not as a kind of philosophy, whereas philosophers are in error when they attempt to solve philosophical problems by relating them to the so-called facts of history. Another essay, 'On the Purpose of Philosophy,' also points to the later moralist views of Tolstoy, for he contends that the purpose is to show man how he should instruct himself in the pursuit of happiness which cannot be found outside himself but only through his own systematic self-improvement.

Self-improvement was Tolstoy's goal once he decided to leave Kazan University to settle down at Yasnaya Polyana. The program of study he drew up for himself seemed like a deliberate criticism of the university's emphasis on specialized education:

> to study (1) the whole course of jurisprudence necessary to pass the final examination at the university; (2) to study practical medicine and to some extent its theory; (3) to study French, Russian, German, English, Italian, and Latin; (4) to study agriculture, theoretical and practical; (5) to study history, geography, and statistics; (6) to study mathematics, the *Gymnasium* course; (7) to write a dissertation; (8) to reach a reasonable degree of perfection in music and painting; (9) to write down rules [for conduct]; (10) to obtain some knowledge in the natural sciences; (11) to compose essays on all the subjects that I shall study.[11]

The rules for conduct which he also meticulously set down, such as rise at five and go to bed at nine or ten, sleep two hours during the day, eat moderately and nothing sweet, walk for an hour, have one woman only once or twice a month, and to do everything possible for himself, were soon multiplied by instructions for the development of the will, memory, and the body; directions to scorn wealth, honours, and opinions of society not based on reason; and to love all to whom he could be useful, to care nothing for the praise of people whom he did not know or disliked; and each day to express his love for all kinds of individuals in some manner or other.

All these ambitious plans were designed to contribute to the young Tolstoy's 'purpose in life' which was nothing less than an ideal of self-perfection. But discouragingly little was accomplished on his program of study and rules of conduct at Yasnaya Polyana, and repeated daily failures were dutifully entered into his diary with lacerating comments.

The same lack of fulfillment appears to have overtaken another endeavor which he had offered as a reason for deserting the university for the country – a humanitarian desire to improve the conditions of his serfs. Though the study of agriculture in his program was intended to equip him for this task, he was hopelessly encumbered by the land-owner's traditional conviction that the enslaved position of the peasantry was ordained by God. His activities at Yasnaya Polyana in these respects were faithfully reflected some years later in the published part of a large novel he never completed, *A Landowner's Morning* (1856). In it the nineteen-year-old hero leaves the university for his estate in the belief that the only way to find happiness is to work for it in others, and he decides to devote his life to the well-being of his serfs. Refusing to believe their poverty is unavoidable, he abolishes corporal punishment, provides schooling and medical aid, and visits them in their wretched hovels in an effort to teach them how to mend their ways and engage in more remunerative work. But all his attempts fail, for the peasants are stubbornly suspicious of his offers of assistance which they regard as tricks of the master to get more labor out of them. Sadly disillusioned by the deception he encounters on every hand, he abandons the experiment.

The hero's experiences no doubt parallel those of the young Tolstoy at Yasnaya Polyana. Many years passed before he came to believe that peasants were the equals or even the superiors of his own noble class. Perhaps the epitaph to this first attempt to improve the lot of his peasants is stated with his usual honesty when the hero's aunt in the story writes her nephew: 'You always wished to appear original but your originality is really nothing but excessive self-esteem.'[12]

The charms of rural existence wore off in less than two years and so did Tolstoy's belief that one could live by philosophizing, self-education, and idealistic rural experiments. He threw it all up and left for Moscow at the end of 1848. Now twenty, he had acquired considerable poise and self-assurance and with the aid of family connections was welcomed among the exclusive social circles of Moscow and St Petersburg. In an excess of fresh devotion to worldly success, which he later came to despise so much, his 'Rules of Conduct' were supplanted by a new set of 'Rules for Society,' among which were such precepts: to seek associations only with men higher in society than himself; to dance at balls only with the most important ladies; never to express his feelings; and to repay double any sarcasm or insult. He joined the English and Nobles Clubs, paid court to well-known dignitaries, and dined and wined with the best families. But he also developed a passion for gambling in which he lost large sums, and often caroused at night with young blades at fashionable restaurants, usually followed by visits to brothels or to gypsy establishments to listen to the haunting melodies of their choruses and to make love to exotic gypsy girls.

Yet this feckless way of life never ceased to trouble his conscience and he repeatedly told himself that he must be a 'practical man.' At times he sought escape by preparing himself for examinations to enter the Faculty of Jurisprudence of Moscow University. But he soon gave up this hope of a career for the idea of becoming a cadet in the Horse Guards, which he in turn surrendered for a nominal post in the Chancellery of the Tula Assembly of Nobles. It allowed him an abundance of time for more carousing and he eventually escaped again to his higher social contacts in Moscow and St Petersburg.

During these several years of sowing wild oats, Tolstoy seemed oblivious of the absorbing political and revolutionary activities in Western Europe (1845–1849) or of their baleful influence on the repressive regime of Nicholas I in Russia. Nor did he appear to be aware of such significant developments as the brilliant efforts of the great critic Belinsky and his followers to direct Russian literature into an effective critique of the abuses of tsarist bureaucracy, or of the fact that the young writer Dostoevsky and others had been arrested and sentenced to exile in Siberia for radical activities.

Summer interludes at Yasnaya Polyana served merely to interrupt temporarily his profligate course in the city. Simple country existence, the kindly influence of Auntie Tatyana, and visits with his level-headed brother Sergei would remind him of his rules of conduct and encourage him to study music, practise on the piano, and to follow a course of gymnastic exercises, for development of the body had become a fetish which he continued for years. With the onset of winter, however, he was off again to Moscow to gamble, he said, to marry, and to obtain a post.

In most respects, during the four years since he had left Kazan University Tolstoy had been leading a form of life that was characteristic of the young men of the gentry, although he led it much more intensively. They grew up on country estates, alternating its rural pleasures with those of fashionable society in the city. The profits of serfdom took care of their financial needs, and they were little concerned with playing an active part in the government or in the social or cultural developments of their country, although they were capable of talking and theorizing endlessly about such matters.

The rare qualities of Tolstoy's nature, however, rescued him from the traditional inertia of Russia's 'superfluous' men. If his relative isolation from practical matters intensified a natural bent for introspection, his thinking and theorizing were concentrated on a deeply felt sense of personal duty as revealed by the workings of his conscience and intellect. Speculation was always paced by an early and consuming ambition to achieve something of importance and by a real, if uncertain, awareness at this time that he possessed the vital powers to do so.

'One cannot live by speculation and philosophy,' Tolstoy wrote his brother Sergei. 'One must live positively, that is, be a practical man.'[13] In truth, during this period of pursuing worldly social success, his letters to the country and his diary are studded with merciless self-criticism of moral lapses and failure to find a practical goal in life. He was almost twenty-three, had become morally sick of his Moscow social existence, and in his struggle for identity had finally caught a glimmer of a new aim in life, that of literature. In this state of mind he desperately felt the need of renewal, and he seized upon the opportunity to accompany his beloved brother Nikolai, who had been home on a furlough, to his battery in the Caucasus far removed from the worldly temptations of Moscow. They left at the end of April 1851.

# 2

# The Caucasus

In Tolstoy's youthful copybook scribblings and diary, one begins to observe, shortly before he left for the Caucasus, fugitive bits of evidence that his thoughts were turning to writing fiction. Among the foreign novelists he read then are Sterne, Goethe, Hugo, Dumas, Eugène Sue, George Sand, and Dickens, who became one of his favourite authors. In a letter many years later, he paid him the following tribute, in English: 'I think that Charles Dickens is the greatest novel writer of the 19th century, and that his works, impressed with true Christian spirit, have done and will continue to do a great deal of good for mankind.'[1] The narratives of older Russian writers are also mentioned, such as Pushkin, Gogol, and Lermontov, and in the thick quality periodicals, he kept abreast of the current fiction of Turgenev, Grigorovich, and Druzhinin. From the point of view of his later concern with aesthetics and religious philosophy, it is interesting that he was deeply impressed at this time by the story of Joseph from the Bible and the Sermon on the Mount.

Further indications of the literary drift of his thoughts in the diary, which he had begun in 1847 and continued with interruptions for years, are quotations from stories, observations on things and people that he might use in fiction, and aesthetic judgments, such as: it is impossible to describe a person but not the effect he might have on you. Then comes a terse entry: 'I intend to write a story of gypsy life should I find the time,'[2] followed shortly thereafter by another: 'To write the history of my childhood.'[3] He did not find the time for the first, but in a few months he began the second, his initial published work.

The budding artist's irresistible urge to observe and describe life had seized him. From his city apartment windows he watched the unfolding comedy and tragedy of street life. He wondered who the policeman was who strolled by and what kind of existence he led. And he asked himself who was in the carriage that drove past and what the passenger was thinking. Or he imagined what an interesting story could be told of the inner lives of the inhabitants in the house across the street.

In the selection and analysis of his own inner experiences in the diary, the young Tolstoy was actually serving an unconscious apprenticeship to the novelist's art. For in dwelling on the suppressed motives of his behavior in an effort to elucidate the subconscious by an application of understanding, we have a suggestion of his later talent in the psychological dissection of imaginary characters.

Perhaps an earnest of his literary intentions, as well as the determination to improve his style, was Tolstoy's attempt to translate *A Sentimental Journey* of Sterne, whose sensibility, story-telling flair, verbal cleverness, and humour fascinated him. Although he never finished the work, as a model it appears to have inspired him to imitate it. For on March 25, 1851, shortly before he departed for the Caucasus, he noted in his diary that he rose at five and worked on his writing until ten. He had begun his first known piece of fiction, a fragment of what was intended to be a lengthy effort under the title, *A History of Yesterday*. It consists of three short sections, the hero's evening at cards with two close friends, man and wife, the description of his sleigh ride home, and the transformation of unexpected and confused associations of thought that enter his head as he falls asleep. Though quite derivative, this fragment has its interest as a Tolstoyan version of Shandian method and manner. There is the familiar Sternian protracted analysis of conscious feelings reacting to particular situations, as well as Sterne's whimsy, asides, puns, digressions, 'posturing' in characterizations, and excessive alliteration in style. Entirely untypical of Tolstoy, it was an approach to fiction that he promptly abandoned.

## II

In the early summer of 1851 Tolstoy's first view of the picturesque Caucasus, already fabled in Russian song and story, thrilled him – the gigantic white mountain masses soaring skywards. He felt all the majesty of their beauty and with it a sense of complete freedom from his past. Quartered with his brother in a village hut of the Grebensk Cossacks settled on the bank of the Terek River, where Nikolai's battery was stationed, Tolstoy quickly adjusted himself to this new frontier existence. The Russians, in their efforts to subdue the fierce

Chechen hill tribes of the region, had erected a series of outposts along the northern banks of the Terek and Kuban rivers and from these they carried on warfare against the natives.

At first Tolstoy was excited by the life and people in these exotic surroundings. He admired the proud, independent Cossack settlers, men who made a cult of bravery and a sacred rite of drinking, and their handsome, well-formed women who seemed to enjoy complete freedom, especially the unmarried girls. And he soon made a 'blood brother' of a native, a 'peaceful' illiterate Chechen, by helping him in his gambling bouts with Russian officers. With the officers, who were typically brave fighters but for the most part poorly educated and passionately addicted to drink and gambling, Tolstoy was at first standoffish as though he feared they would underestimate him or would not recognize that his own standards were beyond their comprehension. 'Once for all,' he wrote in his diary, 'I must become accustomed to the thought that I am an exception, and that either I am ahead of my age or am one of those incompatible, unadaptable natures that are never satisfied.'[4] But his natural conviviality and desire to be liked asserted themselves, and soon the officers were regularly dropping in at his hut for vodka and a chat.

Not long after his arrival Tolstoy impulsively volunteered in an attack on the Chechenians. Later the commander praised his courage under fire and urged him to petition to enter the army. With some misgivings he followed the advice, passed the examinations, and was assigned as a cadet or non-commissioned officer to the artillery battery in which his brother served. In a letter to Auntie Tatyana at Yasnaya Polyana he expressed his delight for – he explained – he had had too much leisure and this had been the principal cause of his faults. The future hater of war also wrote his brother Sergei: 'With all my strength I will assist with the aid of a cannon in destroying the predatory and turbulent Asiatics.'[5]

For months, until the resistance of the hill tribes was broken, Tolstoy took part in the fighting, had several narrow escapes from death, and on three occasions was recommended for decorations. However, the hopeful conviction he had communicated to Auntie Tatyana was of no avail; this carefree army life provided much leisure. He had ample opportunity to resume his city habits of hard drinking, gambling, wenching, and even quarreling with fellow-officers, for because of his prickly nature he bridled at what he considered the slightest offense to his dignity or honor. Short leaves to surrounding towns also provided occasions for dissipation, especially fashionable watering places which he visited ostensibly to take cures.

Tolstoy's diary has frequent brief notations on the Cossack girls he pursued. Every woman's bare legs, he laments, seem to him to belong to a beauty. And in vain he tries to abide by his rule of exhausting himself by hard physical labor and to remind himself that the pleasure is brief and the remorse great. Typical of the repeated litany on sin and repentance is one entry in which he rejoices at having at last exorcised the devils of vice, particularly gambling, but the very next entry tells of losing the large sum of 850 roubles at cards. Then he adds:

> Now I shall restrain myself and live prudently. I went to
> Chervlyonnaya, got drunk there and slept with a woman. All this is
> very bad and troubles me deeply. Indeed, never have I spent more
> than two months well or so that I was satisfied with myself. Last night
> I lusted again. It is good that she would not give herself. Loathsome!
> But I write this as a punishment for myself.[6]

One refuge from the snares of leisure time was to fulfil the determination that he had expressed just before he departed from Moscow – to engage in literature.

## III

In fact, not long after he arrived in the Caucasus Tolstoy began to work, very early in the morning and late at night, on the subject he had mentioned previously in his diary, *Childhood*. He regarded it as the first part of a novel under the tentative title *Four Epochs of Growth*. The slowness and care with which he wrote reflected his anxiety over this initial serious effort to appear in print. The first draft was discarded for a second with a substantially different approach to the narrative, and this was followed by two more drafts containing numerous alterations. The diary records moments of deep dissatisfaction with his progress and uncertainty about continuing. 'Have I talent comparable to that of recent Russian writers?' he asks himself and answers, 'Positively no.'[7] And he warns: 'Without regret, I must destroy all unclear places, prolix, irrelevant, in a word, everything unsatisfactory, even though they may be fine in themselves,'[8] for he was convinced that no addition could improve a work as much as a deletion. Yet there were rare moments of compensation as he indicates in one entry: 'I reread the chapter "Grief" and while so doing wept from my very heart.'[9]

By the beginning of July 1852 the last draft of *Childhood* had received its final polishing and Tolstoy sent it to N. A. Nekrasov, distinguished editor of the well-known progressive periodical, the *Contemporary*. In the accompanying letter authorial anxiety diluted literary pride in the writer of twenty-three. Finishing the remaining parts of the novel, he indicated, would depend on the success of the first. 'I am convinced,' he wrote, 'that an experienced and well-intentioned editor, especially in Russia, by virtue of his position as a constant intermediary between author and reader, can always indicate in advance the success of a work and the public reaction. I await your answer with impatience. It will either encourage me to continue a favourite occupation or oblige me to cease at the very beginning.'[10] And as a final bit of protection he signed himself 'L.N.', the initials of his first name and his patronymic.

Nekrasov's decision to publish and his praise of the author drove him 'silly with joy,'[11] Tolstoy wrote in his diary. But when he read the work in the *Contemporary* (October 1852), he hurried off a sharp criticism of the mutilations of editor and censor. And though he gladly agreed to Nekrasov's offer to print more of his writings at the fair rate then of about a penny a word (Tolstoy had received no payment for *Childhood* as a first published work), he concluded by warning him never again to tamper with his manuscripts.

*Childhood* was very enthusiastically received by the public. Turgenev, who thought it had been written by Tolstoy's brother Nikolai, urged Nekrasov to encourage the author and to convey his interest and praise. And the exiled Dostoevsky in far-off Siberia wrote a friend to ask who was the mysterious L.N. whose recent story had so impressed him. While resting in a hut during the course of a hunt with fellow-officers, Tolstoy came across a recent issue of *Notes of the Fatherland* which contained a highly laudatory review of *Childhood*. One can only guess at his reaction to the reviewer's conclusion: 'If this is the first production of L.N., then one ought to congratulate Russian literature on the appearance of a new and remarkable talent.'[12]

The work is essentially an autobiographical novel based on Tolstoy's childhood experiences disguised as the remembrances of the hero Nikolai Irtenev. The narrative is concentrated mostly on the events of a day in the country and of one in the city, and the whole is interlarded with speculations and generalizations that often reflect Tolstoy's conviction that childhood is the happiest time of life. Though he draws heavily upon memories of his childhood, the work is variously fictionized, especially in the treatments of such characters as Irtenev's mother and father. For example, the exquisitely described scene of the mother's death (Tolstoy's mother died before he was two years old) is an effort of pure imagination. However, Tolstoy's childhood life and that of the family then are wonderfully recreated along with brilliant characterizations of his old German tutor, the extraordinary madman of God, Grisha, and the lovable and loyal servant Savishna.

Later Tolstoy told a friend that when he wrote the work it seemed that no one before him had so felt and depicted all the charm and poetry of childhood. There is a measure of truth in this, whatever previous writers may have influenced him. Tolstoy mentions two himself, the Swiss author Rodolphe Töpffler and Laurence Sterne, although there appears to be almost no dependence on the first, and after the initial draft of *Childhood* he deliberately winnowed out much of Sterne's influence. Yet in the emphasis on sensibility, self-analysis, and frank confession, one detects something of the flavor of Sterne and Rousseau, as well as a touch of the psychological approach of Stendhal, and interesting similarities in the treatment of certain themes between *Childhood* and *David Copperfield* have been pointed out.[13]

By concentrating on two days in the life of his hero Tolstoy achieves an intensifying effect absent in previous publications on childhood. This intensification of the process of recollection adds a special poetic charm to childhood memories and associations only vaguely remembered but when recalled with such feeling seem altogether delightful. The reader, under the author's spell, insensibly agrees with him that childhood is the happiest time of life and man's only period of innocence. Elements of the 'saturation realism' for which Tolstoy was to become noted appear in lush descriptive passages, but he carefully avoids simile and metaphor involving comparisons with remote or improbable objects. And his amazing powers of observation of himself, others, and the world around him are clearly revealed in this first literary effort, as indeed are other qualities of his mature art.

Success and need of money because of gambling losses stimulated Tolstoy to further literary endeavors in the Caucasus. The diary lists expansive plans: to continue his autobiographical novel 'Four Epochs of Growth' (he made progress on *Boyhood* but put it aside for a time); to vary this chronological work with a different project on the daily life of an estate-owner entitled 'Novel of a Russian Landowner' (purpose and plans were set down but only a fragment emerged. *A Landowner's Morning*, published five years later, 1857, and already commented on); to write a series of essays on the Caucasus (nothing of consequence came of the idea); to portray the Cossack way of life of which he had learned much from his friend Epishka Sekhin (this ultimately became the novel *The Cossacks* but was not finished until ten years later); to exploit the current popularity of military fiction in stories of war and the nature of bravery (he did two short stories, *The Raid*, 1853, and *The Woodfelling*, not finished until later and published in 1857).

The two short stories are based on his own army experiences in the Caucasus. In each Tolstoy employs military actions as a background for eliciting information on the nature of bravery among fighting men, why they serve, and the way in which they behave in critical situations. The approach is objective, the narrator rarely intrudes, there is no self-analysis as in *Childhood,* descriptions of nature are kept simple, and characters, modelled on officers and soldiers Tolstoy knew, are portrayed largely externally. In both stories, more so in *The Raid* than in *The Woodfelling* which is less effective as an artistic performance, there is a suggestion of his later antagonism to conventional thinking about military glory. The honest realism of these tales easily elevated them above the romanticized fiction of Caucasian fighting of other writers.

Written also in the Caucasus (1853) is a third short story, *Notes of a Billiard Marker*, which has not been highly valued artistically, but the analysis of the hero's moral disintegration has some autobiographical significance as a revelation of Tolstoy's spiritual distress at this time.


IV

Things literary now occupied much of Tolstoy's thinking in the Caucasus. It afforded him pleasure and profit, he remarked. An article he read on the literary characteristics of genius made him wonder if he were not a remarkable man because of his capacity and eagerness in such endeavors. In some writers, he noted in his diary, 'the fire of inspiration changes into a candle to work by. Literary success that satisfies one's own self is obtained only by working at every aspect of a subject. But the subject must be a lofty one if the labor is always to be pleasant.'[14] He saw little of this devotion in contemporary literature which he felt was debased because authors sacrificed quality to quantity for the sake of commercial gain. 'Better with conviction and absorption to write something good and useful,' he said in his diary. 'One will never grow weary of such a work.'[15] He particularly criticized current literature for its lack of concern for moral problems, and he made the incredible suggestion that 'it would really not be a bad thing in every literary work (as in a fable) to write a moral – stating its aim.' And he followed this in his diary with the proposal 'to edit a periodical, the sole aim of which would be the dissemination of writings morally useful . . .'[16] Although nothing came of the idea, he in effect returned to it after 1880 in his aesthetic theory and practice.

In the towns he visited in the Caucasus Tolstoy read everything he could get his hands on and also sent home for books. He enlarged his knowledge of the Russian and foreign authors already mentioned and added new ones such as Pisemsky, Ostrovsky, Griboyedev, Balzac, Béranger, Stendhal, Thackeray, Fenimore Cooper, and Harriet Beecher Stowe. He read with pen in hand and his diary was the repository of his reactions which often took the form of grandiose but unrealized plans which, however, reflect his thinking at the time. For example, after reading the historians Hume, Thiers, Michaud, and Karamzin, he decided: 'Must compose a true and just history of Europe of the present century. There I have an aim for my whole life. Few epochs in history are so instructive as this one or so little debated . . .'[17] Then Plato's *Politics* and Rousseau's *Contrat social* suggested a still vaster task: 'Will devote the rest of my life to drawing up a plan for an aristocratic selective union with a monarchical administration on the basis of existing elections. Here I have an aim for a virtuous life. I thank thee, O Lord. Grant me strength.'[18]

Nevertheless, at the height of his initial success in writing, Tolstoy burst forth in his Caucasian diary: 'Literature is rubbish and I should like to set down here rules and a plan of estate management.'[19] He could not commit himself unalterably to literature as the answer to his search for a purpose and aim in life, nor did he ever regard himself solely as a literary artist. His fertile, teeming brain would not allow him simply to tell tales for entertainment. There was something in him of the Renaissance man who took all knowledge to be his province.

In truth, during all these months in the Caucasus the incessant question of his future never ceased to shadow Tolstoy's thoughts and activities. At one point he wrote Auntie Tatyana that he had already undergone a moral change, would soon return to Yasnaya Polyana, marry, lead the peaceful country life of his father, and entertain his children with tales of his experiences in the Caucasus. Shortly after, he contemplated turning his back on sophisticated society, for he had come to admire the Cossacks who, as 'natural men,' seemed beautiful, strong,

D

37

and free, and he thought of buying a hut, marrying a Cossack girl, and settling down in the Caucasus.

But dominating the Caucasian diary are Tolstoy's thoughts on the meaning of his life which often become involved in his relentless struggle between good and evil, and at times they assume a striking spiritual expression. One night at camp, soon after his arrival, while trying to define in his diary a view of things, a form of life, he began to pray to God. He later entered in his diary:

> It is impossible to convey the blissful feeling I experienced in prayer. Yet if prayer be defined as a petition of thanksgiving, I was not praying. Rather I was yearning for something lofty and good. What that something was I cannot explain, although I clearly recognized what I desired. I wanted to become fused with the All-Embracing Substance. I besought it to pardon my sins. . . . I could not separate the feeling of faith, hope and love from my general feeling. No, the feeling I experienced last night was love for God, uniting in itself all that is good and renouncing what is bad. [20]

Then Tolstoy adds that not an hour passed before he was listening to the voices of vanity and vice and fell asleep dreaming of fame and women. In another passage he writes: 'I'm tortured with a thirst, not for fame – I have no desire for fame and despise it – but for acquiring great influence for the happiness and benefit of society.' [21]

However young he may have been at the time, it would be a mistake to regard such expressions as anything less than sincere, for moral values never ceased to be the guide of Tolstoy's thought and actions. He insisted in the diary that the first condition of moral beauty is simplicity and conscience, man's most reliable preceptor. 'That man whose purpose is his own happiness,' he wrote in the diary, 'is bad; he whose purpose is the opinion of others is weak; he whose purpose is the happiness of others is virtuous; he whose purpose is God is great.' [22] He tried to do a good deed for others every day and each morning he prayed because he found 'moral solitude' in it. But he had difficulty identifying the idea of God as clearly as the idea of virtue, for the idea of God, he said, comes of man's recognition of his own weakness.

By the end of his second year in the Caucasus he entered in the diary the rather conventional belief he had arrived at: 'I believe in the one incomprehensive and good God, in the immortality of the soul, and in the eternal reward for our deeds; I do not understand the mysteries of the trinity and the birth of the Son of God, but I honor and do not reject the faith of my fathers.'[23] He would not state his faith in quite these words many years later after his spiritual revelation, but he had reached the fixed moral conclusion that happiness depended not upon circumstances but upon oneself, that wisdom consisted in acting in the best possible fashion in the present. On his birthday he laconically, and perhaps with excessive modesty, summed up his state of mind in the diary: 'I'm now 24; yet I have done nothing; I feel that not in vain have I struggled for 8 years with doubt and passion. For what am I destined?'[24]

By this time military life in the Caucasus had lost its novelty for Tolstoy. Camp routine, he thought, could turn one into something of a fool. Maneuvers, drill, and mechanical obedience, he caustically noted, were simply necessary, the discipline essential to the existence of a military class. He had some expectation of promotion and when it was disappointed he put in for a discharge. In the meantime Russia had declared war on Turkey and retirements were forbidden. Tolstoy appealed to his relative, Prince M. D. Gorchakov, head of the Danubian armies, for a transfer to his command and for a furlough. The request was granted on January 12, 1854, and a week later he joyfully set out for Yasnaya Polyana.

Tolstoy later looked back on these two and a half years in the Caucasus as one of the best periods of his life, 'grievous and splendid,' he remarked, a crucible in which his finest qualities had been severely tested, and where he had experienced the first fine rapture of the success of authorship. At twenty-four the qualities of his nature stood out surprisingly well defined, his goals and moral concerns suggested, and the direction of his literary talent more or less indicated.

# 3

## War, Travel, and
## Self-Definition

The furlough was short. Soon Yasnaya Polyana and its bucolic pleasures had to be abandoned for war. Early in March 1854 Tolstoy set out to join an artillery brigade stationed not far from Bucharest. There his light duties enabled him to savor the pleasures of Bucharest and later of Kishinev. Now he had given up his hope of achieving moral perfection; the continued quest for it, he argued with dubious logic, was not incompatible with his failure to be consistently good.

In the meantime, when Britain and France made clear their firm opposition to the designs of Nicholas I in attacking the Ottoman Empire, the Russo–Turkish War was transformed into the Crimean War. A wave of patriotism swept Russia upon the news of this first invasion of the country since Napoleon's. After the bloody battles of Alma, Balaklava, and Inkerman, and the investment of Sevastopol by the allies, Tolstoy, who had been promoted to the rank of sub-lieutenant, was only one of the many young Russian officers of the Danubian Army who petitioned for transfer to the scene of action. He arrived at Sevastopol November 7.

The magnificent heroism of the besieged city's defenders under appalling conditions filled Tolstoy with a surge of patriotism. Here he saw modern warfare involving vast masses of men, so different from the frontier raids in the Caucasus. The carnage sickened him. He approached his superiors with a project for the reorganization of batteries and worked out a plan for the formation of rifle brigades as a means of improving Russian inferiority in small arms. So serious did he regard the army's situation that he drafted a plea for reforms. He bitterly arraigned inhuman conditions of the fighting men and the graft and ineptitude of the officers. A soldier is beaten, he pointed out, if he smokes a long-stemmed pipe, if he wishes to marry, if he dares to notice that his superiors steal from him. Our soldiers are brave, he declared, because death is a blessing for them. 'We have not an army but a crowd of oppressed, disciplined slaves, confessed plunderers and hirelings.'[1] Even this early in his career, Tolstoy had found that exacerbated but persuasive language which later became so pronounced in his frequent attacks on the abuses of government and the Church. Fortunately, perhaps, he had second thoughts about sending this memorandum on army reforms, as he had intended, to one of the Grand Dukes.

Early in March Tolstoy's spirits rose when he was assigned to an extremely dangerous tour of duty at the exposed Fourth Bastion of the Sevastopol earthworks, some two hundred yards from the enemy lines and under almost continual fire. The constant danger was agreeable, he remarked, and he was buoyed by the courage and rough humor of the soldiers and sailors who served with him. This perilous experience helped to inspire his *Sevastopol in December* which he worked away at in a bombproof shelter when not directing the fire of his battery. It appeared in the June 1855 issue of the *Contemporary* and aroused anew the flagging patriotism of an enthusiastic reading public with its vivid genre pictures of the besieged city, an account of heart-rending scenes among the wounded in a military hospital, and its restrained but deeply-felt admiration of the self-sacrificing heroism of the defenders of Sevastopol who were determined that the city must not fall. It was reported that Alexander II, who had succeeded to the throne after the death of Nicholas I in February, read the article with emotion and sent an order to the front to 'spare the life of that young man.'

Not the Tsar's intercession but that of a well-placed relative appears to have brought about Tolstoy's transfer from the death-trap of the Fourth Bastion to the command of a battery on the near-by Belbek River. In the comparative inactivity his patriotic fervor vanished and his growing conviction of the utter futility of war, which had begun in the Caucasus, now took full possession of him. It is brilliantly expressed in his second sketch, *Sevastopol in May*, published in the September 1855 issue of the *Contemporary*. So completely did the censor transform it into a piece of government propaganda for the war that the editor, when the censor insisted it be printed in this mutilated copy, salved his conscience by omitting Tolstoy's name. In the original form, however, *Sevastopol in May* is a powerful condemnation of war. Much more literary than the first sketch, it employs all of Tolstoy's Sevastopol experiences to expose the folly and hypocrisy of those who initiate war and of the leaders who participate in it. He also reveals the vanity of diplomats whose objectives can never be fundamentally achieved by the slaughter of human beings, the vainglory of officers eager to climb to promotion over the dead bodies of fallen comrades, and the supreme pathos of little people, as in the beautifully narrated death of Praskukhin, who are cut down on the battlefield with their story of life untold. There are really no heroes here, Tolstoy implies, and he underscores it in his famous statement in which he declares that the only hero of his tale is truth. In answer to his bitter complaint over the censor's wanton disfigurement of *Sevastopol in May*, Nekrasov echoed the author's indignation and added:

> It is exactly what Russian society now needs: the truth. . . . You are right to value that side of your gifts most of all. Truth – in the form you have introduced it into our literature – is something entirely new among us. I do not know another writer of today who so compels the reader to love him and sympathize heartily with him as he to whom I now write.[2]

As the war drew to a close, Tolstoy desperately sought for release. Was he good for nothing save cannon fodder? he asked himself. 'My service here in Russia,' he noted in his diary, 'begins to madden me as it did in the Caucasus.'[3] When he learned that any surplus, after fixed charges, of the money allotted by the government for the needs of their men customarily found its way into the pockets of the officers, he aroused their ire by steadfastly refusing to indulge in the practice, though at the time he badly needed funds. In general, however, he was well-liked by his comrades for his conviviality, the masterful way in which he told a story, his fine sense of honor, brave bearing, and generosity. At times, they even tried to protect him from his tendency to plunge in gambling by refusing to play cards with him.

Although he wept when, on his twenty-seventh birthday, he saw Sevastopol in flames and the French standards on the Russian bastions, shortly thereafter he eagerly complied with the request of his commanding general to collate various reports of artillery actions on the day the city fell and deliver them, as a courier, to the military authorities in Petersburg. He reached the capital on November 21 and soon sent in his resignation, but before he did so he was promoted to the rank of lieutenant for 'distinguished bravery and courage.' He had ended his career as a militarist and become a pacifist, for Sevastopol had stirred in him an implacable hatred of war.

Before he left Sevastopol Tolstoy had also rediscovered his former view of life, 'the aim of which is welfare and the ideal of virtue,'[4] too long forgotten, he declared, because of his association with military society. His first aim, he promised himself, was to accumulate sufficient money to free his estate from debt and liberate his serfs. And several months before this he had entered into his diary a rather remarkable conception:

> Yesterday a conversation about divinity and faith suggested to me a great, a stupendous idea to the realization of which I feel capable of dedicating my whole life. This is the idea – the founding of a new religion corresponding to the development of mankind: the religion of Christ, but purged of all dogma and mysteriousness, a practical religion, not promising future bliss but realizing bliss on earth. I understand that to bring this idea to fulfillment the conscientious labor of generations towards this end will be necessary. One generation will bequeath the idea to the next, and some day fanaticism or reason will achieve it. Consciously to contribute to the union of man and religion is the basic idea which I hope will improve me.[5]

Tolstoy, at the age of twenty-seven, had at last found a purpose in life, although years were to pass before he devoted all his energies to it.

## II

In Petersburg Tolstoy found himself a literary rather than a war hero. He accepted Turgenev's invitation to stay with him. Sprees, gambling, and visits to the gypsies were varied by the assiduous courting of him by progressive writers clustered around the *Contemporary*, for its editor, Nekrasov, was anxious to retain him as a contributor in the face of competition of other periodicals. Turgenev wrote of Tolstoy's visit to a friend: 'You cannot picture to yourself what a dear and remarkable man he is, although I have nicknamed him the "troglodyte" because of his savage ardor and buffalo-like obstinacy.'[6] There was much more of the troglodyte than the gracious guest in his behavior towards these literary colleagues. Although his forceful bearing and penetrating intelligence won their admiration, he also exasperated both contending groups of Westerners associated with the *Contemporary* by his uncompromising opinions: the moderate liberals, such as Turgenev and Nekrasov, and extreme liberals, such as Chernyshevsky and

Dobrolyubov. In argument he brashly toppled their literary idols: Shakespeare was just an ordinary writer revered by Russians who repeated foreign opinions from force of habit; George Sand disgusted him because of her sheer animalism disguised as poetic; and their exiled oracle Herzen's revolutionary writings were attacked. Tolstoy saw only pose and hypocrisy in the 'democratic haunches' of Turgenev. The so-called 'convictions' of these liberals, he felt, had been invented by the intelligentsia in order to have something to talk about, whereas he tried to live by moral instinct. Nor did he find any more to his liking the conservative 'convictions' of the stern Moscow Slavophils, guardians of undefiled Russianism, whom he visited at this time. He thought the feuding Westerners and Slavophils, to whom many distinguished writers and thinkers gave their allegiance, were simply tilting at windmills.

The conservative poet Fet, one of the few important writers to remain on genuinely friendly terms with Tolstoy, described him then as being involuntarily opposed to all accepted opinions, and the prominent Slavophil Konstantin Aksakov remarked that the reason Tolstoy seemed so unsettled in argument was because he lacked a center in his beliefs. There was some truth in both observations. His pronounced individualism and intellectual pride would not allow him at this stage in his career to subordinate his views to either Westerners or Slavophils. Tolstoy's cross-grained attitude was a measure of his 'dissidence of dissent,' his insistence on originality as a thinker and an artist.

Perhaps the one person in Petersburg capable of exercising a pinch of influence on him was a cousin, Countess Alexandra Tolstoy, Maid of Honour and governess in the family of the daughter of Nicholas I, Grand Duchess Marie. A woman of charm, tact, and high intelligence, whom he jokingly called 'Granny' (she was eleven years older), she was well acquainted with the literary and political life of the capital. During the years their affection deepened, and an extensive and notable correspondence reflects his faith in her judgment and love of truth. She recalled his welcome visits at this time:

> I see him quite clearly as he returned from Sevastopol, a young
> artillery officer, and I remember what a fine impression he made on
> all of us. He was already a public figure. All were enraptured with
> his charming creations, and we were proud of the talent of our
> kinsman, although we did not foresee his future renown.[7]

After six months in Petersburg, unlike the lip-serving progressives of the *Contemporary*, he decided to put into practice his own liberal instincts. More than once he had contemplated the possibility of freeing his serfs. And now, having witnessed how masses of peasants died in the service of their country with courage and humility as though they had a pact with God, he felt that his own deserved a better fate than slavery. Besides, Alexander II, from whom reforms were eagerly expected after the reactionary rule of Nicholas I, had recently warned that it would be better if freedom came to the serfs from above rather than from below.

Tolstoy drafted a project but failed to obtain prompt approval of it from the Assistant Minister of the Interior which elicited an acid comment in his diary on old men in government unfitted for the work of change. Impatiently he left for Yasnaya Polyana to place the plan before his serfs. He called his 309 male heads of families to a meeting and spoke in simple words about the details of the plan. It had been carefully prepared and reflects a degree of business acumen, an ability for which Tolstoy has rarely been given credit. Since the estate was heavily mortgaged, he explained, he could not give them the land outright, and without land their freedom was of little use. He therefore offered each household four and a half desyatins of land. (A desyatin is equal to 2·7 acres.) Half a desyatin would be free but for the rest they must pay five roubles a desyatin annually for thirty years. One rouble of every five would pay off the mortgage and the remainder would purchase for them the four desyatins. At the end of thirty years they would be free of all obligations to him. (During Tolstoy's lifetime the value of the rouble underwent some fluctuation, but in general the pound sterling was worth ten roubles and the dollar two roubles.)

The peasants flatly rejected the offer and justified themselves by a wild rumor that the Tsar would soon free the serfs and give them all the land, and they indicated that their master was trying to force them into a prior disadvantageous contract. The refusal was a keen disappointment to Tolstoy. After his failure and while trying to solve some of the peasants' immediate problems, he wondered whether they really wanted their freedom, and he noted in his diary: 'Two powerful men are chained together; each hurts when the other moves, and there is not enough room for them to work together.'[8] The despotism of landowners, he conjectured, had engendered despotism in the peasants, and he warned a friend in the government that if something were not done soon to remedy the 'peasant question' there would be a bloody outbreak. He had not clearly understood that years of serfdom had developed in the peasantry innate suspicion of the master and deep hostility. Though he experienced a moral duty to free his serfs, his approach to the problem had not been devoid of self-interest. Such contradictions never ceased to trouble him.

Tolstoy spent the rest of the summer at Yasnaya in reading, hunting, and on visits to the homes of his sister, his brother Sergei, and Turgenev. The two hypersensitive authors, though strangely drawn to each other when apart, could never get along well together. Not a little of his leisure time was spent in furtive assignations with peasant girls. Disgusted with himself as usual, he again began to think of settling down and realizing his dream of family happiness. With marriage in mind he began to visit his neighbors, the Arsenevs, whose oldest daughter Valerya attracted him. There was more of the comic than the romantic in the desultory courtship that ensued. At the outset he commented in his diary: 'I fear marriage as well as baseness, i.e., of amusing myself with her. But to marry, much would have to be changed, and I have still a great deal of work to do on myself.'[9] At first he had more criticisms than caresses to offer. Much displeased him – her bare arms, hair, dress, lightmindedness, and her piano playing. She obviously liked him, at first submitted patiently to his wearisome advice on her way of life, and her family and Auntie Tatyana thought it a most desirable match. Perhaps annoyed by his hesitation she even introduced the goad of a rival which both made him jealous and exasperated him. He seemed more concerned with the idea of marriage than with marriage itself, and Valerya lacked the capacity to inspire in Tolstoy a love which he did not initially feel for her. 'I'm not in love,' he wrote in his diary, 'but this bond will always play a great role in my life. If I have not yet known love, then judging by the small beginning that I feel now, I shall experience it with terrible force, and God forbid that it should be for Valerya.'[10]

Thinking that a period of separation would settle the matter one way or the other, he left for Moscow. The first entry in his notebook on arrival was: 'I tried to think of Valerya and thought of brothels; this hurt me.'[11] He went on to Petersburg. The tempo of affection rose in the first days of separation but soon dwindled to mutual recriminations in their correspondence, with him, on the score that he had learned she was still writing to his rival, with her, resentment over his continued parental attitude and insufferable fault-finding. In bowing out he offered her the customary polite explanations, but to Auntie Tatyana his honest feelings: 'I never loved her with a real love. I was carried away with the reprehensible desire to inspire love. . . . It was terrible for me to think of the obligations I should have to perform towards her without loving her. . . . I have behaved very badly; I have asked God to pardon me . . .'[12]

The conclusion of this affair coincided with Tolstoy's long-awaited discharge from the army and he decided to realize a hope he had long entertained – to go abroad. He left Petersburg on January 12, 1857.

III

Tolstoy reveled in Paris; he was made immediately at home there by aristocratic Russian families settled in the city, by touring cousins, and by Turgenev. In a letter to Russia he declared that he could not imagine a time when this great city would lose interest for him, and he singled out especially the social freedom of which he did not even have a comprehension in his own country. Besides visiting the usual tourist museums and sights, he also attended lectures at the Sorbonne, the theater, where only Racine provoked his scorn, and concerts that threw him into ecstasies, particularly the Beethoven, whom the French played like gods, he exclaimed.

Then came the revolt. As one of a crowd of sightseers at the public guillotining of a murderer, he was filled with horror. 'The insolent audacious desire to fulfill justice, the law of God,' he declared in a letter he hurried off to his writer-friend V. P. Botkin. He continued:

> The repulsive crowd, the father who explains to his little daughter the clever, convenient mechanism that does this, etc. Human law – nonsense! . . . I understand the laws of custom, of morality and religion . . . and I feel the laws of art that give happiness always; but for me, political laws are such a horrible lie that I do not see in them anything either better or worse. . . . I will never again look at such a thing and I will never anywhere serve any government.[13]

The next day Tolstoy fled Paris for Geneva. He picked it because Granny (Countess Alexandra Tolstoy) was there with the family of Grand Duchess Marie as the companion of her children. Used to his impressionable nature and extreme sensitivity, she dismissed his tirades on Paris and quickly restored his good humor – they were both enthusiasts, she said, who loved goodness but did not know how to follow it properly. During the next few weeks he visited her often and accompanied her on excursions to Vevey and Salève with her young charges who adored him. They climbed to Glion and at a hotel there, annoyed at what he regarded as the stuffiness of a crowd of English tourists (they 'are morally naked people and go about like that without shame'[14]), he organized an impromptu songfest with the help of Russian friends and directed and accompanied the singers at the piano, much to the delight of the 'stuffy' audience. After, he wrote in his diary: 'I'm so ready to fall in love that it's terrible. If Alexandra were only ten years younger! A fine nature.'[15]

With his base at Clarens, Tolstoy pushed out into the Swiss country-side in the late spring, at one time hiking with knapsack over the mountain roads accompanied by the eleven-year-old son of an ac-quaintance. Tolstoy's *Travel Notes* at this time reveals how extra-ordinarily observant he was of all aspects of nature and the intensely sensuous effect they had on him. The beauty of the twilight view at Clarens, looking across the lake to the mountains beyond, acts on him with the power of the unexpected: 'At that moment I wish to love, and I even feel love for myself, and I regret the past, hope for the future, and there is joy in me at being alive. I want to live forever and thoughts about death are filled with a childishly poetic horror.'[16] But the celebrated view of the Jaman seemed bare and cold and left him unmoved:

> I love nature when it surrounds me on all sides and extends
> unendingly, and when I am a part of it. I love it when I am
> surrounded by warm air, and when that air rolls away into the
> measureless distance; and when those same sappy blades of grass that
> I squash as I sit on them form the green of the boundless meadows;
> when those same leaves that flutter in the wind run their shadows
> across my face and form the line of the distant forest; when the same
> air that you breathe makes the deep azure of the illimitable heaven;
> when you do not exult and rejoice alone in nature, but around you
> buzz and whirl myriads of insects; and beetles, clinging together,
> creep about, and all around you the birds pour forth song.[17]

After a trip to Italy with Botkin and Druzhinin to visit art galleries and Roman ruins, Tolstoy returned to Clarens but soon left for Lucerne. There, at a fashionable hotel, he grew furious when guests, having enjoyed the performance from windows and balconies of a shabby street singer, turned their backs when he begged for money. Tolstoy ran out and brought him into the hotel as his guest and roundly berated any who objected. Granny, who arrived at Lucerne a few days later, found him still highly indignant. But when he told her that he had ordered supper and champagne for the singer, she sensibly remarked: 'I hardly think the guests or even the poor musician himself quite appreciated the irony of this action.'[18]

Tolstoy had intended to continue his travels to Germany, Holland, and to England and return to Russia by way of Constantinople and Odessa. But he got no farther than Baden-Baden where he lost so heavily at roulette that he had to borrow money from friends. At this point he decided to return to Russia and arrived in Petersburg July 30, 1857.

## IV

Tolstoy's eyes filled at the sight of his native birch trees and when he reached his estate he exclaimed: 'Delightful Yasnaya!' But the culture and refinement of Europe had left their impress, for he was soon decrying the patriarchal barbarism, thievery, and lawlessness of Russia. A sense of futility and boredom gnawed at him: 'The ideal is unattainable,' he wrote in his diary. 'I've already destroyed myself. Work, a small reputation, money. What for? Material enjoyment – also what for? Soon eternal night. It always seems to me that I shall die early.'[19] The periodical spiritual depressions that were to haunt him later had already begun.

Tolstoy spent most of his time during the next two years, apart from occasional visits to Moscow and Petersburg, at Yasnaya Polyana where he led the life of a country squire. He attempted to tackle estate management in all seriousness, assuming some of the functions of his bailiff and taking a practical interest in the details of farming. He even tried his hand at ploughing and professed to relish this hard labor. And he set out to improve the value of his timber land by tree-planting. In fact, he drew up a plan for large-scale reforestation in the district but failed to obtain government permission to carry it out. He also began now a regular policy of allowing his serfs to buy their freedom, and at a meeting of landowners he signed a resolution that favored emancipation of serfs with a just allotment of land. The city was a diversion, the country his solace, and he was never happier than when coursing the fields and woods in his favorite sport; in fact he almost lost his life at this time in a bear hunt. At night he played the piano, read, or enjoyed the old-fashioned company of Auntie Tatyana. Spring in the country, he wrote Granny, 'acts on me so powerfully that I often catch myself in the full blaze of dreaming I'm a plant that is just about to put forth its leaves with other plants, and will go on growing simply, calmly and happily in God's world.'[20]

Part of his contentment in the country may be attributed to his affair with a pretty married peasant girl, Aksinya Bazykin, which developed into an attachment more serious than the customary transient liaisons of master and serf. There are cryptic references to her in the diary: 'Today, in the big old woods. I'm a fool, a brute. Her bronze flush and her eyes . . . I'm in love as never before in my life.'[21] A son was born.

This illicit union, which tormented him with a sense of guilt amounting at times almost to physical suffering, was part of the reason for his trips to the city, for now more than ever he felt that he must marry. Though there were abundant opportunities with the daughters of fashionable families where he was a welcome guest, something still made him hesitate. However, he did remark to a friend about a charming little girl, daughter of the court physician, A. E. Bers, who took delight in the lively amusement he provided her: 'If Sonya were sixteen and not fourteen, I would propose to her at once.'[22] He had unwittingly singled out his future bride.

Tolstoy varied his social activities in Moscow with seeing close literary friends, such as Fet and the brilliant philosopher and jurist B. N. Chicherin who urged him to take an interest in science. He began to read geology and the curious scientific works of Michelet. After a vigorous argument with Chicherin on Christianity, Tolstoy set down the following comment which he would have found no reason to change during the remainder of his life: 'Christ did not impose but revealed a moral law that will always remain as a standard of good and evil.'[23]

Another religious interchange took place with Granny. At Easter he wrote her that he had tried the experiment of going to church but could not stand the motley crowd or the priest's unintelligible mumbling, and he jokingly asked her to impart to him a moiety of her own Orthodox faith. A deeply religious woman, as he was well aware, she sharply replied, with a touch of sarcasm, that he seemed to combine in himself 'every idolatry of heathendom. While adoring God in a sunbeam, in an aspect of nature, or in one of the innumerable aspects of His glory, you never understand that you must rise to the source of life to be enlightened and purified.'[24] She accused him of pride in disdaining simple worshippers and the priest and concluded on a note of love for him and with a prayer that he would find true humility which teaches more than all the so-called sublime thoughts and cravings for God.

The letter moved Tolstoy and he replied that he had been at fault. Then he tried to explain why he had long since put aside the traditional faith of his childhood. But in his spiritual struggle in the Caucasus, he added: 'I found that immortality exists, that there is love, that you have to live for others in order to be eternally happy.' He realized that these discoveries were in conformity with the Christian religion, yet when he searched the Gospels, he asserted, he did not find in them his conception of God. At moments, he wrote, he had a gleam of faith but no religion or dogma. 'Further,' he continued, 'with me religion is the outcome of life and not the reverse. Whenever I lead a good life, I feel religion near at hand and am quite ready to step into this blissful world; but when I lead a bad life, there seems to be no need for religion.'[25] In short, he could win his way to spiritual faith only through experience and his own intellectual conviction, a position which in most essentials he continued to adhere to in the future.

In his emotionally and intellectually troubled existence after his return from abroad, Tolstoy derived some comfort from literature. At the time of the widespread popular reception of *Sevastopol in December,* he had noted in his diary: 'Have only now reached a period of real temptation through vanity. I could gain much in life if I wished to write without conviction.'[26] The second Sevastopol sketch is evidence of his emphatic rejection of the temptation. When the article appeared in mangled censored form, a diary entry indicates his anger and his thought of abandoning writing, but he promptly adds: 'My sole and chief occupation, dominating all other inclinations and activities, must be literature. My aim is literary fame, the good that I can accomplish by my writing.'[27]

*Boyhood,* which lacks the evocative charm of *Childhood* yet contains some superb things such as the chapter on the storm, appeared in 1854 and was followed by its sequel *Youth* (1855, 1857), the least aesthetically satisfying of the three parts of Tolstoy's autobiographical novel (the fourth 'epoch' of the original plan never materialized), although there is much fine writing in it.

The third and last of Tolstoy's war sketches, *Sevastopol in August,* did not appear until he had left the Crimea (1856). Here he is much more a fiction writer than a war correspondent, for he tells the story of the Kozeltsov brothers whose contrasting natures in the face of varying military situations are admirably portrayed. In the manner of narration and the structure of the story one may discern influences of Thackeray whom Tolstoy had been avidly reading at this time. To connect the three Sevastopol sketches with as vast a novel as *War and Peace* may seem pointless, but there can be little doubt that in the treatment of war and in the characterization of military figures they do represent steps in the direction of his masterpiece.

In this same year (1856) were also published the short stories: *The Snowstorm*, *Two Hussars*, *Meeting a Moscow Acquaintance in the Detachment*, and *A Landowner's Morning*. Only *Two Hussars* deserves special notice. It reads well but is somewhat marred by the contrived contrasts of the father and son, and here again one may observe the possible influence of Thackeray. By this time Tolstoy felt that his literary position was strong enough for him to publish two volumes of his collected works, *Childhood and Boyhood* and *Army Tales*. The little notice they received upset him. The fact that the contents had previously appeared in a periodical probably had something to do with the reaction but even more so did the coolness of the liberal Petersburg writers and critics whom he had offended upon his return from Sevastopol. His chagrin is reflected in a diary entry: 'How I long to have done with magazines in order to write in the way I'm now beginning to think about art: awfully lofty and pure.'[28]

The several stories he wrote abroad and shortly after his return, which were intended to exemplify his new approach, brought him further disappointment. *Lucerne* (1857), based on the incident of the unrewarded street singer, sacrifices the conventional appeals of fiction to a didactic insistence on the incompatibility of organized society and the virtues of morality and art. It chilled his admirers and made them wonder what had happened to the author of *Childhood*. And so did *Albert* (1858) – at first rejected by Nekrasov – the story of a drunken violinist, which was apparently designed to reveal to 'conviction'-ridden *Contemporary* authors that society was really unable to understand and protect genuine art. *Three Deaths* (1859) definitely fortified the critics in their belief that Tolstoy's artistic powers were failing him. Intended to demonstrate the moral truth of pure art, the story contrasts the deaths of an aristocratic lady, a peasant, and a tree in an effort to exemplify dissonance with nature in the self-pitying old lady's passing and harmony with creation in the death of the peasant and the tree. There is more substance to his longer tale, *Family Happiness* (1859), Tolstoy's first treatment of love in fiction. The enchanting opening, an idyllic picture of dawning love in the young heroine, soon gives way, after her marriage, to the husband's patent preaching on a wife's obligation to subordinate her personal concerns to the larger duties of the family. His lordly admonitions recall Tolstoy's behavior in his courtship of Valerya Arsenev, an experience that no doubt had some influence on the writing of *Family Happiness*. Tolstoy sensed the story's failings, called it a shameful abomination, and tried – too late – to prevent its publication, at which point he decided he was finshed as a writer.

In considerable measure Tolstoy tended to relate the decline of his literary reputation to the current insistence on themes of social and political significance which, he felt, was undermining public taste for art. He thought of starting a magazine that would become the public's teacher in the matter of taste, but only in that. There were no supporters of the idea. In a brief speech on the occasion of his induction into the Moscow Society of Lovers of Russian Literature (February 4, 1859), he said in part: 'The majority of the public has begun to think that the problem of all literature consists only in the denunciation of evil, in the debate and correction of it, in short, in the growth of civic feeling in society.' Without utterly dismissing this approach, he nevertheless maintained: 'A literature of the people is its full, many sided consciousness, in which must be equally reflected popular love for goodness and truth, as well as popular contemplation of beauty in a given epoch of development.' And he ended with a statement that bears a striking resemblance to his main position in *What Is Art?* many years later: 'There is another literature, reflecting eternal and universally human interests, the most precious, sincere consciousness of the people, a literature accessible to every people and to all times, a literature without which no single people, gifted with strength and richness, has ever developed.'[29] The organization's president coldly replied that the literary artist must be a man of his own times and that in the present historical moment self-indictment acquired a special significance which every writer must realize.

In reality, Tolstoy's disillusionment with literature was simply one aspect of an intense intellectual and spiritual turmoil that had been working within him during the last seven years. His experiences in the Caucasus, the Crimean War, and his contacts with the culture and civilization of Western Europe had not so much changed him as they had tremendously accelerated his development. Varied reading had included more of the works of his old favorite writers of fiction and poetry, and some new names were added to the list, such as Rabelais, Cervantes, George Eliot, Goncharov, and Saltykov-Shchedrin. But his perspective was broadened and deepened more by sterner stuff – the Gospels, religious works of Khomyakov, Proudhon's *Qu'est-ce que la Propriété,* and various scientific, social, and historical works. Comments in the notebooks indicate the seminal nature of some of the ideas he garnered from this reading. For example, Proudhon's beliefs that private property is theft, government of man by man is oppression, and the union of order and anarchy is the highest form of society clearly reflect some of Tolstoy's views years later. He says of him in the note-books:

> While reading the logical, material Proudhon, his mistakes were as
> clear to me as the mistakes of the idealists to him. How often does
> one see the powerlessness of one's mind – always expressing one
> side; but it is better to see this one side in past thinkers and workers,
> especially when they complement each other. From this comes love,
> uniting all these views into one, and this is the simple infallible law of
> humanity.[30]

The observation points forward to Tolstoy's conception of universal love, and the notebooks suggest that he was already beginning to reckon with its principal obstacle – modern civilization. For he writes: 'Nationality is the one single bar to the growth of freedom,' and further, 'the absence of laws is possible, but there must be security against violence.'[31] He also condemns now the shedding of blood for any political gain and questions the very relevance of socialism. Then, suddenly, at this early stage, he advances the proposition that was to torment him in his old age: 'All governments are in equal measure good and evil. The best ideal is anarchy.'[32]

Tolstoy, full of bewildering contradictions, had by the age of thirty quite fully defined his personality and suggested the future direction of his thought and art. What followed was intense development of all aspects of the image that has already been presented. Subsequent emphasis, therefore, will be on the major activities of mind and art that define the greatness of his genius. In Tolstoy's progress, there was no 'continual extinction of personality,' which T. S. Eliot argues in his account of the artist's development, no widening of the chasm between 'the man who suffers and the mind which creates.' Quite the contrary, there is a very intimate connection between the facts of Tolstoy's life and nearly everything he created or did, whether it be in art or in moral, social, political, or religious writing or activity. In considering his main achievements, these connections will be briefly noted whenever they seem significant.

# 4

## Educator

I

At the end of his first European tour, in 1857, Tolstoy wrote in his diary: 'The idea came clearly and strongly into my head to start a school in my own village for the whole district, and general activity of that kind.'[1] The intention was forgotten during the next two years of absorption in literary endeavors, but he returned to it in 1859 when he grew disillusioned with his writing. For whom did Russian authors write? he asked. For themselves, for the cultured few. Masses of Russian peasants were illiterate. If they could not read his writings, then he would teach them. This, he now believed, was the first essential step towards the creation of a 'literature for the people,' an objective that would satisfy his desire for activity and moral influence.

Tolstoy started his school in a large room of the manor house at Yasnaya Polyana in the autumn of 1859, and some twenty village youngsters responded to his announcement that there they could receive instruction free. At that time rural education was mostly limited to the few children of parents who could afford to hire a village priest or an ex-soldier to teach the rudiments of reading and writing. Learning was by rote, blows were frequent, and little progress was made. Tolstoy insisted that education should be voluntary and free, and he tried to develop a pedagogical approach that was quite unique.

After six months of effort he wrote a friend, whose brother was Minister of Education, of his exciting experiment which had grown to fifty students and that the number was still increasing. Since only one per cent of seventy million people were literate, he pointed out, the value to Russian progress of roads, the telegraph, literature, and the arts was highly dubious. And he proposed the establishment of a Society for National Education which would set up public schools, design courses of instruction, train teachers in suitable educational methods, and publish a journal devoted to its own pedagogical ideals. Tolstoy hoped the friend would influence his brother to consider this project.

Nothing appears to have come of the idea, but perhaps he anticipated at this time writing for such a publication, for fragments of articles have survived among Tolstoy's papers, one of which begins: 'For every living condition of development, there is a pedagogical expediency, and to search this out is the problem of pedagogy.'[2] Like Rousseau, he calls for a fresh look at the whole development of education and its rationale. If he was influenced by Rousseau's emphasis on permissiveness in teaching methods, he rejected his belief that the general will of society, manifesting itself through the teacher, must in the end define the educational directions of students. Basically this is an anti-individualistic position, whereas for Tolstoy education had no ultimate aim and its primary expression was to be found only in individual freedom.

Aware that Western European and especially German educational theory dominated what Russian thinking there was in the field, Tolstoy soon grew convinced that he must inform himself of both the theory and practice of it at the source. His first session of teaching ended when his young peasant charges had to help their parents in spring farming, and Tolstoy took advantage of the interruption to set out for Europe in the summer of 1860. Another motive for the trip, on which his sister and her three children accompanied him, was to visit his beloved older brother, Nikolai, who was undergoing treatment for tuberculosis in Germany.

II

During the ten months that Tolstoy spent abroad on this occasion, he did not undertake what could be considered systematic modern research in depth in Western European educational theory and practice. Moreover, an objective approach to the various problems was difficult because of his own preconceived notions on education, his paradoxical and contradictory turn of mind, and his determination, which has already been stressed, of following his own independent and often original thought. However, he visited a considerable number of classrooms and queried administrators, teachers, and students in Germany, France, Switzerland, Belgium, and England, talked with educational theorists, made extensive notes on his experiences, collected quantities of the latest textbooks to take back to Russia, and read much in relevant or near-relevant material from Plato, Luther, Francis Bacon, Rousseau to Herbert Spencer, Pestalozzi, Friedrich Froebel, Wilhelm Riehl, and F. Diesterweg. The reactions of a peculiarly abrasive but powerful intellect to these many encounters with foreign educational theory and practice were bound to be significant.

It should be added that there were interruptions in Tolstoy's researches, such as a sightseeing trip to Italy, pleasant visits with the exiled Herzen in London and Proudhon in Brussels, stays with his sister and her children and his very sick brother. Finally, Nikolai's death at Hyères profoundly affected him and for weeks killed interest in everything else. Tolstoy wrote Fet that Nikolai awoke shortly before he died and whispered with horror: 'What is that?' And Tolstoy continued:

> That was when he saw it – the absorption of himself into nothingness. And if he found nothing to cling to, what then will I find? . . . As soon as man reaches the highest degree of development, then he sees clearly that it is all nonsense and deceit, and that the truth – which he still loves better than all else – is terrible. And when you look at it well and clearly, you awake with a start and say with terror, as my brother did: 'What is that?'[3]

Short, sharp comments on visits to schools in Leipzig and Kissingen pepper the diary – prayers for the king, everything learned by rote, terrified, beaten children, all seemed terrible to him. But the zest of the chase had seized him and he noted that the idea of experimental pedagogy agitated him so that he could scarcely contain himself. If the account of a conversation he had with Julius Froebel, nephew of Friedrich Froebel the celebrated founder of the kindergarten system, is any indication, Tolstoy's attitude towards his foreign sources of information must have been a disturbing combination of the polite eager searcher for knowledge and an arrogant chauvinist. For he made it clear that he belonged to no school of thought, had his own point of view on most educational problems, and that anyway Europeans did not understand the real failings of their own civilization. 'Progress in Russia,' Julius Froebel quotes him as saying, 'must come out of public education, which among us will give better results than in Germany, because the Russian masses are not yet spoiled by false education. . . . If education is good, then the need for it will manifest itself like hunger.'[4]

Tolstoy went on to visit schools at Soden, Geneva, and Marseille, and at all of them he was critical of the subjects taught and the dull, unimaginative way of teaching them. When he quizzed pupils they answered well what they had learned by heart but failed badly when he asked pertinent questions slightly off the beaten path. Pupils seemed unable to think or to apply the facts they had learned. However, after spending some time roaming about the streets of Marseille talking to youngsters and workers, he found them intelligent and surprisingly well informed. In such talks he gathered that they learned history from exciting popular novels, and politics and much other useful knowledge from newspapers, magazines, and discussions in their social organizations. He decided, in one of those provocative half-truths which he frequently invoked in his theorizing, that here was an unconscious school undermining a compulsory school and making its content almost of no worth. 'What I saw at Marseille,' he wrote, 'and in all other countries, amounts to this: everywhere the principal part in educating a people is played not by schools but by life.'[5]

Light praise tempered Tolstoy's usual asperity on things educational during his London sojourn. Although the temperament of the individual Englishman, so different from his own, annoyed him, he shared the continental admiration of the country's just laws, liberal thought, and democratic government. Some years later, for example, infuriated by a legal conflict he had with Russian authorities, he contemplated moving his whole family to England where, he asserted, everybody's freedom and dignity were assured. He lavished praise on the Kensington Museum and especially on free lectures by experts there, the themes of which had been suggested by practical questions of visitors (utility, he believed, was a primary consideration in education); he was enraptured by a lecture on education given by his literary idol Dickens; but he thought a three-hour speech by Palmerston in the House of Commons 'boring and meaningless' – Tolstoy read English well at this time, but it is doubtful that he could have passed secure judgment on the contents of a lengthy speech or lecture that he listened to.

He lost no time in applying to the Office of the Department of Education for permission to visit schools and his success in obtaining it may have been aided by Matthew Arnold, an inspector of schools then, whose acquaintance he seems to have made. In a later article, Tolstoy tells of one of his visits to a London school. For his edification the teacher offered an object-lesson exercise on the subject of cotton, and the pupils did well on a set series of questions. Guessing that the questions had been limited and the answers learned by heart, Tolstoy obtained permission to ask some questions directly on the subject and they stumped the students. He concluded that the object-lesson method was wrong since its scope was limited by the teacher's knowledge-preference and its ideal application would involve an impractical number of subdivisions of science. Tolstoy left London loaded down with more than fifty English textbooks and educational journals which have turned up in his library, many of them containing his notes.

Back on the continent, Tolstoy had a last fling at German schools, this time visiting several at Weimar and Gotha. He asked one instructor to explain his method of teaching history; requested the pupils in a class on composition to provide him with copies of their writing on an assigned theme; and he scornfully commented on the operation of a kindergarten class. In Berlin he made a point of meeting the minor German novelist Berthold Auerbach whose work, *Ein Neues Leben*, he had recently read with great enthusiasm. It is the story of a devoted rural schoolteacher who devises his own methods of instruction, believes that the purpose of education is to make prisons and coercive laws unnecessary, and allows his pupils to come and go and behave as they wish in the conviction that everything must be done to encourage in the student a feeling of his own worth. Here was an approach to education very close to Tolstoy's heart and one that undoubtedly had some influence on him.

After hiring a young German mathematics teacher to instruct at Yasnaya Polyana, Tolstoy set out on the return trip in April 1861. He had written his brother Sergei that he had been determined to learn everything of significance on foreign pedagogy so that no one in Russia would dare question his authority in this respect. His experiences abroad had convinced him that the French, English, and even the Americans, as well as the Russians, were much indebted to German educational theory, but in this scheme of things he believed that theory came first and the children were its victims. In fact, he had grown weary of theory and wanted to get back to teaching. 'My one aim,' he wrote in his notebook, 'is education of the masses. My one faith, which I dimly feel, binds me to the career of education.'[6]

III

Now, with a permanent operation in mind, Tolstoy obtained permission from Tula authorities to establish a private school at Yasnaya

Polyana at his own expense. For the purpose he provided a two-storey building connected with the manor house. It contained two large classrooms and additional space for an office, a science laboratory, a tiny museum, a workshop, and a few pieces of gymnasium equipment. Above the school entrance was the inscription: 'Enter and Leave Freely.'

There were three teachers besides himself, two lower classes and one advanced, and attendance averaged about thirty to forty peasant boys between the ages of seven to thirteen. A few girls came and occasionally several adults. The majority of the students were from Yasnaya Polyana but a few came from other villages. Absolute beginners were not encouraged to attend, and all instruction was free. Tolstoy remarks that some parents, because they did not approve of the methods of teaching and lack of discipline, took their children out and sent them to other village schools (where they had to pay) which the government promoted after the Emancipation Act of 1861. On the other hand, students continued to come to Yasnaya Polyana, often from distant villages, because they heard that excellent free instruction could be obtained there. Tolstoy frankly admits, on the basis of his conviction that a school and its methods must be adapted to the peculiar condition of the students, that his school might be the worst possible model for schools elsewhere.

Twelve subjects were initially offered: mechanical and graded reading, writing, penmanship, grammar, sacred history, Russian history, drawing, mechanical drawing, singing, mathematics, talks on natural sciences, and religion. But this program, he insisted, could always be modified on the basis of experience and in conformity with student needs, for he saw nothing sacrosanct in curricula. In fact, the teachers kept diaries on their school activities which were discussed at Sunday meetings, and often the program for the next week was substantially altered.

For almost two years Tolstoy worked with zeal as guiding spirit of the school, teacher, and as editor and frequent contributor to *Yasnaya Polyana*, a pedagogical periodical which he founded. It appeared monthly between February 1862 and March 1863. Apart from a few pieces by the other teachers and an occasional student, the bulk of the issues consists of twelve articles, some of considerable length, and a series of notes by Tolstoy which offer a detailed picture of the functioning of the school, as well as a presentation of his views on the theory and practice of education.

In these articles he ranges widely and freely over all levels of contemporary institutional learning in a spirit of irritated and irritating condemnation. He decries compulsory state schools abroad, curiously making a partial exception of the United States because its educational system had been imposed by democratically elected representatives of the people. The Russian tendency to adopt Western European educational ideas, he says, is like trying to feed meat to a horse. And he voices his opposition to newly contemplated national schools in Russia, to the old *Gymnasium*, and to the university because of their degree of compulsion and conformism, reverence for status, uniforms, punishment, stultified curricula, and their alienation from life and the needs of the people. Moreover, he makes a series of striking but often arbitrary judgments, such as the following: if one compares a peasant boy, who has had no education, with a gentleman's son who has been tutored for five years, superiority of mind and knowledge is on the side of the peasant; the peasant or workman is a much better specimen of humanity than the university-trained person who cannot get anywhere with his education; curricula should be changed if students want them changed; instruction ought to be an answer only to questions put by life; schools are presently established not for the convenience of children to study but in order that teachers may teach in comfort; the demand and form of education should emanate from the people rather than from governments; schools ought to be an implement of education but at the same time they should be an experiment for the younger generation, constantly giving new results.

In one of his long periodical articles, Tolstoy conveys the school's character and prevailing atmosphere by describing a typical day. On a cold winter morning the bell rings at eight and children emerge from their village huts. There is no dallying on the way. They carry no books, for homework is not assigned, writes Tolstoy, so they bring with them only their impressionable natures and the belief that it will be as jolly in school today as it was yesterday. While waiting for the teacher some play around the porch or slide on the hard snowy crust of the road, others go into the schoolroom. The teacher enters to begin a reading lesson. Yelling children struggle on the floor, shouting:

'The heap is not large enough!'

'You're squashing me, kids!'

'Don't pull my hair!'

'Good morning, Peter Mikhailovich!' several shout while continuing their roughhouse.

The teacher begins to distribute books to those who have followed him to the shelf. Some, still wrestling on the floor, also cry out for books. By degrees the heap becomes smaller, and when the majority have their books, the rest leap up and run to the shelf, shouting: 'Me too, me too!' If by chance a couple of children continue their noisy grappling on the floor, the others yell at them: 'You there, don't bother us. We can't hear a thing. Cut it out!'[7] The pair cease, run for their books, and still out of breath continue to swing their legs from unalloyed excitement as they search for the page number.

The martial spirit takes flight and the reading spirit reigns in the classroom. They sit wherever they please – on benches, tables, window sills, or the floor. There is no whispering or giggling, and it would take as much effort, remarks Tolstoy, to tear any one of them away from his book as it did to get him away from wrestling on the floor.

The two lower classes meet in one room and the advanced class occupies the second. Though the schedule may call for four lessons on different subjects before noon, there may be only three or two, and on entirely different subjects from those planned. At times teacher and students are so carried away that instead of one hour the class lasts three. Pupils shout for more and scold those who are tired of the lesson.

Ordinarily the teaching day consisted of seven one-hour classes, but with recesses and the long break during the peasant dinner at two, after-noon sessions might last until eight or nine. On the other hand, some-times before holidays or if a lesson proved to be boring – and there were many, Tolstoy confesses – several boys in an afternoon class might abruptly announce that they were going home. The sudden urge of a few quickly turns into a spontaneous exodus of all, despite the feeble protest of the teacher who had prepared for his lesson. Tolstoy remarks that such desertions did not happen often.

Since a high degree of permissiveness was a basic principle of his school, Tolstoy speculates at some length on the matter. He defended the student's right not to come or not even to listen to the teacher. The further students progressed educationally in a non-compulsory school, he contended, the more they themselves experienced the need for order and the greater the teacher's influence in this respect. The school, he said, ought not to interfere in that part of education which belonged to the family, nor did it have any right to reward or punish. Pupils should have as much freedom as possible to settle their own disputes as best they can. Although it might be disagreeable for the teacher if his students elected to go home, Tolstoy argued that such an occurrence only proved the significance of the many classes they voluntarily attended with pleasure.

A certain amount of disorder in the classroom, he believed, was useful and perhaps necessary. Children, like adults, were more receptive when in an excited state and therefore it was a mistake to regard the happy spirit of children in school as an obstacle. And he pointed out that students ordinarily became dissatisfied when disturbed in their lessons and were quite capable of taking their own measures to remedy it. When the instructor left the room in a strictly disciplined classroom in Germany, he observed, the children broke into an uproar and played all kinds of pranks. When he tried the same experiment, and eavesdropped, his undisciplined students behaved as though he were still in the room; they walked about freely, praised or corrected each other's work, or became entirely quiet, absorbed in their studies. The result seemed entirely natural to him among children who were not obliged to come to school, remain, or pay attention. Only in the absence of force or compulsion, he maintained, could entirely natural relations between teachers and pupils be established.

In fact, such natural relations appear to have been a most important factor in the success of Tolstoy's school. He discouraged persistent quizzing of an individual student before the class as inimical to such relations, and he tended to eliminate the practice of grading work and eventually abolished examinations as injurious, a deception, and an obstacle to instruction. Though he tells of pulling a student's hair once because of his inability to solve a simple arithmetic problem, he was firmly opposed to punishment. When the children decided to punish a pilfering pupil by sewing the label 'thief' on his jacket, Tolstoy could not bear to witness the boy's sufferings from the mockery of his play-mates and tore the label off, for he saw in this revenge rather than punishment.

Tolstoy's psychological understanding of the needs of students and their claims on attention inspired his youthful teachers in their work. In his pedagogical periodical are fetching accounts of his personal relations with these peasant lads. The bell rings, the lesson is over, and it is time to eat. He challenges the class to race him outdoors. The screaming, laughing children pelt him with snowballs and clamber on his back in an effort to pull him down and cover him with snow. Or on a moonless winter night he walks a few of them home on a roundabout way through the woods. In an atmosphere scary with thoughts of wolves, he tells of hair-raising Caucasian adventures. And he tries to answer their endless questions, such as why do they have to sing at school, why draw pictures? And they begin to speculate on such matters and reach a kind of conclusion that not everything exists for use, that there is also beauty, and that this is worth caring for. At the doors of their huts the boys are loath to part with him. Then there are memorable trips to the circus at Tula which they had never seen, and at Easter and Christmas he gathered them all together for entertainment and various gifts and goodies. But what they most enjoyed, when school was over at the end of the day, was to gather on the terrace of his house and listen to his army stories or his near-fatal bear hunt. Nor did he fail to prompt them into telling village tales of wizards and ghosts. Sometimes the conversation became serious, about belief in the supernatural, the horrors of killing in war, or even whether he should become a peasant, marry a village girl, and work the land as their fathers did. One suspects that this devotion to the master was an important factor, in a non-compulsory situation, in motivating these children to go to school and to learn.

## IV

Tolstoy regarded his school as a kind of pedagogical laboratory in which an emphasis on experimentation should be guided by a search for fundamental laws of life. Though curriculum and methods of teaching concerned him, in the end he began to wonder whether method was anything more than persistent trial and error. The important thing was to realize that teaching was an art and hence the struggle to perfect it must continue endlessly.

Accounts of experiments in the selection of curriculum and methods of reading fill many pages of the pedagogical periodical, but only the briefest mention of them can be given here. In the beginning classes made little progress in mechanical or graded reading. Student interest lagged despite several approaches employed by the teachers. Then, prompted by a spirit of competition with an older boy who read excellently, others, anxious to understand their texts, pledged that they would learn to read as well as he. They worked hard at the subject individually. More students were similarly stimulated and soon considerable progress was being made by most of the class. The experience drew from Tolstoy the generalization that the more convenient a method of instruction is for the teacher, the more inconvenient it is likely to be for students, and that the correct method is the one which satisfies the student. It also suggested to him the individuality of learning, that a method which is difficult for one may not be for another. Ultimately the several methods commonly employed then in conventional schools were used. What Tolstoy fails to comment on is whether the varying ages and previous preparation may have contributed to the problems encountered in teaching reading.

Writing was taught in a competitive fashion, somewhat the way grown-ups might teach a game to a group of children and it went along merrily. At first, pupils were instructed in how to recognize and draw letters of the alphabet in block fashion, then to spell and write whole words. Next one student would dictate anything that came into his head and the others tried to write it. Soon the outer walls of the schoolhouse and their huts were covered with letters and words, and finally they enjoyed the great satisfaction of composing whole sentences. Script was not insisted upon at the beginning; it should be learned, Tolstoy said, in a natural manner, a few letters at a time, under the guidance of older pupils. At first practising penmanship proved boring to the younger class. Then a few students in the advanced class, who had taken to copying out stories from sacred history in their exercise books, asked to take them home, perhaps to read to their parents. Soon the exercise books were torn, soiled, and scribbled over, and one of these students asked for fresh paper on which to recopy his stories. In no time the whole school was demanding clean paper, and a fashion for penmanship developed in which pupils competed with each other, the model alphabet in front of them, in copying out stories, eager to correct faults in one another's writing.

Though various experiments were tried to enliven instruction in the difficult Russian grammar, children went to sleep or even deserted the class. Tolstoy finally rejected the subject. Neither man nor child, he declared, likes to give up the living word to mechanical dismemberment. 'It seems to me,' he wrote, 'that grammar comes of itself as a mental, unprofitable gymnastic exercise, and language – the ability to write with skill and to read and understand – also comes of itself.'[8] He insisted, however, that his school regarded all known methods of teaching language as legitimate and they were used to the extent that they were cheerfully accepted by pupils.

Tolstoy makes the observation that to the teacher instructing in composition the simplest and most general approach appears to be easiest, whereas for students only the complicated and living are easy. The teachers quickly learned that compositions assigned on the description of a simple object aroused opposition. A pupil who will weep over a composition on a bench or a tree will excellently describe in his own words the story of the Biblical Joseph which he has heard or read. Accordingly, pupils were encouraged to select their own subjects, or themes were suggested on the description of an incident, the relations of persons, or retelling a story they had heard. Composition became a favorite and individual writers began to express themselves so definitely that the teachers introduced a popular experiment of asking the class to guess the names of the pupils whose compositions were read.

In one of his articles Tolstoy gives a striking example of his own inspirational teaching in composition. He suggested to the class that they write a story based on the proverb: 'The spoon feeds but the handle sticks in the eye.' One boy proposed that he write the story in competition with the class. He began it and soon two pupils were hanging on the back of his chair, looking over his shoulder, and criticizing what he wrote. They offered differing ways of continuing the tale, and he was so surprised by their imagination and sense of proportion that he urged them to dictate and he would write. The joint effort went on for some time and was continued the next day. Through a schoolboy prank the unfinished manuscript was destroyed, but aware of his keen disappointment, the two pupils offered to reconstruct what had been written and finish it themselves, which they did. Tolstoy was amazed at this discovery of such artistic and creative ability in two peasant lads, and after some revising he published the tale in the pedagogical periodical. The experience prompted him to offer advice in instructing children in composition: children cannot be taught to write and compose but only how to go about writing; suggest a variety of themes, not designed especially for children but only subjects that seem serious and interesting; give them only children's compositions to read and use as models, for they are likely to be more correct and more moral than those of adults; and never criticize penmanship, spelling, the logic or structure of the sentences, or the cleanliness of the copybook.

The main problem in teaching sacred history to children, according to Tolstoy, was that the standard Russian readers consisted of dull, incomprehensible retellings of Biblical stories. He taught the subject directly from the Bible, especially the Old Testament, which, he said, opened up a new world for his pupils. No other work united all sides of human thought in such a compressed poetical form as the Bible. When he read from it, he wrote, he completely took possession of the children; they fell in love with the book, with the study of it, and with him. He came to regard the Bible as an ideal text with which to begin the study of sacred history, suggested that it could serve as a model for children's readers in general, and made the interesting proposal that a translation of the Bible should be made into idiomatic Russian.

No such success attended the subject of universal history. Pupils had no interest in the ancient past and saw no reason why it should be thrust upon them. Even old Russian history left them cold. Then the experiment was tried, which students favored, of having one instructor give the early history of the country and Tolstoy the more modern until they met chronologically. His accounts of the Crimean War and Napoleon's 1812 invasion of Russia enraptured his pupils. Their pleasure, he realized, was rooted in an instinctive nationalist sentiment, and he concluded that historical interest in learners made its appearance after the artistic and that even then historical phenomena had first to be personified, just as tradition or life itself personify them. Although extensive efforts were made, neither could student interest be aroused in the study of geography beyond their natural curiosity in the geographical location of their own village. Travel, Tolstoy reasoned, and some knowledge of natural sciences might help. But he eventually came to the conclusion that formal teaching of both history and geography ought to be postponed until the university.

Some of the most interesting yet characteristically paradoxical theorizing in the pages of the pedagogical periodical concerns Tolstoy's views on teaching the arts to peasant children. He asks the basic question: Have children of the masses the right to art? And his simplistic answer is: Yes, because there are only thousands of us and millions of them. Then he goes on to assert that nearly all contemporary art is intended for people of leisure and artificial training and is useless to the masses whose demand for art is more legitimate. He rejects the stereotyped notion that in order to appreciate the beautiful a certain amount of preparation is necessary:

> It is only an excuse, a way out from a hopeless situation into which we have been led by the false direction of our art produced by one class alone. Why are the beauties of the sun, the human face, the sounds of folk songs, or an act of love and self-sacrifice accessible to all, and why do they demand no preparation?[9]

Nor did he hesitate to question whether the lyrics of Pushkin or the symphonies of Beethoven were as absolutely and universally good as art as the songs of the folk. The interests and efforts of his peasant pupils had taught him that the need to enjoy art was inherent in every human being and that this need had its rights and should be served. Moreover, he insisted that in art the teacher should always be prepared to give the 'younger generation a chance to work out something new, both in form and content.'[10] Here were ideas he was to return to years later in his treatise, *What Is Art?* (1898).

In introducing drawing and music, Tolstoy first had to overcome prejudices of his teachers who saw little point in subjecting peasant children to the appeals of art. At the most they believed that instruction should be limited to mechanical drawing and, in music, to the elements of church choir singing. In teaching drawing, Tolstoy thought it useless to oblige beginners to copy complete figures or pictures when they had no notion of their evolution. The child who does not learn to create himself, he asserted, will always imitate and copy in life because very few, once having learned to copy, are able to make an independent application of such knowledge. His own method was to evolve figures on the blackboard by drawing horizontal and vertical lines, dividing them into segments by dots and then connecting the parts. Pupils were asked to criticize the lines and the relation of one to the other as he drew them. Often they were requested to add lines or even to invent the shape of the figure. Soon they moved from symmetrical figures to shades and shadows and curved lines. Eventually, the best pupils, according to Tolstoy, were able to achieve a clear and correct handling of the pencil and created not only straight-lined figures, but also the most fantastic compositions of curved lines.

The Chevé System of teaching music to children, popularized but not invented by Emile Chevé, which Tolstoy had seen applied in Paris classes, markedly influenced his approach to instructing in this field. He used numerals in place of notes to indicate sounds and taught rhythm separately from pitch. After a few lessons the brighter students, he remarked, were able to write out the melodies of songs they knew, and to a limited extent they were able to read music at sight.

Unfortunately, Tolstoy left no accounts of his experiences in teaching two other subjects which he admitted into his curriculum – mathematics and 'talks on natural sciences.' He omitted all his material on them in the pedagogical magazine because of lack of time and of space. There is simply a passing reference to the fact that his students evinced a horror for the study of mathematics and analysis.

## V

Tolstoy had introduced his pedagogical periodical with a note to readers in which he invited criticism. A few progressives attacked him for denigrating the advanced ideas of their favorite Western European theorists, and several conservative educators dismissed his views as altogether too extreme. Apart from these and some thin praise on certain features of his school, his periodical was little noticed. It is safe to say that if the majority of professional Russian educators had been aware of Tolstoy's theory and practice and the freedoms he advocated in teaching children, they would have regarded him as excessively radical, verging on anarchy, and a positive threat to national education and the authority of the state. In truth, the government, aroused by rumors of subversion about Tolstoy and his young teachers, ordered a police search of Yasnaya Polyana during the absence of the master. All that turned up was that the resident passport of one of the young instructors was a bit out of order. And in October 1862, the Minister of the Interior complained to the Minister of National Education that the general direction and spirit of Tolstoy's pedagogical periodical perverted fundamental values and morality, and he requested that the censor's attention be directed to this. Happily, the Minister of National Education took a more enlightened view, for he advised that Tolstoy's published educational ideas might better be corrected in professional journals than by the prohibition of the censor. Perhaps the fears of the Minister of the Interior had some justification, for in his articles Tolstoy had been stressing society's false morality and declaring his conviction that the mass of people could exist without the educated class and government, but the educated class could not exist without the masses.

Despite the cloud of official suspicion over Tolstoy's concern for peasant education, by the end of the next year thirteen rural schools had been set up by peasants in the neighborhood of Yasnaya Polyana with government encouragement. Peasants in the Tula district appealed to Tolstoy to help them find teachers, and he recommended a number, most of them young men who had been dismissed from their universities during the radical student movement of 1862. They became eager disciples of his pedagogical approach, and from statements of some of them, they grew passionately devoted to him, for he inspired in them a love for these peasant children and set an example of self-sacrificing service in the cause of educating them.

Towards the end of 1862 Tolstoy's zeal for his Yasnaya Polyana school began to wane. One reason, no doubt, was his courting an eighteen-year-old-girl, Sofiya Andreyevna Bers, whom he married on September 23 of that year. In addition, this extensive and absorbing educational experiment had unintentionally contributed to his further career, for in the end it acted as a kind of catharsis of his literary disillusionment three years before and left him once again anxious to resume his artistic writing.

## VI

Educational activity, however, had gained too firm a hold on Tolstoy to be dismissed for good, perhaps because he felt that his ideas in the field had never received the recognition they should. After ten years of marriage, absorbed with rearing a family, estate improvements, and the writing of *War and Peace*, his thoughts turned once again, in 1872, to opening a school at Yasnaya Polyana. The fact that he now had children of his own to educate may have had some influence on his decision.

Connected with the endeavor was a project that had been in his mind for some time: 'First Book for reading and a primer for families and schools, with direction to teachers, by Count L. N. Tolstoy.' Soon published as *ABC Book* (1872), it was based on the pedagogical theories he had developed and was designed, he said, for the teacher who loved both his students and his calling. A complete curriculum for beginners, the work has sections on reading and writing with drawings and typographical devices to aid in spelling and pronunciation, and sections on natural sciences and arithmetic. He stresses the importance of effective examples and exercises which he restricts in scope and difficulty according to the limitations of the pupils and their daily lives. In the reading selections he labored over the style and artistic effects of folk tales, legends, and historical narratives many of which he translated from foreign languages. Some of the stories are his own and are told with much of the artlessness of the literature of the folk. Two of them, *A Prisoner of the Caucasus* and *God Sees the Truth but Waits*, he later asserted were among the best of his works.

Tolstoy hoped for success after so major an effort, but critics, deciding that the *ABC Book* was an attack on accepted educational methods, damned it for opposing to a pedagogical system of reason one of faith, to a system of science one of instinct and imagination, and to a system of conviction and ideas one of moral principles. In the first few months the book sold only four hundred copies. He was deeply disappointed and returned to teaching in his school which served as a proving ground for the methods he advocated in his *ABC Book*.

Shortly thereafter (June 1873), he turned again to the public in matters educational with a letter to a Moscow newspaper to object to certain aspects of the German *Lautiermethode*, the phonetic system widely used by Russian schools to teach children to read. And he also invited a group of village teachers to Yasnaya Polyana to induce them to apply his own method.

One result of this renewed activity was a polite request from the Moscow Committee on Literacy to appear before them and their guests to explain his educational ideas. He accepted. About a hundred people were present, many of them eminent pedagogues, who were no doubt more attracted by Tolstoy's name as the celebrated author of *War and Peace* than by any réclame he had achieved as a specialist in education. With a sudden show of temperament he refused to favor this distinguished audience with a forthright exposition of his methods of teaching and restricted himself to answering questions which appears to have thwarted their quest for illumination. However, he did agree to a practical demonstration of his teaching in a Moscow school, which also proved to be inconclusive. Then the Committee on Literacy proposed a test of both approaches to which he agreed. Two groups of illiterate Moscow children of similar ages and social backgrounds were provided. An expert in the prevalent phonetic system of reading was designated to teach one group and a Tolstoy-trained instructor the other for a period of seven weeks. At the conclusion the decision of the examiners was not unanimous, but a majority voted that pupils taught by the conventional approach excelled in all three subjects – reading, writing, and arithmetic.

Tolstoy was present when the full Committee on Literacy met to appraise the results. He protested – and with some justification from his point of view – that the competition had been conducted under the worst possible conditions. And on this occasion he did present a detailed account of his system of teaching in which he declared at the end that he had learned from peasant youngsters and not from pedagogues what and how to teach successfully. Schools, he insisted, must satisfy the needs of the people and not what theory-ridden educators think they need.

This interesting but hardly favorable experience with a group of recognized authorities prompted Tolstoy to attempt to set the record straight on his own views before a much larger audience. He wrote a lengthy article, *On National Education*, in the form of a letter addressed to the Committee on Literacy, and took the precaution to publish it in the popular periodical *Notes of the Fatherland* (September 1874). In most respects it is a reaffirmation of his position expressed in his various pedagogical articles twelve years before. With uncompromising tenacity he excoriated both the phonetic and visual methods, employed in Russian elementary schools, and their teachers, influenced by German pedagogical theory, who failed to understand the needs of the Russian masses. He dogmatically asserted that teachers had no right to offer subjects other than those which parents wanted their children to learn. As for how to teach, he repeated his old formula: the only criterion for pedagogy is freedom, the only method is experience.

Unlike all his previous articles on education, this was the first to attract widespread attention and to provoke a large number of public reactions and letters. With few exceptions the experts damned him as a 'pedagogical nihilist,' but there were many sympathetic responses from laymen.

Elated with this degree of public recognition, Tolstoy quickly endeavored to exploit it by publishing (February 1875) a *New ABC Book*, shorter, cheaper, more practical, and – he indicated in the foreword – adaptable to any method of teaching. This was not an admission of failure, for multiplicity of methods, based on experience, had been his position all the time. Now he achieved a signal success, for the Ministry of National Education recommended the work and it was widely adopted by schools and ran into large editions. He soon followed this up by publishing four children's *Readers*, compiled largely from material taken from the first *ABC Book*. The variety, charm, and artistic appeal of these tales, and no doubt the inexpensive price of the *Readers*, won a vast audience.

Tolstoy's old dream of exercising a real influence on Russian elementary education now expanded. He inquired of the Minister of Education whether the government would consider two plans he had in mind, one on instruction in the schools, and another for training teachers. While waiting for an answer, he accepted an appointment to the Educational Committee of the County Council, in itself some measure of official approval of his expertise in these matters. For a time the official task of inspecting schools in his district absorbed him. According to his own testimony, he found a world of poetry in this work which brought him face to face with multitudes of ragged children, thin, dirty, with bright eyes, and with such angelic expressions that he was seized, he said, with the anxiety and terror he would have experienced in seeing people drown. He could not tear himself away from these living creatures to bother about imaginary ones, he remarked when taxed with failure to complete *Anna Karenina* because of his preoccupation with schoolchildren.

Not until 1876 did the Ministry approve of Tolstoy's plan for a teachers' training seminary at Yasnaya Polyana, for he strongly believed that teachers of peasant children should be trained to provide the kind of education that would not instill alien desires in their pupils or render them unfit to perform the duties which their position in life required. It never seemed to occur to him that he was advocating a kind of aristocratic doctrine of class stratification, one inevitably opposed to social progress. But then he was no believer in the religion of progress. Outside of faith, he said, nothing proves the necessity of progress. He called the proposed teachers' seminary his 'university of bast shoes.' Tula government officials promised financial assistance in return for a number of tuition-teaching scholarships. And Tolstoy had one wing of the manor house renovated to provide classrooms for the opening in September 1877. However, only twelve candidates applied. The small number discouraged him and he refused to open his 'university of bast shoes.'

This was Tolstoy's final effort to contribute to education in Russia on his own terms. A long and arduous chapter of eighteen years in the history of his civic conscience had come to an end. He never regretted the activity. Six years before his death he wrote of his teaching experience: 'The brightest period of my life gave me not female love, but love for people, for children. This was a wonderful time, especially in contrast to the preceding gloom.'[11]

And for a number of students he taught and the teachers he influenced, it also seemed to have been an unforgettable experience. One of his favorite pupils, looking back over a span of fifty years, recalled his schooldays at Yasnaya Polyana:

There I am a ten-year-old schoolboy, there is young, jolly Leo Nikolayevich; there I am sliding down the steep hill, romping with

Leo Nikolayevich, covering him with snow, playing ball, walking in the woods and fields, and having conversations on the terrace, telling our tales about the wizards. . . . The remembrance of those happy, bright days of my life I have never lost and never will. The love for Leo Nikolayevich that burned within me then still burns brightly in my soul and illumines my life.[12]

## VII

Was it Tolstoy's capacity to inspire love among his students and teachers that made his pedagogical world go around? Or like any born teacher – and he certainly was that – would he not have succeeded if he had never had a theory and method to rub together? In the circumstances there was something arrogant in his pretensions to evolving a systematic theory of education which, if adopted, would improve if not transform the whole pedagogical practice of Russia. In actuality, there was nothing very systematic or comprehensive about his educational writings, surely nothing that could be correctly described as a philosophy of education. Nevertheless, Tolstoy made a significant contribution to the subject which must be pieced together from a mixture of often brilliant, pragmatic and romantic thinking, from keen psychological observations, and from the practical experience he accumulated in directing and teaching in a small and quite special country school.

Though he considered education as history and therefore without any final end, he defined it variously: a knowledge of facts and their correlation; that activity of man which has for its base the need of equality and the invariable law of educational progress – by equality here he meant that success in learning a given subject is obtained when the pupil achieves equality in the instructor's knowledge of the subject. He deprecated the commonly held belief that a student should be educated to conform to the *mores* of the society in which he lives. Rather, he maintained, a student should be educated to prepare himself for a creative life in terms of the inherited values of society and, if necessary, to reshape that society to meet new needs and challenges. But what he found most objectionable was the compulsory aspect of state-dominated education and the fact that the student, who should be the chief concern, was lost sight of by administrators and teachers. All authoritarianism and imposed discipline that creates fear in the student, he deplored.

Curriculum should be dictated by student needs and not by tradition or convention. Courses selected must take into consideration the realities of the student's world. Though courses should not be designed to prepare him for a specific vocation, they should have some relation to skills which all must acquire. Nor did Tolstoy see any virtue in completeness or comprehensiveness in the structuring of a curriculum.

For Tolstoy the best teacher was one who knew the explanation of what bothered the student. He was less interested in the teacher's scholarship than in his human qualities, and he expected him to be something of an artist with sharp psychological insights. The teacher must also be independent, original, and an educational improviser, capable of stimulating students in those aspects of culture which he thought valuable. In the classroom the teacher should be a free agent, teaching what he wished and as long as he thought necessary. He must listen and modify what he hears from his students and not simply talk at them. Nor should the teacher confine the process of education to assigned material but rather endeavor to emancipate the mind and emotions of the students during teaching and after it has ended. A primary fault that Tolstoy detected in conventional schools was the teacher's failure to relate learning to life in general, and he expected his own teachers to be vitally aware of the real world and to prepare students to grow and flourish in it.

Perhaps Tolstoy's most radical innovation was his conviction that students must become the central focus of all educational planning which should be based on a psychological understanding of their needs. His own educational hypotheses were formulated by the exercise of common sense, psychological observation, and his trial-and-error experiments among the students of his school. He never lost sight of the fact that he was dealing with children, essentially good, curious, eager to grow up, youngsters whose individual interests and desires should be encouraged, rather than distorted or evaded, and whose spirit and originality should be maintained and enriched by education. Throughout his theorizing he stressed that the student's psychological reactions to the learning process were the best indicators of what and how he would study, as well as the teacher's surest guide in directing the youngster's learning. He had one aim in education, to attain the greatest harmony possible in the child in the sense of truth, beauty, and goodness. The everlasting error of all pedagogical theories, he remarked, is to neglect this harmony by pushing the thing the student makes most progress in and mistaking it for the sole aim.

In Tolstoy's relations with students the feature that provoked most criticism during his lifetime was permissiveness. In this connection he maintained that to develop what he called the 'spirit' of a school was all-important and that once achieved he cautioned his teachers to avoid destroying it. Spirit, he said, is always in inverse relation to compulsion and order and communicates itself from student to student and even to the teacher who ought to strive to stimulate it. When animation is so strong that it interferes with the teacher's conduct of a class, Tolstoy argues that nothing could be more desirable if the animation is connected with the subject being taught. But if it is caused by something else, then the fault is the teacher's for not managing the animation properly.

One hesitates to claim too much for Tolstoy's influence as an educational reformer. However, his more commonsensical aims and the values that underlie them, especially his belief that learning should be intrinsically enjoyable to students, antedate by several decades the well-known views and practice of the pragmatists in the development of 'progressive education' by John Dewey and his disciples. More significant are the striking similarities between Tolstoy's thinking and practice in the field and those of many experts involved in the sweeping revolutionary changes in education today. Present theorizing on a purely student-oriented education, opposition to subordinating the whole educational way of life to centralized administration, the demand that schools and their staffs be held responsible for failures in learning, the close relationship of life and education, and the encouragement of permissiveness in the classroom – these and other modern emphases reflect Tolstoy's program. An American expert plainly echoes Tolstoy when he declares that the time has come to give up asking students to adjust to their educational institutions but rather to adjust the institutions so that they will fit the needs of the students.

In fact, one of the answers to the turmoil today is to set up schools that will serve as models for so-called 'alternative education,' such as the 'free schools,' which are frankly influenced by Tolstoy, as well as other experimenters, in using methods that are based on observed needs of children's growth. Like Tolstoy's school at Yasnaya Polyana, they are kept small so that pupils and teachers can have ready access to one another, personal relationships replace arbitrary discipline, the absence of coercion makes room for the development of morality and ethics and these in turn foster human relations which are the proper setting for the growth of the young. Nor are the methods and spirit in the new

British Infant Schools, which have inspired a similar movement in the United States, unrelated to the theorizing and some of the methods and psychological practices of Tolstoy.

In truth, Tolstoy would feel quite at home in the demand today for radical educational change in the Western world, but then he was destined ever to be a prophet in his original endeavors instead of what he most wanted to be – an influence for good in his own time.

# 5

## *War and Peace*

Vasily Botkin, concerned with Tolstoy's desertion of artistic work in his preoccupation with educational problems, wrote their mutual friend Fet: 'Without some firm ground under one's feet, it is impossible to write. That is the reason why he cannot write, and this will continue to be the case until his soul finds something on which it can rest.'[1] There was an element of truth in this judgment, for in marriage Tolstoy's soul found something on which it could rest – an ideal of family happiness which had been one of his objectives for years.

A pretty, inexperienced city-bred girl, Sofya (Sonya) Andreyevna Bers found it hard at first to become accustomed to country living at Yasnaya Polyana. Before marriage he had given her his diary to read, probably a misguided test of her love for him. His various past affairs with women recounted there she forgave him. But she was understandably hurt and also jealous, a feeling she never quite got over. Almost twice her age, Tolstoy's well-worn bachelor ruts of self-sufficiency annoyed her at times. And with his conservative ideas on marriage, he seems to have expected Sonya to make herself over in his image. However, they were deeply in love. The commonplace reality of daily life in the country quickly banished her romantic storybook notions of marriage. Soon she was happily and efficiently running the estate office and taking charge of all the accounts, while he busied himself with agricultural improvements such as bee cultivation and sheep herding. For he now looked forward to becoming a family man: the first of thirteen children, a son Sergei, was born nine months after their marriage. They had surmounted the early trials of adjustment and their love gradually began to assume a new aspect of greater calm and strength. Tolstoy's strong emotional impulses had been localized and the family happiness that he had eventually realized temporarily resolved the inner struggle of his nature. The school was discontinued and now that his thoughts and energies had once again been freed, he entered upon the greatest creative period of his life.

## II

Shortly after his marriage Tolstoy finished a short novel, *Polikushka* (1863), which his educational activities had interrupted months before. A powerful performance, his first to deal solidly with the peasantry, it is the tale of a wayward serf in whom the mistress of the estate, against all advice, continues to show faith. His joy over her willingness to entrust him with an errand to town to fetch a sum of money is transformed into utter despair when he accidentally loses it on the way back. Aware that no one in the village will believe him if he tells the truth, he commits suicide. The tragic incident gains impressive credibility by virtue of Tolstoy's remarkable realistic handling of Polikushka, the other characters, the events involved, and the whole village setting reeking with peasant superstition. Here Tolstoy is the pure story-teller, eschewing autobiographical elements or personal thesis-solving, bent solely on bringing out the moral irony of life's twists of fate. And for the first time he adapts his language in a consistent and effective manner to the speech patterns of characters not of his own class. It is little wonder that Turgenev, after reading *Polikushka*, wrote Fet that he marvelled at the strength of Tolstoy's huge talent: 'There are pages that are truly amazing. . . . He is a master! A master!'[2]

At about this same time (1862), Tolstoy also completed his short novel, *The Cossacks* (1863), which he had conceived ten years earlier and had been pecking away at ever since. Perhaps it would never have been finished if he had not desperately needed a publisher's advance to pay off a gambling debt. Originally planned as a long novel designed to give a truthful picture of the Caucasus and its people which would correct the conventional Russian image, *The Cossacks* went through many alterations before it reached the final shortened form we now have.

It is largely the story of Olenin, who, in 1852, seeks escape from the boredom of fashionable Moscow society to live among the Cossacks in a Caucasian village. Olenin's struggle between the social and moral values of his former sophisticated way of life and those of simple, amoral Cossacks resembles Tolstoy's during his stay in the Caucasus. And the characters Olenin becomes involved with are based on natives Tolstoy knew well: the old reprobate Daddy Eroshka who thinks it no sin to have fun with a pretty girl, scorns all religion as a fraud, and lives nostalgically on memories of dashing deeds of war and dangerous feats of hunting; the fiery young Cossack Lukashka who kills Chechens, steals horses, and gets drunk; and his sweetheart, the beautiful Maryanka, who rejects Olenin as a non-Cossack incapable of identifying himself with their emancipated life. Like Tolstoy, Olenin is unable to merge himself with these Cossack 'children of nature.' For a time their unspoiled existence transforms him into a philosophical reasoner, a kind of Rousseauistic 'natural man' who seeks personal happiness in terms of self-sacrifice and love for others, but in the end he reverts to type, leaves the village, and returns to his regiment.

*The Cossacks,* a very superior accomplishment, concluded Tolstoy's first literary period. It is a well-told story, peopled with a number of memorable characters, and richly varied stylistically and descriptively. Though some radical reviewers criticized the lack of social content and its attack on the cultured society to which Tolstoy himself belonged, most readers praised it highly. Fet raved over it. Turgenev pronounced it the best thing in the language, and Tolstoy's close friends hailed his return to print.

It should be mentioned that at about this same time (1863) Tolstoy also wrote *Strider, the Story of a Horse,* which was not published until 1885. It is an attractive and unusual short story of the life and death of an old piebald gelding, told mostly by the horse. Tolstoy, in a remarkable manner, humanizes the animal by projecting himself into its consciousness, in the course of which the evils of modern society are satirized.

At this time brief comments in Tolstoy's diary reflect a mounting artistic urge to create something truly formidable. In one entry he mentions that it would be natural for him to tackle a work of epic proportions; in another, that he could not remember having such a powerful desire to write; and shortly before the birth of his first son he jotted down that he had been reading in Goethe and that thoughts for fiction fairly swarmed in his mind. Tolstoy's creative energies were already prepared to grapple with the elaborate design of *War and Peace.*

## III

Though E. M. Forster, like so many distinguished novelists and critics, thought *War and Peace* the greatest novel ever written, he also regarded it as an 'untidy book.'[3] The judgment of untidiness seems a bit harsh in terms of the finished product's inner harmony or, for that matter, in terms of the conception and gestation of the novel, and the infinite pains Tolstoy took in all details of planning, characterization, and style during almost seven years of labor, in the course of which he accumulated discarded drafts and notes that print up to more pages than the huge novel itself.

The planning of *War and Peace* as reflected in the early drafts is very complex, thematically and chronologically, and the confusion has resulted in differences of opinion among those who have studied the novel's genesis.[4] As early as 1857 Tolstoy appears to have contemplated a novel on the Decembrist Revolt of 1825 which was crushed by Nicholas I, but anything he may have written on the subject then has disappeared. In 1863 he returned to the subject which he now conceived as a trilogy. The first volume was to center on 1812, a time in which the future Decembrists imbibed liberal fervor from the West during their service in the Napoleonic Wars; the second volume was to concentrate on 1825, the year of the revolt; and the last volume was to concern the return of a Decembrist hero from Siberian exile in 1856, when the conspirators were amnestied by Tsar Alexander II. Now, in 1863, Tolstoy elected to begin this grandiose project with the third or 1856 volume. He wrote four fascinating chapters on the return of his exiled hero, who might well be considered as a kind of reformed revolutionary, Pierre Bezukhov at the age of sixty-five, for it may be remembered that at the end of *War and Peace* the stage is being set for Pierre's involvement in the Decembrist Revolt of 1825, which presumably would have been the subject of the second volume of the trilogy. There is some evidence that what Tolstoy had in mind at this stage was a contemporary political novel, and he may actually have regarded this emphasis as providing him an opportunity to respond to what he considered the liberal political cant of writers associated with the periodical the *Contemporary*.

In the early drafts of *War and Peace*, Tolstoy tells us that he discontinued this initial effort on the Decembrists because he could not identify himself emotionally and factually with his aging hero of 1856 and felt it necessary to probe his thoughts and activities during the period of his youth, a process of historical devolution to a point in time where *War and Peace* begins. Soon he was involved in a conception and characters quite different from those with which he had started. Something of his uncertainty about where to begin, chronologically, as well as his continued enthusiasm for the subject, are suggested in a letter to Granny on October 17, 1863: 'I have never felt my mental and even all my moral faculties so free and ready for work. And this work now exists. It is a novel covering the years from 1810 to 1820 which has entirely occupied me since autumn. . . . Now I am an author with all my soul. I write and meditate as never before.'5 (Actually, *War and Peace* concerns the years from 1805 to 1820.)

However, the more than dozen drafts of the first chapter and of others that followed in his altered design indicate that the political emphasis connected with the novel on the Decembrists was not easily eliminated, for it still mingles with attempts to begin with social characterizations of the earlier period he was now concerned with. But gradually political content was pushed more into the background and happy scenes of family life took center stage. During the first year and a half of writing, little space was devoted to war and then not in terms of its philosophical or historical implications but in its effect on his characters. And in the early drafts there was more sensationalism in events and the emotions expressed are more extreme than those in the final version of the novel. Old Prince Bolkonsky has a serf mistress and several illegitimate children, Natasha is really seduced by Anatole Kuragin, even the very proper Nikolai Rostov has a mistress, and it was hinted that Helene had incestuous relations with her brother. Though he early outlined in his notes most of the main fictional characters, a few such as Prince Andrei and Karatayev do not appear to have occurred to him as yet, and in some instances the relations of characters to each other were considerably altered to conform with later developments in the action. In fact, when the first thirty-eight chapters of the work appeared serially in *The Russian Messenger* (February and March 1865) under the simple title *1805*, Tolstoy insisted in an unpublished introduction that the work in progress was not a novel in the conventional sense in which the genre was understood in Europe. In this he was partly right, for what he was writing added dimensions of time and space, seriousness and imagination, and a richness of variety in thought and emotions that transcended the genre as it was then known. He literally was on the way to creating a new form of the novel.

Nor did the publication of the next installment the following year, which carried the story only through 1805, give a clear indication of the great historical sweep and the many complications in the lives of the characters that were to come, although in what he had published up to this point he had gone much beyond the early drafts in developing techniques of narration and in perfecting his style in the full spirit of the final version. Yet his notes propose an ending quite different from the one he ultimately used and which would have brought the work to a conclusion much earlier. In fact, he expected to complete the novel as early as 1867 and planned to publish it under the title *All's Well That Ends Well*.

It is difficult to ascertain from the extensive notes and drafts precisely when Tolstoy grasped the final design, external limits, and ultimate historical purpose of his masterpiece. A diary entry on March 19, 1865, very possibly hints at fresh inspiration and a new emphasis and direction:

> I read with delight the history of Napoleon and Alexander. At once
> I was enveloped in a cloud of joy; and the consciousness of the
> possibility of doing a great thing took hold of my thoughts – to
> write a psychological novel of Alexander and Napoleon and of all
> the baseness, phrases, madness, all the contradictions of these men and
> of the people surrounding them.[6]

Further entries reaffirm this purpose, and at about the same time Tolstoy began attending Moscow gatherings of intellectual friends where there was much discussion on the philosophy of history, especially on the relation of individual freedom to historical necessity and the factor of causality in history. No doubt Proudhon's works, including *La Guerre et la paix,* which Tolstoy knew, were also discussed at these meetings. Although it may be argued on the basis of early drafts that the War of 1812 and the struggle between Napoleon and Alexander had been part of the design from the beginning, it seems more likely that this may have been so then because of their relevance to the prior plan for a trilogy on the Decembrists. However, the treatment of these subjects from the point of view of Tolstoy's developing theory of history seems to be a later and most significant alteration of his original conception of the novel. In any event, the new emphasis expanded the scope of the work, which he now finally entitled *War and Peace*. Serial publication was abandoned for the book, but the final volume did not appear until 1869.

Tolstoy's absorption in the work was intense as though (as his wife said) this greatest creation of his genius must be superb. The amount of historical research he did has perhaps been exaggerated, but he read quantities of material and impressed members of the Bers family in

Moscow to read for him in the libraries there and take notes. And he made an excursion to Borodino to go over the field and even drew up his own plan of the battle there in 1812. Though he did not hesitate to borrow directly from books and articles, the amount of historical background and local color obtained from published sources was not extensive. Often he depended on archives of the Volkonsky and Tolstoy families, and life at Yasnaya Polyana and of his wife's family in Moscow provided settings and scenes for country and city existence of the Bolkonskys and Rostovs. Tolstoy's family, relatives, and friends were drawn upon directly or in a composite manner for characters in *War and Peace*: close parallels may be discerned between grandfather Volkonsky and old Bolkonsky, Tolstoy's father and Nikolai Rostov, his sister-in-law Tatyana Bers and Natasha Rostov. Not a little of Tolstoy himself is reflected in the characterizations of both Prince Andrei and Pierre Bezukhov, especially in the moral conflict between them which recalls the inner struggle that had been going on in Tolstoy since his youth. He distrusted writers who invented 'reality'; he always contended that it was more difficult to portray real life and people artistically than to invent them.

At first Sonya grew jealous of her husband's total absorption in his massive novel, but when he asked her to make clear copies of his nearly illegible manuscripts she soon developed a passionate interest in *War and Peace*. Besides copying, she corrected grammatical slips, offered criticism of the work in progress, and before long became an invaluable assistant in Tolstoy's literary endeavors. The consciousness of serving a genius and a great man, she wrote in her diary, gave her strength for anything. Sonya needed the strength, for by the time *War and Peace* was finished in 1869, she had borne three more children, and in addition to helping on the novel, often copying revised chapters a number of times, she also continued to supervise the affairs of the household and the estate and tried to protect her husband from all outside interruptions and cares while he wrote daily for hours at a time in his study. These years were perhaps the happiest in their long married life. In the autumn of 1864, Tolstoy entered in his diary: 'Relations between Sonya and me have been strengthened, consolidated. We love, that is to say, we are dearer to each other than all other people in the world.'[7] Indeed her aid and the ideal atmosphere she created contributed to the successful completion of her husband's great masterpiece, and her reward was their mutual joy over the national acclaim that greeted its publication.

## IV

Despite the magnificence of *War and Peace,* detractors were not lacking in his own day and since. Some have complained that there is no single hero. Tolstoy would have answered that for the artist who elects to treat man's relation to all sides of life, there can be no heroes, only men. Others regret that there is no subject in the novel other than life itself, which is not an unusual characteristic of some major classics of Russian fiction. But if what is meant by subject is the absence of conventional plot, Tolstoy appears to have a substitute for it which does perform the function of aesthetically unifying his vast design. In the drafts is an unusual introduction to the novel where he declares: 'I shall write a history of people freer than statesmen . . .'8 – people, he adds, whose faults go unmentioned in the chronicles of history. A little later, in replying to Fet's comments on the early published chapters, Tolstoy explains that apart from conflicts of characters he is concerned with a much more complicating factor, a historical one. Then, in 1868, he wrote to the historian M. P. Pogodin: 'My thoughts about the limits of freedom and independence, and my views on history are not a mere paradox that has occupied me in passing. These thoughts are the fruits of all the intellectual efforts of my life. . . .'9 That is, to write a history of the people, thinking of history as a theory of knowledge and the principal integrating factor in articulating a wealth of material, is the real object of *War and Peace.*

Aware that this unusual emphasis in a novel would aggravate some readers and be misunderstood by others, Tolstoy tried to anticipate criticism by publishing an article, 'Some Words About *War and Peace*' (1868), which contains a brief statement of his views on the philosophy of history. He asserts that there are two kinds of actions, some that do and others that do not depend on a person's will, and that in a certain kind of action man's consciousness of freedom in the commission of it is erroneous. The less connected a person's activity is with that of others the more free it is. Accordingly, when he describes historical events in which this law of predetermination is obvious, he is unable to attribute importance to the actions of those who thought they control-led the events without realizing that they had introduced less free human activity into them than all the others who had participated. The activities of such people, Tolstoy declares, interest him only as an illustration of the law of predetermination which, in his opinion, guides history in addition to the psychological law that compels a man who acts under compulsion to supply in his imagination a series of retrospective reflections to prove his freedom of action to himself.

Tolstoy's misgivings were correct. The exposition of his theory and his interpretation of historical figures and events in the light of it, which run through many pages of *War and Peace*, have aroused much criticism and have often been considered a major artistic flaw in the work. Yet he regarded his efforts to resolve these problems involved in his theory of history as the core of a work written to contrast the reality of the life of individuals and communities with the unreality of historians. His attack on historians, although entirely destructive, is executed with intellectual brilliance and persuasiveness. He argues that since there are no genuine laws of history, then he must know what history consists of and recreate only that because he is searching for the truth. In order to understand the process of history, Tolstoy points out in his novel, one must start not with the deeds of supposed great men, but with the integration of infinitely large numbers of actions of innumerable people, often fortuitous or independent of their own will, what he calls the 'differential of history.' In his conviction that man lives consciously for himself, but is an unconscious instrument in attaining the historical, universal aims of humanity, Tolstoy deflates the historical reputations of celebrated figures, such as Napoleon, Alexander I, and many military leaders, who have been credited with shaping great events beyond their active control. A deed done, Tolstoy contends, is irrevocable, and its results, coinciding in time with the actions of millions of people, assumes a historic importance. The so-called great men are simply labels giving names to events. To fix responsibility for what occurs in life, as historians so often do, on the heroic virtues or vices of famous personalities or on causes, genius, or chance is plainly the result of ignorance.

If any major historical figure among the military escapes these strictures, it is the Russian commander-in-chief Kutuzov. As Tolstoy portrays him, Kutuzov recognizes the impossibility of controlling events. In his simplicity and lack of hypocrisy and affectation, Kutuzov takes his place with the common folk, the peasantry, and gentry as a representative of the unconscious spirit of the nation which Tolstoy identifies as the true historical force in a time of national crisis. In his 'intuitive wisdom' he realizes that all is controlled by an inexorable historical determinism that renders him obedient to the natural law which presides over the lives of human beings no less than all the processes of nature itself.

The tendency has been to dismiss Tolstoy's philosophy of history expounded in *War and Peace* as something of a mental aberration and a product of his corrosive skepticism. On the other hand, Sir Isaiah Berlin, who has analyzed the theory in his little book, *The Hedgehog and the Fox*, with impressive learning and scholarly objectivity, points out its significance in the history of ideas and its importance for an understanding of Tolstoy's intellectual and moral development, as well as being an integrating factor in the structure of a novel that set out to be a 'history of people.' Generalizing from a line of the Greek poet Archilochus, 'The fox knows many things, but the hedgehog knows one big thing,' Sir Isaiah suggests that Tolstoy was by nature a fox, but believed in being a hedgehog. That is, he concludes, 'Tolstoy perceived reality in its multiplicity, as a collection of separate entities round and into which he saw with a clarity and penetration scarcely ever equalled, but he believed only in one vast, unitary whole.'[10]

Tolstoy was not entirely original in the formulation of his philosophy of history in *War and Peace*. Sources have been indicated for this or that aspect, especially in the writings of the Savoyard diplomat Count Joseph de Maistre. Sir Isaiah Berlin points out striking similarities in the thinking of both men on the interpretation of events by conventional historians. And there are passages in the novel in which Tolstoy either avoids historical evidence or distorts it to support his thesis, especially in the portrayal of Kutuzov who is idealized biographically, and accounts of his activities in the war are sometimes unhistorical. Nor is it difficult to discover inconsistencies in the argument of Tolstoy's theory, which arise largely from the uncompromising rigidity of his views. For example, he was finally forced to admit in *War and Peace* that the multiplicity of individual small actions which, he believed, determined how things actually happened was unknowable in its totality. Though he arrived at no conclusion on how to resolve the dilemma, he insisted that it was better to be fully aware of this fact rather than depend upon the delusions of historians who, not knowing it, thought they were telling the truth, perhaps one of the more positive contributions of his theorizing on the philosophy of history. In a larger sense, however, his theory bears the stamp of uniqueness, and its relevance to the grand sweep of life, to the thought, action, and characters of *War and Peace*, is indubitable.

## V

Tolstoy realized the risk he ran of boring readers of *War and Peace* because of the many pages devoted to explication of his theory of history and to discussions of imponderables in understanding the first causes of wars and the fatuous assumption of directive control by so-called great leaders of them. But he was too instinctive a literary artist to surrender the boundless appeal of imaginary characters to the shrunk shanks of historical theorizing. And one suspects that his own vital interest, as that of his readers, was not in the purely historical emperors and generals who for the most part serve as two-dimensional illustrations of debatable points of his theory, but in the pulsing daily existence of the full-bodied members of the five major families he created – the Rostovs, Bolkonskys, Bezukhovs, Kuragins, and Drubetskoys. Though critics accused Tolstoy of confusing art with problem-solving in his novel, he kept them separate in his own mind as a letter to a literary friend at this time indicates:

> The aims of art are incommensurable (as they say in mathematics) with social aims. The aim of an artist is not to resolve questions irrefutably, but to compel one to love life in all its manifestations and these are inexhaustible. If I were told that I could write a novel in which I could indisputably establish as true my point of view on all social questions, I would not dedicate two hours to such a work, but if I were told that what I wrote would be read twenty years from now by those who are children today, and that they would weep and laugh over it and fall in love with the life in it, then I would dedicate all my existence and all my powers to it.[11]

If fictional characters such as Tushin and Karatayev, whose fates are determined by their actions in war, are also swept into the vortex of Tolstoy's theory of history, in their case he noticeably avoids arguing his thesis on the limitations of man's conscious will. The same may be said of Natasha, Nikolai, Sonya, Pierre, Princess Marya, Prince Andrei, and scores of others whose actions are conditioned by the same lack of freedom. The point is that although fate, chance, accident, or decisions thrust upon them may determine crucial events in their lives, they still enjoy the illusion of freedom, the consciousness that they are directing their own destinies. Unlike the historical figures, these vividly portrayed and wonderfully alive characters, as already indicated, were based on people whom Tolstoy knew. The artistic process involved in their creation has been aptly described by R. F. Christian as that of an intensifying rather than an inventive genius.[12]

Though there are contradictions, faults of chronology, and errors of fact and history in *War and Peace*, probably no novel has ever received such enduring and universal acclaim. So numerous and varied have been Russian and foreign appreciations that it no longer seems possible to offer a 'new word' of praise or blame. Almost the only substantial and penetrating piece of adverse criticism of its artistic aspects by a distinguished writer is to be found in Konstantin Leontiev's *Analysis, Style, and Atmosphere in the Novels of Count L. N. Tolstoy* (1890),[13] and even this is written in a spirit of profound admiration.

In its incredibly rich tapestry of life, the novel's chief glory, as so many have pointed out, is Tolstoy's characterizations of his imaginary men and women. Their total personalities are revealed as they would be in real life. That is, we meet them first in customary settings and our initial impression of their external appearance is usually limited to what Tolstoy conveys in a few descriptive touches. Though we learn little more at this point, as time goes on, often a matter of years and many pages, our knowledge of them gradually grows through innumerable small actions and intimacies, conversations, self-examinations, and especially by the remarks of others about them, until finally we obtain a complete image of each.

If art in intention is mimesis, as Auden asserts, the reader here never quite realizes the resemblance. Or as Percy Lubbock puts it, these men and women in *War and Peace* do not appear to inhabit a world of their own, rather they appear to inhabit our world in the same sense that we identify with them because of the universality of their human appeal. Tolstoy's approach to characterization is subtly flexible in his capacity to adapt it to the way of life of the person he is describing. In the case of Prince Andrei and Pierre he employs mostly an internal, psychological approach which brings out their dissatisfaction with life as it is through dialogue, self-examination, and reflection on their reactions to life's experiences. In this process of analysis, however, Tolstoy does not preside over their destinies. What they think and do always appears to be psychologically necessary, even though their consciousness of freedom of choice in the Tolstoyan sense may be illusory. One never suspects the author, except perhaps in the case of Platon Karatoyev, of manipulating his imaginary creations as one sometimes does with the more important historical personages where he fails to abide by his rule that the artist should portray and not judge. Tolstoy's extraordinary psychological insights reflected in his characterizations create in the reader a feeling of intimacy with his men and women, possibly because his points of reference in analysis of thoughts, feelings, and actions are nearly always to the reality of life and not abstractions. You can invent anything you please, he once said of Gorky's fiction, but you cannot invent psychology.

However, if the impression he wishes to convey of the human nature of a character is that of a man or woman devoid of inner passion and moral or spiritual substance, his approach is that of externalization. Take, for example, his introduction of Princess Helene at Anna Pavlovna's soirée at the opening of the novel. The meticulous description of her clothes, beautiful figure, face, shapely shoulders, back and bosom, and her vapid smile to all and sundry pinpoints her as a mindless and soulless woman who lives only to dazzle all by her beauty. And whenever she appears, her meretricious gleaming white shoulders become the appropriate symbol of her being, just as the Princess Bolkonsky's pretty upper lip and Napoleon's soft white hands are the repeated external symbols of beings who have no inner spiritual or moral substance worth troubling about.

A Western critic once remarked that if life could write it would write just as Tolstoy did. Certainly some such fanciful impression cozens the mind when confronted with scores and scores of exquisite scenes, involving so expansive a range of human experience, as are scattered throughout the hundreds of pages of *War and Peace*. It would dizzy the arithmetic of memory to recall them but the effort brings back remembered pleasures upon first encountering one's favorites. And these scenes, along with the characters in them, describe an elaborate pattern of juxtapositions and alternating contrasts which serve to create the impression of ceaseless movement throughout the novel's amazing thematic multiplicity. With the juxtaposition of war and peace are associated large areas of human experience identified with public affairs and the peaceful manifold activities of the family. Within the framework of war are alternating contrasts of Napoleon, Alexander I, a variety of military leaders who think they are controlling events and brave, simple, selfless officers and men of the ranks who are concerned only with doing their duty. In the domain of peace there are the juxtapositions of city and country life with their striking contrasts between the cynicism, cultural snobbery, and bureaucratic crassness of the city and the unpretentious pleasures of country existence; between

91

the aristocratic reserve of the Bolkonskys and the genial demonstrative-ness of the Rostovs, or the unselfish patriotism and service of these two families and the self-seeking careerism of the Kuragins and Drubetskoys. Contrasting pairs of characters are numerous, and in individuals, especially in the case of Pierre and Natasha, Tolstoy stresses the manner in which the conflicting attributes of their personalities helped to determine their actions.

In writing *War and Peace* Tolstoy sensed that he had achieved what he thought was the primary business of the novelist: to create life, without beginning or end, with all its ceaseless ebb and flow. Perhaps the most thorough and discriminating contemporary criticism of the novel, running to four articles, was that of N. N. Strakhov, who was later esteemed as a distinguished thinker. His final judgment of the work was: 'A complete picture of human life. A complete picture of the Russia of that day. A complete picture of what may be called the history and struggles of peoples. A complete picture of everything in which people find their happiness and greatness, their grief and humiliation. That is *War and Peace*.'[14] After reading this review, Tolstoy remarked to his wife with an air of self-assurance: 'N. N. Strakhov has placed *War and Peace* on the pinnacle where it will remain in the opinion of society.'[15]

# 6

## *Anna Karenina*

Turgenev once remarked that the hounds of thought hunted Tolstoy's head to exhaustion. After the prolonged effort on *War and Peace* the hours seemed dead and Tolstoy promptly plunged into a special study of philosophy. Hegel struck him as an 'empty collection of phrases' and Schopenhauer as 'the greatest genius among men.'[1] Zeal for philosophy was quickly displaced by a passion for drama. He gobbled up scores of them, contemplated writing one, and then decided it could hardly fail to be an insignificant thing after *War and Peace*. So he next turned to the idea of writing another huge historical novel, this one on the period of Peter the Great. Though he did extensive research on the subject and strained vainly at one beginning after another of the novel, he eventually dropped it, convinced that he could not recreate in his imagination so remote a historical period. Actually, he had interrupted his preparation by still another enthusiasm, the study of Greek, which he claimed to have learned in three months, and after reading in the classics he declared that 'without a knowledge of Greek there is no education.'[2]

These feverish and fruitless efforts after the long concentration on *War and Peace* were not so much the cause as the symptom of a physical and emotional letdown. To pause in vital activity meant to dwell upon intense self-analysis which nearly always brought Tolstoy to a point of spiritual despair. And the situation was worsened by a growing coolness between husband and wife. After her fifth child, Sonya suffered an illness that proved almost fatal. The prospects of another pregnancy frightened her and she told her husband. With his strict views on the duties of marriage, such an attitude deeply offended him. In poor health and disturbed in mind, in the summer of 1871 he was advised to take a *kumys* cure (fermented mare's milk) among the Bashkirs in the Samara steppes.

The treatment improved Tolstoy's health and also his relations with his wife. During the six-weeks' separation, the longest since their marriage, their correspondence was tender and loving. Upon returning to Yasnaya Polyana, still seeking to anchor his thoughts and energies on some fixed occupation, he reopened his village school and busied himself with teaching and writing his ABC books. (See Chapter 4 for an account of this activity.) During this time the couple experienced their first real mutual sorrow – the death of their sixth child, Petya, when he was only a year and a half old. If one of the family had to go, he remarked, it was better that it should be the youngest. But he deeply sympathized with the grief of the mother, that wonderful and highest manifestation of Divinity on earth, he said.

Both parents spent considerable time with their children. Though some of the guiding principles Tolstoy formulated for teaching peasant youngsters were applied to his own, in deference to the social circle in which they would later move they were not allowed to lack for governesses and tutors from whom they learned manners and French, German, and English. And Sonya and he also took a hand in their instruction. The children loved to be in his company, vied with him in sports, and he was endlessly inventive in devising games and entertainment for them. Happy people, he declared, had no history, and at this time at Yasnaya Polyana they were all happy.

## II

Tolstoy's cheerful frame of mind combined with certain odd circumstances to release once again his literary energies, and this time the effort resulted in the creation of his next great masterpiece – *Anna Karenina*. As early as 1870 he had mentioned to his wife a theme for a novel; a married woman of high society who commits adultery. His intention, he explained, was 'to represent the woman as not guilty but merely pitiable.'[3] It was not exactly an original subject for fiction, but then his positive ideas on women, marriage, and sex promised that his approach to the theme would hardly be that of the conventional writer of romances.

Distracted by renewed educational activities, Tolstoy did nothing about the proposed novel for a couple of years at which time he was gruesomely reminded of it by being called upon to attend the postmortem of a neighbor's mistress who had thrown herself under a train because her lover had deserted her for another woman. Tolstoy, in effect, had the conclusion of his novel, but as usual he had much difficulty with a beginning. Then reading by chance one day an unfinished tale of Pushkin, he expressed admiration for the bold way in which the writer started, *in medias res,* and Tolstoy was promptly inspired to begin his novel in this manner. Sonya dates in her diary that he began *Anna Karenina* on March 19 or 20, 1873.

In the early stages of the work Tolstoy accumulated a complex mass of outlines, notes, drafts of chapters and variants of these which, unlike similar material in the genesis of *War and Peace*, does not easily fall into a pattern of sequential development. Obviously the story-line in the early drafts differed considerably from the final version, and key characters underwent striking transformations during the course of writing what turned out to be a long novel on the contemporary scene. At first the liaison of wife and lover was well underway when the story opened and divorce and marriage eventually followed. Unlike the later Karenin, the original of the husband has marked redeeming traits sufficient to arouse real sympathy for his marital misfortune, and the lover has little in common with the later Vronsky. In particular, the initial conception of the heroine bore no resemblance to the later Anna; in fact, she was singularly unattractive in appearance and behavior. And it appears that the important contrasting couple, Kitty and Levin, had not at all figured in Tolstoy's planning in the early drafts.

As far as one can discover, the introduction of Kitty and Levin in later drafts coincides with radical alterations along the lines of the final version. Like Dostoevsky, who also engaged in elaborate planning and trial flights in the early stages of his major novels, Tolstoy's ultimate shaping went on constantly in the actual course of writing when many of his most significant changes occurred to him. In its final version the core of *Anna Karenina* is the story of the heroine's adultery expanded into a consideration of problems of marriage, in which the subplot of the love and marriage of Kitty and Levin underscores the tragic moral of the *mariage de convenance* of Anna and Karenin.

In a feat of artistic planning little short of miraculous, Tolstoy integrates with this core theme layers of contemporary society observed in their manifold activities in the two capitals, in the countryside, and even abroad. And he peopled the domain he created with numerous characters (one mathematically-minded critic has tabulated 143), many highly individualized and all contributing to the development and illumination of the action of his story. Confronted with this amazing outpouring of knowledge of human experience, one recalls 'God's plenty' in *War and Peace*. In some respects the two novels bear comparison, but there are more differences than similarities. More tragedy, striking scenes, poetry, and grandeur are to be found in the earlier novel, and less psychological eavesdropping in *Anna Karenina,* where analysis is at times more precise and maturer and achieves a more organic and subtle connection with the development of action. Moreover, there is a greater inner unity in *Anna Karenina*, perhaps because Tolstoy was not concerned with demonstrating the applicability to his main theme of so abstract a thesis as his philosophy of history.

The first of the eight parts of *Anna Karenina* began to appear serially in *The Russian Messenger* in 1875. Then Tolstoy suddenly became disgusted with the work and, despite pleas of enraptured readers, he retreated again to his pedagogical activities. Another installment, however, was published the next year, and the last in 1877. The whole work came out in book form in 1878.

## III

Though commonly regarded as one of the greatest love stories of world fiction, *Anna Karenina* has its detractors. The most familiar types, especially during the nineteenth century, were those who, while praising the novel as a consummate work of art, strenuously objected to the heroine's apparently willful betrayal of her marriage vows. If Matthew Arnold, with Victorian predictability, was the first to set this moral tone in the West in his well-known essay, *Anna Karenina*,[4] Russian critics had preceded him in this respect. Nor has this position entirely vanished, though perhaps with a different emphasis, in the euphoric emancipation from morals today. In a radio program not long ago the present writer recalls a distinguished novelist dismissing Anna as 'just a little bitch.'

Another type of critic is censorious of Tolstoy's attitude towards Anna, as though he condemned her for her adultery. In this connection some ambiguity may derive from the quotation from St Paul used as an epigraph to the novel, 'Vengeance is mine, I will repay,' which could imply that Tolstoy doomed Anna to death under the wheels of the train for deserting her husband Karenin and running off with Vronsky. Anna's death, as we have seen, was decided by Tolstoy before he began writing the novel and the epigraph had been thought of in the very early stages of the work. Certainly he believed in the sanctity of the family even to the extent of arguing for the necessity of prostitution as a protection of the institution of holy matrimony, an incredible position in the light of his later views and one which had been partly suggested to him in his reading of Schopenhauer. Moreover, he sees only evil in the destruction of the family by either a husband or wife who indulges in the egotistic love of affinity which, as in Anna's case, leads to the ruin of her life as well as that of Vronsky. Nor can one ignore the contrast between the loveless situation of Anna and her husband and the mutuality of pure love of Kitty and Levin achieved by sacrifice, forgiveness, and the desire to make each other happy. Such moral values, however, are not unaccompanied by contradiction, for Tolstoy's attitude towards adulterous lapses of others in the novel, especially to such indiscretions of the amiable Stiva Oblonsky, seems to be one of sufferance.

The point is that Tolstoy allows his men and women freedom and avoids as much as possible passing overt judgment on their actions. He does not condemn his beautiful, warm-hearted, radiant Anna, with whom he was obviously a bit in love himself, and his contempt for the other characters in the novel who do is implied if not expressed. What he appears to be indicating is that it is not for them, sinners that they are, to cast a stone. Only God can condemn her, which no doubt was his final understanding of the meaning of the novel's epigraph. Tolstoy's undeclared sympathy for his heroine is artistically implicit in the total characterization, and it somehow conveys itself to all but the rigidly righteous, even to Matthew Arnold who, in praising the special quality of the work as superior to the 'petrified feeling' of Flaubert's *Madame Bovary*, perceptively stresses Tolstoy's 'treasures of compassion' for Anna. One might say, to paraphrase Leontiev, that Tolstoy's element of subjectivity in portraying Anna is objectivized, whereas the reverse is true in the case of some of the characters in *War and Peace*.

In the endless disharmony between life as it is and life as it should be, Tolstoy directs his art, as did Chekhov, to the problem of rebellion against reality in pursuit of an unrealizable ideal. In a practice common enough in those days, Anna as a girl was thrust into an arranged loveless marriage to Karenin, a man whose self-esteem was matched by his utter imperviousness to the human factors involved in the daily business of living together. Tolstoy ironically says of him that in devoting his entire life to his government duties he even lacked the human weakness necessary to fall in love. For Anna, it is a dull but socially secure

relationship, eventually made tolerable by force of habit and particularly by her devotion to her young son Seryozha. Chance throws her
into the company of Vronsky, a handsome young Guards officer. They
are attracted to each other. Some, reflecting on Anna's moral scruples at
this point, criticize her seemingly quick and easy capitulation to Vronsky.
It was neither easy nor sudden. Tolstoy, with uncanny psychological
skill, analyzes the conscious and unconscious elements of Anna's
nature and the planned and fortuitous circumstances of her daily
existence which step by step transformed what might have been merely
a passing flirtation into a deeply serious love. And this dawning
emotion is answered by Vronsky's persistent attentions which are an
outgrowth of his equally sincere love for her. Anna's ultimate surrender
comes only after long heart-searching into what her marriage with
Karenin had been and would continue to be, and in the full tide of
a mature woman's yearning to alter that life with a love she had never
experienced.

If Anna had engaged in the kind of 'affair' freely sanctioned by the
*mores* of fashionable society to which she belonged and had conducted
it with the requisite discretion, it would have been gleefully accepted
and her social reputation would have remained untarnished. It may be
recalled that Vronsky's mother regarded a liaison with a beautiful
married woman such as Anna as a factor of social distinction in her
son's career. The only one hurt would be the husband, the traditional
sacrifice in such matters. But Anna was passionately, publicly in love
and so was Vronsky. She was prepared to leave her home, risk the loss
of her son, and suffer the cruel condemnation of her own social world
because she flouted its conventions. This was the higher morality, one
suspects, that led Tolstoy to describe the adulterous heroine to his wife
'as not guilty but merely pitiable.'

The cause of the slow, relentless moral deterioration of Anna after
she cast her lot with Vronsky has been the subject of much debate. A
guilty conscience, separation from her son, the ostracism of society,
archaic divorce laws, the inadequacy of Vronsky to meet the supreme
challenge of her love – these and other reasons have been cited to
explain the breakdown of all the vital forces of Anna's radiant nature
which finally brought about her suicide. Although one or all of these
may have been the reason, Tolstoy avoids offering any explanation or
justification for Anna's tragic failure. For example, in the matter of
Vronsky's so-called 'inadequacy,' though Tolstoy apparently disliked
the code by which he lived, he portrays him as noble-minded, loyal,

gentle, and deeply loving and solicitous of Anna despite her eventual insane, provocative, and causeless jealousy.

One may conjecture that Tolstoy, with keen artistic insight, intentionally left the 'why' in Anna's tragic history unanswered, much as Dostoevsky avoided any definitive explanation of why Raskolnikov murdered. Perhaps it is the artist's realization that among disturbed natures under terrible human stress there never is any definitive reason why a crucial final action is taken, and it may well be that, psychologically, there can be none. Tolstoy, like Dostoevsky, was concerned primarily with stating with consummate skill all the problems involved in the simple or complex lives of his men and women.

## IV

Though for Tolstoy the novel was an art form superbly designed to create life, he also thought of it as an ideal instrument for conveying knowledge, and throughout the extensive background material of *Anna Karenina* he provides much information on the contemporary Russian social and cultural scene. Yet this variegated matter is artistically used to advance the novel's action and develop its characters. Levin is the focus for vivid pictures of country life but he is also deeply involved in practical agricultural questions that agitated the gentry and peasantry after the emancipation. Like Tolstoy, Levin tended to believe that the gentry's failure to improve their landholdings by introducing modernized methods of cultivation and stock breeding would result in their ruination as a class and their eventual economic displacement by the peasantry.

On this slender basis and other rather insubstantial evidence in Tolstoy's writings and activities, Soviet Marxian critics have rhapsodized about him as a symbol of the peasant revolution. Their views are epitomized by the outstanding Hungarian Marxian literary critic George Lukács, who spent some years in the Soviet Union. Lukács appears to believe that Tolstoy makes the exploited peasant the central problem of his fiction. In his analysis of the characters the main question, Lukács indicates, was in what way they depended on the receipt of groundrents and on the exploitation of the peasants and what problems this social basis creates in their lives. Even the celebrated mowing scene in *Anna Karenina*, when viewed in terms of Levin's 'un-Marxian' relations with his peasants, becomes for Lukács simply an expression of his 'sentimental attitude to physical labor.'[5]

Though the argumentative positions taken by various characters in *Anna Karenina* on other controversial issues, such as divorce laws, spiritualism, women's education, military service, and the Serbian revolt, are consistent with their developing personalities, Tolstoy's views on these matters are implicit if not directly stated. In fact, his mounting antagonism to governmental abuses and the failings, vices, and hypocrisy of high society flows through the novel and enriches it with a superior intellection and the vibrant quality of his personality. But his interest in the classes and in social problems was by no means inclusive. If he concentrated in *Anna Karenina*, as he had done in *War and Peace*, on the upper classes and seemed uninterested in merchants, the lower class, and the proletariat of the cities, it was because he found such people 'unattractive' and 'boring' as he declares in an unused chapter in *War and Peace* where he goes on to explain why he prefers to limit himself to the upper classes in his fiction: 'I belong to the very highest class of society, and I love it. . . . I am an aristocrat by birth and by habit and by situation.'[6] And in this list of 'unattractive' and 'boring' people, he also included the peasantry. Moreover, at heart he remained an aristocrat, something that Soviet Marxian critics tend to overlook. In reality, peasants play only a small part in the total corpus of Tolstoy's fiction, and he rarely stresses their class opposition to the landed gentry. Whatever may have been his spiritual identity with the peasantry later, he never became one of them, as is so commonly assumed.

If any one character in *Anna Karenina* acts as a mouthpiece for Tolstoy, it is Levin. More than this, there is a considerable element of the autobiographical in his portrayal. The courtship, marriage, and the life together of Kitty and Levin closely resemble Tolstoy's experiences. Again like Tolstoy, Levin in his metaphysical wanderings seeks relief in association with the land, in the poetry of working it, which inspires his unforgettable meditation at harvest time. But it is the poetry of fact whose imaginative quality and freshness derive from Tolstoy's own contacts with nature. However, Levin could no more become a peasant than the intellectual Olenin in *The Cossacks*, or Tolstoy himself. Levin also manifests Tolstoy's strident quality of dissidence as exemplified by his rejection of conventional moral values, his dislike of hypocritical high society and government bureaucracy, and his condemnation of the government for thrusting the Russo–Turkish War on a populace which knew nothing of the issues. Levin's obdurate questing for faith, for life's higher meaning, soon troubled his married life as it did Tolstoy's. Neither the character nor his creator could be contented in the face of the unanswerable questions of life and death. At the end of the portrayal one gathers the impression that Levin, though partially satisfied with the results of his philosophical quest, will continue to grope for the kind of solution to life's impasse that Tolstoy eventually discovered in the spiritual crisis that overtook him about the time he finished *Anna Karenina*.

The relation of art to life had been a vital concern of Tolstoy ever since he had begun to write and it is not surprising that he should accord the subject significant attention in *Anna Karenina* where it is most effectively interwoven into the narrative in the episode in Italy concerning the dedicated painter Mikhailov and Anna and Vronsky. During the course of the conversation in the artist's studio before his masterpiece, several favorite ideas of Tolstoy are deftly brought into the discussion: his contempt for the fashionable reaction to art which fails to perceive that it must not be invented, that it must be inspired directly by life and society. Like Mikhailov, Tolstoy believes that the artist's aim is 'to strip off the layers' and reveal the inner substance, to show people and things – as Chekhov might have put it – not as they appear to be but as they really are.

Nowhere have Tolstoy's artistic ideals and techniques been so completely realized as in *Anna Karenina*. As in *War and Peace,* there are slips in chronology and in the sequence of actions of some of the characters, and critics have offered adverse opinions, often with little justification, on matters of structure, characterization, psychology, and style. But the magnificence of the whole artistic accomplishment dwarfs these strictures into insignificance. The structure, somewhat like that of *War and Peace*, is built upon on a series of contrasts and parallels involving the three main groupings of characters – Anna and Vronsky, Kitty and Levin, Dolly and Oblonsky – in which the development of plot, the personality traits of participants, and factors governing their action are made infinitely more meaningful through the interaction of the groups in which the ironies and coincidences of life play their part. The closely knitted structure refutes the not infrequent criticism that there are really two novels in *Anna Karenina*, one about Anna and Vronsky and another about Kitty and Levin. As for style, critics are not always aware of Tolstoy's enormous labor over it. In *Anna Karenina*, despite some occasional lapses, the style is a perfect instrument for conveying meaning with lucidity and the tonal qualities and speech traits of the characters. For example, in the famous passage where Anna, before her suicide, reads the book of her life by candlelight which wavers and then goes out for ever, the force of the passage is not in the symbolism of the rather commonplace image, but in the rhythm and suggestiveness of the language. For power and grandeur there are few passages to compare with it in Russian literature. And in the psychological analysis of the characters it is, if possible, more effective than that of *War and Peace,* for added to it is a deeper and more searching moral probing. But beyond the display of extraordinary knowledge of human nature in *Anna Karenina,* there is a still rarer quality, especially for fiction in the nineteenth century – Tolstoy's complete and compassionate understanding of a fallen woman.

# 7
## Spiritual Crisis and Religious Faith

At about the age of fifty Tolstoy underwent a major spiritual crisis and the religious conversion that followed dominated the remaining thirty-two years of his life. The experience seemed almost predestined. That is, it was not so much an abrupt change as a gradual peaking of moral and spiritual demands in his nature which, as we have seen, had begun to manifest themselves from his early youth. A marked acceleration of the process took place during the years after *War and Peace* and especially in the period when he was completing the last part of *Anna Karenina*. This development was no doubt influenced then by deepening concern for his own form of life, as well as by the Populism movement among conscience-stricken gentry and educated progressives determined to 'go to the people' to aid the vast grey masses of peasantry living in ignorance and poverty in a country controlled by an oppressive government and a parasitic minority well endowed with the world's goods.

The story of events that led to the intensification of Tolstoy's spiritual agony and brought about his crisis is told in *Confession* (written 1879–1880, banned in Russia, and first published in Geneva in 1884), a short work of the highest art and most profound sincerity. It is narrated in a pure, simple style filled with Biblical cadences, and is easily comparable to the finest 'confession' literature whether it be that of St Augustine or Rousseau.

At the beginning of *Confession* Tolstoy recalls many moments of spiritual anxiety in the past which he had lightly brushed aside or satisfactorily rationalized. He compares the situation to that of a man who suffers slight afflictions to which he pays no attention. But as time passes the illness grows worse and suddenly he is confronted with what has become more important for him than anything in the world – death! Soon Tolstoy feels compelled to ask himself the reason for everything he does and can find no answers except the truth that life is meaningless, that there is nothing before him save physical extinction. Although he apparently has everything to live for – a happy family existence, fame, and fortune – none of it gives him contentment for it does not seem to have any purpose. Has someone played a cruel, stupid joke by placing him on this earth? And he begins to think of suicide.

Nor can Tolstoy take pleasure any longer from the two things that had hitherto most diverted him from the awful conclusion he had arrived at – family happiness and artistic creation – for neither is able to provide him with an explanation of the meaning of life which death does not destroy. Realizing that the question incessantly gnawing at him had been asked in one form or another by thoughtful people since the beginning of time, he made an eager search for the answer among philosophers, scholars, scientists, and theologians. None he lists in *Confession* brings him any comfort; they are all pretty much variants of Solomon's answer, namely, that everything in the world – folly and wisdom, riches and poverty, and mirth and grief – are vanity and emptiness; and that when man dies nothing is left.

In this impasse in a matter so desperately crucial to him, Tolstoy's unshakable conviction in the primacy of reason as the fruit of life may well have prevented him from parting with it. For now reason led him to see that he had been generalizing on his terrible problem solely from the point of view of his own learned and leisured class, which had lost any sense of the meaning of life, and not from the outlook of millions of common folk who support the burden of their own lives in terms of their faith. But he could not accept the Russian Orthodox faith with all its paraphernalia of the supernatural which for him was a denial of reason. Upon further consideration, however, he decided that his initial error was in ever expecting an examination of finite things to supply a meaning to life, for the finite has no ultimate meaning apart from the infinite. Both, he declares, must be linked before one can find an answer to life's problems. This fresh illumination eventually leads him to the following conclusion: The meaning life has that death does not destroy is union with eternal God. Though he still insists that faith remains irrational, it alone gives mankind a reply to the question of life and consequently makes life possible.

Having come to an understanding of faith consistent with his reason,

Tolstoy devotes the latter part of *Confession* to a moving account of his search for a form of religion in which he could believe. He first turned to the Russian Orthodoxy of his own circle but its devotees repelled him because their lives, quite different from the altered form of life he had begun to adopt, did not correspond with the Christian principles they espoused. Next he drew close to simple folk, peasants, monks, sectarians, and pilgrims. Though he realized that among them Christian truths were mixed with superstitions, he believed they possessed a real faith which was necessary to them and gave their lives meaning. The more he came to know these people in the course of two years, the more he loved them. He notes in *Confession* that a perceptible change came over him. The life of his own circle grew distasteful to him but the faith and meaning of the mass of laboring people gave to life something he could accept. Suddenly he recognized that for years he had been searching for God only to be frustrated again and again by insisting upon propounding metaphysical or realistic definitions of Him. Now he rejoiced to discover that one need only be aware of God to live, for God is life.

Though Tolstoy had come to believe as he thought the common folk did, renounced upper-class pleasures, and prepared to be humble, to labor, to suffer, and be merciful, his reason still would not allow him to accept those rituals inseparably bound up with their simple faith, such as the sacraments, fasts, and adoration of relics and icons. He faithfully attended services and attempted to abide by the infallibility of the Church in all its beliefs and practices, but he could not resist visiting learned theologians and revered elders of monasteries to question them sharply on such matters. What particularly outraged him was their brushing aside his queries about the reasons for the marked divisiveness of Christian religion and the Church's support of war in the name of Christian love, since he himself believed that truth in religion lay in union through love. Though he agreed that the explanation of every-thing must be concealed in infinity, he insisted that anything that is inexplicable should present itself to him as necessarily so and not as something he was arbitrarily expected to believe. In the end, he decided that not all was true in the religion he had joined, and that even in the faith of his favored peasants much falsehood was mingled with truth.

Tolstoy concluded *Confession* with a promise to continue his investigation of religion in order to discover what is true and what is false in it. At about this time he entered in his diary, which he had neglected for a number of years, the following:

There are light people, winged, who rise easily from among the crowd and again descend: good idealists. There are powerfully winged ones who, drawn by carnal desires, descend among the crowd and break their wings. Such am I. Then they struggle with broken wings, flutter desperately, and fall. If my wings heal I will fly high. God grant it. There are those who have heavenly wings, and purposely – out of love for all mankind – descend to earth (folding their wings) and teach men to fly. When they are needed no more, they fly away: Christ.[1]

## II

Probably before he finished *Confession* Tolstoy had already embarked on the rather extensive work he promised at the conclusion of it – *A Criticism of Dogmatic Theology* (1880). His intention was not solely to expose Church dogma which would not stand the simple test of logic, but also to come closer to those Christian truths which he felt he could live by. He realized that he could not publish such a book in Russia (the first edition in Russian appeared in Geneva and not until 1891), and that he actually risked prosecution for writing it. The field had been ploughed by many others before him, but his approach, not unlike that of some religious modernists today, was inspired by a desire to bring the Church closer to the needs of life. If he lacked the expert theologian's profound scholarship for such a task, although he possessed a substantial amount of it, he had compensations of a deeply sincere religious intention and a genius for literary expression that communicated a remarkable intensity to his performance.

Tolstoy began by endeavoring to demonstrate that the Church's dogma diverts men's minds from the very principles of faith that Jesus most emphasized. He used both Greek and Russian texts in interpreting the Bible and later learned Hebrew in order to read the Old Testament in that language. Unlike many medieval Biblical commentators who believed in order to understand, he sought to understand in order to believe. If in so arcane a matter he seems at times to place excessive faith in his own reasoning, his conclusion that Church dogma is often false and an insult to human intelligence is well sustained.

Tolstoy's analysis concentrates on the Gospels, especially the Sermon on the Mount which had long been a favorite of his although some passages had never ceased to puzzle him. For example, against the background of his own rearing and gentleman's code, 'Resist not him that is evil. But whosoever smiteth thee on the right cheek, turn to him the other also' (Matt. 5: 39), always seemed to him unreasonable, senseless, and confused his understanding of the personality and teaching of Christ. Then it suddenly dawned on him, he tells us in *A Criticism of Dogmatic Theology*, that Christ had meant this statement to be taken literally. The idea obliged Tolstoy to reconsider the meaning of the Sermon on the Mount and convinced him that it was a recapitulation of serious practical advice, a conclusion that brought into a different focus the whole teaching and example of Christ as he had never before understood them.

From Christ's teaching Tolstoy accepted five commandments which, put in brief form, are: Do not be angry; do not commit adultery; do not bind yourself by oaths; do not defend yourself by violence; and do not go to war. They are incontrovertibly supported by Christ's teaching, he said, they clearly relate religion to daily life, and they guided all his future religious writings and behavior. He had found the answer to the stubborn question that had brought about his spiritual crisis: What is the meaning of my life? 'There is a power,' he wrote, 'enabling me to discern what is good; I am in touch with it, my reason and conscience flow from it, and the purpose of my conscious life is to do its will – that is, to do good.' [2]

Begun during the same years as *A Criticism of Dogmatic Theology*, but probably not finished until the next (1881), is another long work, *Union and Translation of the Four Gospels*. After admitting the well-known fallibility of an author's appreciation of his own writings, Tolstoy later declared this work to be more important than any book he had ever done and a turning point in his whole life. It consists of the Greek text, the Russian version, and his own translation arranged in three parallel columns, but much space is devoted to comments on the texts, especially on the authorized Russian version, and to his various explanations and criticisms on the commentaries of Gospel exegetes. The performance is nothing if not original, for Tolstoy determines the order of chapters and verses to suit his own sense of the fitness of things and arbitrarily omits whatever he disapproved of or did not readily comprehend. Perhaps because of his impeccable literary taste, his translation of the Gospels is a consistent and absorbing narrative that strikingly reflects Christ's teaching and personality as Tolstoy assumed them to be. The Christ that emerges is the humble sectarian, not that of the theologically sophisticated commentators. Though Tolstoy fearlessly contends with the scholars, not always convincingly, in their own proper domain, the chief thrust of his translation and interpretation is to spell out what the Gospels really mean by a very close reading of the text, particularly where exegesis has traditionally stumbled, and always in accord with his inner consciousness of what is right or wrong. If at times he displays an unscholarly impetuosity in sweeping away sophistries, his pronounced rational bent nearly always compels him to emphasize clear meaning above hair-splitting. One result is that more often than not he sheds a great deal of light on vexed points. He assumed that the authors of the Gospels intended to make sense and his approach to textual problems is a commonsensical one. And unlike so many theological experts in the field, the main point of his endeavor is to seek in the Gospels rather than from the dogma of the Christian Church practical guidance for the life of man.

It should be added that a family tutor, wishing to copy out Tolstoy's work on the *Union and Translation of the Four Gospels,* was able to finish only the summaries of the chapters without the translation. In this extremely shortened form it eventually appeared in print, *The Gospel in Brief,* to which Tolstoy wrote a preface, and it became much more popular than the longer work.

III

Tolstoy's religious writings up to this point were necessary preparation for *What I Believe,* a long book which he finished in January 1884. It is one of the most popular and widely translated of his didactic works. So anxious was he to see it published that he attempted a familiar dodge to avoid the censor. He had an expensive private edition of fifty copies printed in the hope that the work would be certified because it was obviously not intended for general circulation. The ruse failed. The head of the Moscow Civil Censorship reported that *What I Believe* 'must be considered an extremely harmful book as it undermines the foundations of social and governmental institutions and wholly destroys the teachings of the Church.'[3] And on the basis of the report of the spiritual censor, the Procurator of the Holy Synod, K. P. Pobedonostsev, ordered all copies of the book to be burned. Actually, not one copy was destroyed. The whole edition was sent to Petersburg and illegally distributed to high government and Church officials and their friends.

It is hard to imagine a more maddening, uncompromising profession of religious faith than *What I Believe,* yet it is a work of utter sincerity and is expressed in that lucid literary style, adorned with balance and

measure, and enlivened by fresh, homely illustrations, of which Tolstoy
was such a master. Whether one accepts or rejects his convictions, the
tremendous inner struggle that led to them glows with an incandescent
human quality compelling attention.

At the outset Tolstoy tells how he found the key to Christ's teaching
through a clear literal interpretation of his commandment in the
Sermon on the Mount on non-resistance to evil by force. Since all know
that the meaning of Christ's teaching is based on love to man, he
declares, then 'resist not him that is evil' means never resist him that
is evil, that is, never do an act of violence, an act contrary to love,
whatever the insult or harm you may bear. He points out that the
previous circumstances of his life were based precisely on what
Christ's commandment rejects – the law of an eye for an eye, a tooth
for a tooth.

In insisting on this commandment as the core of Christ's teaching,
Tolstoy is fully aware of the extreme sacrifices it may require from all
who actively profess it. For he repudiates the common notion that
Christian teaching relates only to personal salvation and not to public,
political, social, and economic questions. His new faith requires that all
who profess it, within their personal limitations, strive to practise it in
life's endeavors. In any conflict between the law of God and the law
of man, one must abide by the law of God. His contention is that progress towards the welfare of mankind is made not by the persecutors but
by the persecuted, that only goodness, confronting evil, conquers it in
the end.

The central portion of *What I Believe* is devoted to an elucidation of
the five commandments in the Sermon on the Mount accompanied by
sharp criticism of the Church's compromises with them or failure to
observe them. In the analysis Tolstoy makes use of his linguistic knowledge and a library of Biblical commentators to probe the difficulties
of interpretation or to correct errors which he believes have crept into
the language of the Gospels. At times his readings of puzzling passages
seem more plausible than traditional ones. He remarks that if the
Gospels had survived half burnt or obliterated, it would have been easier
to discover their meaning than it is now because of manifest attempts to
pervert or hide the sense. He ends the section in an ironic flight of fancy,
in which he imagines the whole of Christendom rearing the young
according to the five commandments instead of on regular church
attendance, prayers, abstinence from flesh on Fridays, and fasting
every Lent. For fulfillment of Christ's teaching as expressed in his

commandments aims at establishing the kingdom of God on earth which would bring the highest blessing attainable by man – peace.

Tolstoy anticipates obvious objections to trying to live one's life in conformity with Christ's commandments whatever the consequences. People always say that strict observance of Christ's teaching would surely bring about the kingdom of God on earth, but since observance is impossibly difficult the teaching is impracticable. Tolstoy's simple answer is that man's rational activity has always been directed to ascertaining what is best among the contradictions that fill an individual's life. That being the case, then it would be in accord with human nature to live by Christ's teaching which all agree is the best guide. It is the dogma of the Church that has convinced man to deny the practicability of that which they admit offers them blessedness. The Church has created the further illusion, that if man merely has faith in Christ and believes he has redeemed him from sin, then he no longer need shed the light of reason on his path through life because he is already sinless, that is, completely good. But the divine light of reason that dwells in man, says Tolstoy, must be continually served by him, for it is by its aid that he seeks for what is good. Nevertheless, he protests, the Church, science, and public opinion continue to say that the life we lead is bad and yet persist in believing that the teaching which would enable us to become better is impracticable.

Nor does Tolstoy hold out for sinning man the beatitude of life after death. He demonstrates to his own satisfaction that in the Gospels Christ never asserted a personal resurrection or immortality for man. Though the life of God is eternal, that of man is mortal. What is important, Tolstoy writes, is not that he shall die, as everyone else, but that the life and death of all will have a meaning and serve the salvation of everyone, which is what Christ taught.

Having thus far mentioned in passing in *What I Believe* that personal life gains meaning only by fulfillment of the will of God, Tolstoy now dedicates a chapter to discussing why action is the most essential aspect of fulfillment. In a paraphrase of a declaration of James, he affirms that the only signs of faith are the works which flow from it, otherwise faith is merely the desire to believe something. It was a principle he had already begun to act upon, hoping that his example might affect the conventional Christians he was surrounded by who lived by faith alone. The emphasis he placed on faith was that which he derived from the teaching of Christ, who nowhere demanded faith in himself but rather faith in the truth.

The tendency of man to regard the search for truth defining human life as a useless occupation inspired one of the most provocative of the later chapters of *What I Believe*. Tolstoy makes the sharpest distinction between the truth of Christ's teaching and the so-called truth of the teaching of the world. He asks every reader to recall honestly his whole life and then he will see that never once has he suffered from obeying Christ's teaching, whereas all his misfortunes have come about because, contrary to his own inclinations, he has followed the world's teaching. And he calls to witness the unhappiness of his own life and further illustrates the point by citing experiences of numerous people of high and low degree. If you test life by the measure of what all men have described as happiness, he claims, you will see that this life is terribly unhappy. Then he asks and answers: What are the chief conditions of indisputably earthly happiness? One is man's union with nature, and he pictures in detail the unpleasant artificial city existence of those who, in increasing numbers, have been deserting the natural healthy life of the countryside. Work which one is fond of and is voluntary and physical labor which gives one an appetite and sound sleep is another condition of happiness. But how many are there who do not have to work and infinitely more who do work they hate? But these and other conditions of happiness, such as a good family life, amicable intercourse with different people, and a painless death, Tolstoy qualifies by his now familiar touchstone that the higher one advances in worldly success the less is real happiness accessible to him.

We need not be martyrs in Christ's name, Tolstoy interjects here, for that is not what he teaches. He simply asks us not to torment ourselves by following the world's false teaching. Yet people do not even try to fulfill Christ's teaching because the Church instructs them that to do so will cause them suffering. So conditioned have people become to this state of affairs, says Tolstoy, that Christ's teaching that a man's happiness cannot depend on power, on his estate, or his social position, seems like a demand to sacrifice for the sake of future bliss. Christ does not call upon us to make sacrifices, he adds, but only to do what is better for us here in this life. If men live without property and resisting others, Christ teaches, then they will be happier. However, Tolstoy affirms, a man who lives in accord with Christ's teaching must be prepared to die by the violence of others or by cold or hunger. Although we may regard this as a demand for sacrifice, it is no more than what every man may expect.

Perhaps nothing so disturbed Tolstoy as what he regarded as the

Church's apostasy as the legatee of Christ's teaching and as the perpetrator of a religious fraud on the people in his name. Much of his previous religious writing had been concerned with this conviction, and in the penultimate chapter of *What I Believe*, symbolically entitled 'The Dead Church,' he returns to the charge. With fresh evidence drawn from official catechisms and prayer books of Russian Orthodoxy, he attempts to prove that the Church, while acknowledging Christ's teaching in words, has rejected it in life. As centuries passed in the history of the Church, Tolstoy writes, instead of being the guiding spirit in advocating Christ's truth, it followed the life of the world and then devised allegories to show people that they were living in accord with Christ's law whereas the reverse was true. Eventually, he argues, it was not the Church but the people who 'abolished slavery, which the Church justified, religious executions, the power (sanctioned by the Church) of Emperors and Popes, and have now begun the task that will come next in turn: the abolition of property and the state'[4] (in part, a rather striking prophetic insight on the Russian Revolution thirty-three years later).

Again anticipating religious modernists today, Tolstoy concludes that the Church's teaching has no relation to life; 'it has nothing left but Cathedrals, icons, brocaded vestments, and words.' All that really lives in our European world, he adds, has rejected the Church. State institutions, science, and the arts, which formerly served the Church, either ignore it or have contempt for it. If the Catholic, Orthodox, and various Protestant churches still exist, it is only because people fear to break a vessel which once held precious contents.

With sorrow Tolstoy points to the Church's failure to be concerned with people's harmful way of life; in fact, he accuses it of acquiescence to their follies. All the evils that exist, it explains, exist by the will of God as a punishment for the sins of the world. It teaches that every Christian must submit to the tsar, to all officials appointed by him, defend by violence their own and other people's property, and fight, execute, and endure execution at the will of these authorities. Though he has questioned hundreds of Christians as to why they do things contrary to their faith, no one gives him a direct, forthright answer. Each replies about the salvation of the Church and the whole of humanity. Even the average man, if asked why he continues to live the kind of life he condemns without doing anything to improve it, answers only in generalities. The policeman will say: How will law and order get on if, to improve my life, I cease to take part in them?

He and all the others, writes Tolstoy, have no philosophy of life and no man can live without a philosophy of life. If these men have any religion at all, he decides, it is a religion dedicated to existing authority.

There is no rational conception of law, Tolstoy points out, which is made obligatory on everyone by his inner convictions, just as there are no clearly expressed moral principles. On the contrary, there is a strange belief that moral principles are not even needed and that religion consists in certain words about a future life and about God, a few ceremonies useful for saving one's soul in the opinion of some people and of no use in the opinion of others, and that life goes on of itself and requires no principles except that one must do what is ordered.

Tolstoy calls for a rebirth of the Church in the spirit of Christ's teaching as he understands it. If you consider it irrational to kill people in war, to benefit from the labor of the poor, to imprison men, to live in the infected atmosphere of cities, then he calls upon all to avoid these things. Since Christ's teaching provides mankind a way of life which is not novel but long familiar, Tolstoy returns to the five commandments and urges that nothing the Church requires of a believer prevents him from fulfilling what Christ has revealed to be necessary for his welfare.

The last chapter of *What I Believe* offers the fullest statement of the articles of Tolstoy's new faith. Formulated with unquestioned integrity, they constitute an amazing program of action, especially as coming from the great literary artist of *War and Peace* and *Anna Karenina*. In many respects, however, the position he reached seems to mark a logical development of his unusual qualities of mind and spirit. The form his statement on faith takes is a merciless renunciation of his past and a commitment in detail to his new credo in terms of Christ's five commandments. Only the briefest summary can be attempted here.

He begins by confessing that only a true understanding of Christ's teaching had saved him from submission to the teaching of the world and enabled him to perceive that human welfare lies in unity with all men. The first temptation he learned from Christ is that anger destroys the good of life and that he must no longer bear ill-will to others, justifying anger by considering himself important and wise and other people insignificant and senseless. He now knows that that man alone is superior to others who humbles himself before others and is the servant of all; that what he formerly regarded as good and lofty – honors, fame, education, riches, food, and dress – he now regards as mean and bad, whereas peasant life, obscurity, poverty, and simplicity of surroundings have become for him good and noble.

The second temptation he had learned from Christ's teaching is the harmfulness of adulterous lust, which he formerly palliated. He will no longer serve this end, for Christ forbids as divorce the desertion by man or woman of the first person with whom he or she mated. Nor will he seek those amusements which inflame lust, such as novels, poetry, music, theater, and balls. Though he does not make distinctions between unions called marriages and those not so called, he regards as holy only the first union of man and woman.

The oath is the third temptation that contributed to his unhappiness. In the past he justified himself because he thought this action did no one any harm. Now he will never swear an oath again, for one must not obey anyone but God. Tolstoy stresses the many evils that can follow from swearing an oath to the government, the army, or to any institution. It is an acknowledgment of an obligation to submit to the will of others, however evil the demand may be, and which may involve one in actions contrary to conscience.

The most important temptation Christ revealed to him was resistance to evil by means of violence applied to others. He cannot, as he did formerly, condone this evil on the grounds that it is essential for his defense or that of others. It is a delusion that life can be secured by defending oneself and one's property. Man's welfare is possible only when he labors for others and not for himself. Tolstoy seems to imply here that violence will wither away, so to speak, if each – as he himself now proposed to do – seeks poverty and humiliation, renounces property, and refuses to defend himself and others or to serve the government in any capacity in which force or violence are required.

The fifth and last temptation which Tolstoy had learned from Christ's teachings was that which leads a man to separate his own country from others. He has now come to recognize that his differentiation is false, a kind of delusion, for one's individual welfare is bound up with that of all peoples of the earth. Such a union cannot be severed by frontiers, for all men everywhere are equals and brothers. Recalling all the evil he has done, seen, and suffered in war between nations, he now contends that the cause of it all 'is the gross fraud called patriotism and love of country.' Hostility to other nations is unnatural and the result of an insane education. So he opposes love of the Fatherland and refuses to take part in quarrels between nations, to pay taxes for military armament, or serve in the army or help others to do so.

Tolstoy concludes *What I Believe* with a reaffirmation of his new faith and reassures those who will most certainly reject its practicability. To live by this faith, he writes, will endow his life with the only possible, joyful meaning that is indestructible by death. What had once dissuaded him from accepting Christ's teaching, the risk which unbelievers had held out to him of privations, suffering, and even death, is now what confirms for him its truth. Once he understood the meaning of Christ's 'The truth will make you free,' he felt himself completely free. All evil that criminal men may do him will be evil for themselves and thus should do him good. For if men to whom the truth is unknown do evil to him while considering it good, he will show them the truth. But to do so, he must renounce all participation in evil and acknowledge the truth by his actions.

To those who object that fierce foreign invaders will slaughter him if he does not defend himself, he replies that if a Christian society harms no one and gives the surplus of their work to others, no enemy will kill them. No man will be so foolish as to deprive of good those who serve him. Or if one objects that the government will severely punish a Christian, who knows the truth, for refusing to do obligatory service, Tolstoy answers that the government's demand is that of people who do not know the truth and hence the persecuted Christian is afforded the opportunity to witness the truth, not in words but in deeds. Every act of violence by war, robbery, or execution is not a result of irrational forces of nature, but is committed by erring people deprived of knowledge of the truth, and a Christian can impart that knowledge only by refraining from error, by returning good for evil. Man can make the truth known, declares Tolstoy at the end of *What I Believe*, only by deeds of truth.

## IV

After *What I Believe* Tolstoy continued to write on religious subjects, with diminishing emphasis, until almost the end of his life. His persistence is all the more striking because of numerous difficulties in publication. In most cases printing in Russia was out of the question, but some of these writings were distributed by adherents in clandestine mimeographed or hectographed copies. Most of them were published abroad in Russian and in foreign translations and were smuggled back into Russia in quantity for wide circulation.

One may observe the swift development of a characteristic Tolstoyan style in his didactic writings, in which the eloquent expounder of doctrine makes use of the devices of the literary artist. For the compelling persuasiveness of the best of his didactic works is not unrelated to those qualities of his fiction which reveal a deep concern for the universal activities of humanity. The brilliant realism and descriptive power of the novels reappear often in his non-fiction, and the moral preoccupation of major characters of his stories bears a clear analogy to the intense personal search for moral truth that so strikingly illuminates his religious and social writings.

The remaining religious works are relatively short pieces with one important exception, *The Kingdom of God Is Within You*, which will be treated separately later. The various shorter pieces usually concern religion in terms of some related subject, such as morality, reason, patriotism, the state, but they do not alter in any essential degree the position on faith which Tolstoy had arrived at by the time he wrote *What I Believe*. Occasionally they are epistolary articles, a form which he tended to favor in answering letters on religion which impressed him. The remaining religious writings briefly commented on here are those which seem to have some significance for the development of his beliefs.

In the light of repeated charges that Tolstoy did not live his personal life according to his new faith, it is perhaps worth noting an epistolary article which he wrote at the time he was working on *What I Believe*. It is an answer to a letter and a manuscript article against the Orthodox Church sent to him by a university student, M. A. Engelhardt, who had been exiled for political activity. In the answer, after an explanation of his theory of non-violence, Tolstoy writes:

> It seems to me that if Christ and his teaching had never existed, I myself would have discovered this truth – it now appears to me so simple and clear and convincing. . . . The significance of Christianity consists of pointing out the possibilities and the happiness of fulfilling the law of love. . . . Now another question directly and involuntarily follows from this: 'Well, but you, Leo Nikolayevich, how do you practise what you preach?' And I answer that I do not preach and I cannot preach, although I passionately desire to do so. I can preach only by deeds, and my deeds are bad. What I say is not a sermon; it is only a refutation of a false understanding of Christian teaching and an explanation of its real meaning. Its meaning is not that we should in its name rearrange society by violence; its significance is to find the meaning of life in the world. The fulfillment of Christ's five com-

mandments gives that meaning. .... Teach me how to escape the nets
of temptation that have ensnared me, help me and I will fulfill them;
but even without help I wish and hope to do so. Blame me – I do that
myself – but blame me and not the road I follow, and show it to
those who ask me where in my opinion the road lies. If I know the
road home and go along it drunk, staggering from side to side, does
that make the road by which I go the wrong one? If it be wrong,
show me another; if I have lost my way and stagger, help me,
support me in the right path as I am ready to support you; and do not
confuse me, do not rejoice that I have lost my way; do not cry out
with delight: 'Look at him! He says that he's going home yet he's
slipping in the bog!' Do not rejoice at that, but help and support
me.[5]

*On Life* (finished in 1887), one of the more substantial studies of this
later period, is a closely reasoned philosophical analysis of the major
premises on which Tolstoy's new faith was based. The rather discursive
style in which it is written, recalling that in passages on the theory of
history in *War and Peace*, is fortunately relieved by frequent attempts to
explain abstruse doctrinal pronouncements in terms of homely illustrations from the real world of plant and animal life and incidents
drawn from daily existence. Yet its philosophical content has no doubt
contributed to its being one of the least read of his religious writings,
which is a pity for the work is important for an understanding of his
beliefs.

*On Life* is fundamentally an investigation of an aspect of the theory
of knowledge. Tolstoy vigorously opposes the assumption of experimental science, history, and political science that we know what we
cannot know and that we cannot know the one thing that we really do
know. These disciplines, he says, unaware of the central contradiction
of human life, mistakenly concentrate on the study of man's animal
personality and its welfare without reference to the chief object of
knowledge which is the subordination of man's animal personality to
the law of reason in order to attain the good of the true life. The true
life of man, though manifested in time and space, is not determined by
conditions of time and space but only by the degree of subjection of the
animal personality to what he calls 'reasonable consciousness.' He
claims no originality for his position which, he says, was held by all the
great sages of the past who perceived that the whole advance of
humanity has consisted in man's renouncing his animal personality in

order to live by that pure welfare which strife, suffering and death cannot destroy.

The inevitable awakening in man of reasonable consciousness Tolstoy connects with Christ's declaration that man must be born again. And in that state the feeling that will resolve all life's contradictions and provide the greatest good is love, the fullest experience of which is the sacrifice of self, the capacity 'to love thy neighbor as thyself.'

The work's last section is concerned with the relation of life to death. With a touch of mysticism in Tolstoy the rationalist, he argues at some length that men who have subdued their personality to reason and devoted their lives to love cannot accept the possibility that death destroys life. Because of their relationship to the world, they leave behind them after death a force which continues to act on others as it did in their lifetime. And knowledge of this gives them a confident faith in the stability, immortality, and eternal growth of life.

Among the few noteworthy shorter pieces, 'Religion and Morality' (1893) is concerned with the familiar question: What is religion and can it exist apart from morality? Tolstoy's answer may be summed up in his concluding words: 'Religion is a certain relation which man has worked out between his own personality and the infinite universe or its Source, whereas morality is the constant guide to life which emerges from that relation.'

As a kind of warning to disciples who discussed matters of faith in terms of mysticism or revelation, Tolstoy wrote a brief epistolary article 'Reason and Religion' (1894), in which he pounds away on a familiar theme, namely, that man had received direct from God only one instrument that would enable him to know himself – reason. Therefore, he insists, man must be expected to use the whole strength of his mind to clarify for himself the premises that should ultimately determine his faith.

In the separate 'Preface' (1898) to his unfinished *Christian Teaching*, which apparently Tolstoy had intended to be a systematic presentation of his religious faith, he offers a summary of the doubts and difficulties he encountered in arriving at his beliefs. The 'Preface' is a kind of recapitulation of the detailed account of these matters in *Confession* and therefore stands as a brief introduction to that work.

Among the remaining short pieces that directly concern religion, such as *How to Read the Gospels* (1896), *What Is Religion?* (1902), *An Appeal to the Clergy* (1902), which repeats Tolstoy's attack on the

Church but this time in very forceful language, *The Restoration of Hell* (1903), *Church and State* (1904), and *The Teaching of Jesus* (1909), he adds little that is new.

One item, however, does deserve comment because of its historical importance and is, in effect, a statement of Tolstoy's final position on religion. This is *A Reply to the Synod's Edict of Excommunication* (1901). In the course of time his Christian anarchism, which had become widely known abroad as well as in Russia, increasingly alarmed the Orthodox Church and the government, of which the Church was simply an arm. Moreover, at this time (1901) political unrest was prevalent in the country, especially among progressive university students, and Tolstoy's opposition to the whole political and social order was a matter of common knowledge among the educated and was feared by the government. There is reason to suppose that secular authorities, hesitant to take action against the internationally known Tolstoy, were prepared to allow the ecclesiastical hierarchy to do so on the assumption that it would at least win support in a matter of religious faith from masses of Orthodox believers.

On February 24, 1901, there appeared in the *Church Gazette,* official journal of the Holy Synod, an edict signed by seven leading churchmen, in which Tolstoy's heretical beliefs were duly listed and he was excluded from the Church, although the door was left open should he repent of his heresies. Perhaps to the surprise of both the Church and government, the action aroused a wave of national and international sympathy for Tolstoy. Street demonstrations occurred, letters and petitions of protest signed by hundreds of people were sent, and many citizens visited him to express their indignation. So numerous were the communications that Tolstoy finally had to send a letter to the press 'to thank all those people from high officials to simple workers,'[6] for their sympathetic messages.

Aware that the edict was designed by the Church and government to combat his influence among people, Tolstoy sent a reply to the Holy Synod which it published in the *Church Gazette,* but with significant deletions that the censor found impossible to print 'without offending the religious feelings of the faithful.'[7] After pointing out what he considered to be true and untrue in the Synod's edict, he also indicated that he did not accept what the Church said it believed in, but did believe in much that it tried to persuade people he did not believe. 'I believe in this,' he wrote:

I believe in God, whom I understand as Spirit, as love, as the Source
of all. I believe that He is in me and I in Him. I believe that the will
of God is most clearly and intelligibly expressed in the teaching of the
man Jesus, whom to consider as God and pray to, I consider the
greatest blasphemy. I believe that man's true welfare lies in fulfilling
God's will, and His will is that men should love one another and
should consequently do to others as they wish others to do to them –
of which it is said in the Gospels that in this is the law and the
prophets. I believe therefore that the meaning of the life of every man
is to be found only in increasing the love that is in him; that this
increase of love leads man, even in this life, to ever greater and
greater blessedness, and after death gives him the more blessedness
the more love he has, and helps him more than anything else towards
the establishment of the kingdom of God on earth: that is, to the
establishment of an order of life in which the discord, deception and
violence that now rule will be replaced by free accord, by truth,
and by the brotherly love of one for another.

At the conclusion of his answer Tolstoy writes with simple eloquence:

Whether or not these beliefs of mine offend, grieve, or prove a
stumbling block to anyone, or hinder anything, or give displeasure
to anybody, I can as little change them as I can change my body.
I must myself live my own life, and I must myself alone meet death
(and that very soon) and therefore I cannot believe otherwise than as
I – preparing to go to that God from which I came – do believe. I do
not believe my faith to be the one indubitable truth for all time; but
I see no other that is plainer, clearer, or answers better to all the
demands of my reason and my heart; should I find such a one I shall
at once accept it; for God requires nothing but the truth. But I can no
more return to that from which with such suffering I have escaped,
than a flying bird can re-enter the eggshell from which it has
emerged. [8]

## V

Tolstoy's individual quest for a new religious faith seems like an
intensely personal and lonely experience. In his attacks on the contemporary Church and its 'revisionism' of Christianity, he worked
within a hoary tradition of religious dissent which no doubt influenced

him for he was quite familiar with it. Some of the teachings of Christ, which he reformulated in his own way, had evidently been held and practised, with a different emphasis to be sure, as early as the first century of the Church. With later modifications they also appeared in the teachings and practice of various Russian and Western European sects. And in Tolstoy's own lifetime, he could hardly have remained uninfluenced by Russian utopian communal movements and the reform program of the Populists. Nor was his new faith unaffected, in a negative sense, by the materialism flooding into Russia from the West on the heels of Darwinism, which tended to remove contemporary science still further from any concern with religion. Such formative influences, however, do not reflect markedly on the originality of Tolstoy's achievement. The powerful force that compelled him to undertake his memorable journey of religious discovery was a profound inner spiritual need to resolve the incessant problem of the meaning of his life. But unlike those who had preceded him in dissenting from worldly formalism of the Church, he went on to advocate constructively and on the basis of the Gospels the universal significance of Christ's teaching more vigorously than he condemned the Church.

Though there has been a great deal of specialized writing on Tolstoyism, so far as I know there has never been a definitive study of the subject which would objectively test its validity in theory and practice as a religious philosophy of life. Part of the reason is the seemingly extreme unreality of his total doctrine in terms of the normal experience of human nature as nearly all people understand it or – as Tolstoy might say – compromise with it. So often in argument he gives the impression that everyone is as obsessed as he is with an agonizing search for first causes or with an uncontrolable desire to know what is the meaning of his life, whereas experience indicates that nearly everyone is cheerfully unconcerned with such matters, at least in a serious way. One is reminded of the coteries of novelists, psychologists, and sociologists today who convey in their writings the notion that all of us are passionately absorbed with the question of personal identity, of discovering who we are and why we are here.

It is also true that at the center of Tolstoy's doctrine is a large element of religious anarchism in his evaluations of the conduct of human affairs by absolute moral standards, although it must be said that more than once he admitted the impossibility of realizing such standards. This practice led him to oversimplify observance of the five commandments he professed and of the problems that grew out of them, particularly in connection with violence and the operations of government, law, and property. But behind his rigidity in this respect was his conviction that any surrender to compromise or expediency meant ultimately a total loss of principle and sincerity in the practice of faith. If all would scrupulously abide by duty to their conscience and to God, he believed that the best results would follow for mankind.

An attempt at a point-by-point refutation or justification of the various articles of Tolstoy's faith would go well beyond the modest purpose of this book. It may be said, however, that if his moral philosophy seems like an exercise in futility today in the light of civilization's tremendous advances since his death, it would still be a bit premature to imagine, as many do, that Tolstoy diagnosed the ills of his time correctly but prescribed an incantation for a cure. In fact, one is bound to be impressed by the extraordinary relevance and immediacy of his moral criticism of what passed for progress in his time while contemplating the crisis of confidence in the enormities of so-called progress in our own day. As years passed without fundamentally altering his religious views, the rigidity of his position somewhat softened. He began to place less emphasis on the exact wording of the Gospels and on the importance of the personality of Christ. For the moral teaching of goodness, he eventually stressed, was the core of all great religions, in fact, of the whole spiritual life of humanity. And a slight variation may be observed in his later view of life after death, which he had at first dismissed. Without in any way asserting personal immortality, he felt that after death one became part of the infinite, but what form of existence this would take he wisely refused to say since it was beyond the knowledge of man.

To the end, however, Tolstoy clung to the central conviction which he had reached early in his search for faith and which really went to the ultimate root of all religion: that we are all part of a moral universe and only to the extent that we discern such an order and adjust ourselves to it has life any meaning and purpose that is not defeated by death. Moreover, his constant belief that man owes a duty to a higher power that reveals itself through his reason and conscience is a fact of personal experience confirmed by testing among the world's leading religions. His was a faith closely and peculiarly linked to daily life in which each individual was confronted with moral responsibility for his actions, a responsibility based on the law of love. If in its practice

he condemned out of hand all those actions of institutions of government, property, law, and commerce that did not square with his faith,
one can only point to the ceaseless violations of the natural rights of
man sanctioned by these institutions in Tolstoy's day and more so in
ours. In his lifetime, and long after, Tolstoy's religious writings and
activities inspired many people all over the world to reorganize their
lives in keeping with his faith.

# 8

## *What Then Must We Do?*

I

Between 1880 and 1886, during which time Tolstoy produced most of his major religious writings, he began the difficult process of trying to transform the whole pattern of his life to conform to his new beliefs. Constantly in his mind was fear of the charge of hypocrisy for failing to live up to the spirit and letter of his faith, and the mental and spiritual anguish he underwent seemed to alter his personality. In fact, the struggle never really ceased and in it may be observed the tragic chronicle of the last thirty years of his life.

The first real trial of conscience arose out of the assassination of Emperor Alexander II on March 1, 1881, by a group of terrorists who belonged to the revolutionary organization, Peoples' Freedom. Six were apprehended, including one woman, and were condemned to death. Though revolted by this act of violence, Tolstoy's conscience was also tormented by the thought of the executioners assigned to hang the murderers. He awoke one day from a vivid dream in which with horror he saw himself as the executioner, and he at once wrote a letter to Alexander III, son and successor of the murdered monarch. It is an amazing performance, combining humility, hopeless idealism, and bold political prophecy. Tolstoy writes of the horror of the crime and admits the possibility that adherents of the terrorists, 'for the sake of the imaginary good they seek, must wish to kill you too.' And he can well understand, he says, the Tsar's desire for vengeance on his father's murderers. Then, quoting the Gospel passage on love your enemies, he implores Alexander III to return good for evil. If you pardon them, he declares, 'the hearts of thousands, of millions, will throb with joy and tenderness at this example of goodness shown from the throne at a moment so terrible for the son of a murdered father.' To this he adds: 'I do not know how others would react, but I, a poor subject, would be your dog, your slave. I would weep from tenderness, as I now weep every time I hear your name.'

In an eloquent and frank conclusion, Tolstoy writes:

Who are these revolutionists? They are people who hate the existing order of things; they find it bad, and they have in mind the establishment of a future order that will be better. It is impossible to contend against them by killing and destroying them. Their number is not important, but their thought. To struggle against them one must struggle spiritually. Their ideal is a sufficiency for all, equality, and freedom. To oppose them one must oppose their ideal with one that is superior to theirs and includes it. . . . There is only one ideal that can be opposed to them. And that ideal, the one from which they start – though not understanding and blaspheming it – and which includes theirs, is the ideal of love, of forgiveness, and of returning good for evil. Only one word of forgiveness and Christian love, spoken and fulfilled from the height of the throne, and the path of Christian rule which is before you, waiting to be trod, can destroy the evil that is corroding Russia. As wax before the fire, every revolutionary struggle will melt away before the man-tsar who fulfills the law of Christ.[1]

Through intermediaries, the letter apparently reached the ruler. His response, how authentic is uncertain, was: 'Concerning this letter, Alexander III commanded that Count L. N. Tolstoy be told that if an attempt had been made on his own life, he could pardon it, but he did not have the right to pardon the murderers of his father.'[2] When the powerful Procurator of the Holy Synod, Pobedonostsev, conveyed to the Emperor his fear that Tolstoy's letter might influence him, Alexander III reassured him: 'Be calm, no one will dare to come to me with such proposals; I guarantee *that all six will be hanged*.'[3] And so they were.

This first of a number of failures to persuade government officials and institutions to be guided by the law of Christ should not necessarily be regarded as political naïveté on Tolstoy's part. He understood only too well the nature of the coercion that obliged individual members of organized society to submit to forces inimical to the teaching of the Sermon on the Mount. This did not lessen his conviction of the need to protest. No doubt his largest service to humanity was just this insistence that violation of moral law caused most of mankind's suffering.

Implicit in his letter is the realization that the evils of established government and its revolutionary opponents were caused then, and always will be caused, by the absence of moral values in striving for political and social ends.

Not only public actions, including a refusal to do jury duty, but also private efforts to alter his daily mode of living, began to make friends and even members of the family wonder whether Tolstoy had not lost his mind. He dressed often in peasant style, and soon gave up hunting, a beloved sport of forty years' enjoyment, liquor, meat, and smoking, the latter only after a hard struggle. Money he distributed to the poor and investigated their trials and tribulations in visits to law courts, jails, and recruiting stations. Pilgrimages were made to monasteries and he sought out celebrated holy men for religious discussions. Moreover, this aristocrat, who had dropped his title of Count, now dispensed with the attention of servants and tried to do everything possible for himself: he cleaned his room, emptied the chamber pot, cut wood, drew water, and even made his own boots after taking lessons from a shoemaker. To the family it seemed like proletarian play-acting, to him it was the only way to lead a personal Christian life so he would not be a parasite living on the backs of the working class. Under this regimen all noticed that he grew thin and lost much of his natural ebullience and sense of fun.

At the end of 1881 his wife Sonya decided that the family should move from the country to Moscow, for the oldest son, Sergei, was ready for the university, the daughter Tanya was old enough to come out in society, and the younger children could benefit from city education. A large house was rented at first but later one was bought. Tolstoy regarded the move with foreboding. His worst fears were quickly realized. In the city their close-knit country existence together lost its simplicity, artlessness, originality, and both husband and wife and the older children felt a growing family estrangement. The new life according to God that Tolstoy wished to live had nothing in common with traditional aristocratic city ways. Despite Sonya's careful management, expenses mounted alarmingly in a milieu where social caste and custom made excessive demands. Five tutors and governesses lived in and as many more teachers were employed to give special lessons to the children. Eleven servants worked in the house, outside, and took charge of various family vehicles. At a time when Tolstoy had begun to wonder about the religious scruples of possessing any money at all, the costs of food alone for twenty-six members of the household seemed like an unmitigated evil. He jotted down in his diary: 'A month has passed. The most miserable in my life. The move to Moscow. All are busy arranging – when will they begin to live. Nothing is for the sake of living, only in order to be like other people.'[4]

Soon the news got around that the Tolstoys were living in Moscow and the house was deluged with callers, many of them people of distinction who wanted to talk with the great author of *War and Peace* and *Anna Karenina*. He received them with quiet but affable simplicity. Some having heard of his 'new religion,' tried to draw him out on it, and then vigorous arguments ensued. Not a few callers were comrades in Christ, some of whom had already anticipated one aspect or another of his beliefs, such as T. M. Bondarev and V. K. Syutayev, two unusual peasant sectarians to whose moral influence he paid tribute, a poverty-striken schoolteacher V. F. Orlov, and the saint-like librarian N. F. Fyodorov. These spiritual fellow travelers were nearly always joyfully received by Tolstoy and were not at all surprised to find him engaged in household chores or, in one of the two sparse rooms he kept for himself upstairs, pounding wooden pegs into a new pair of shoes he was cobbling. Infinite talk would follow for he was keenly interested in the views and way of life of these enthusiastic disciples. More often, however, the house would be full of socialites and friends of the young. To escape the hubbub and 'wasteful life,' he would hurry off to the Sparrow Hills across the river to saw and split wood with peasant acquaintances, or wander gloomily through the slums of Moscow and give coins to begging derelicts.

During the summers the whole family deserted Moscow for Yasnaya Polyana. The welcome reprieve from city living rejoiced Tolstoy. As always, his spirits rose in communion with nature. In the country his daily program of physical labor expanded, not only because it was the healthy thing to do, but now because he felt it a duty sanctified by Holy Scripture. It included not only work for himself but also for hard-pressed peasants who needed a helping hand – this was 'bread labor,' for one could not serve man while consuming what others labor to produce. He ploughed, reaped, carted grain, manure, and timber. Or one could see him helping a poor widow repair her hut, astride a roof beam, cutting notches for cross-rafters, chisel stuck in his leather belt, a saw hanging from his waist, and his graying beard shaking with each blow of the axe. Tolstoy secretly hoped that his example and zeal would influence the family, and at times they did put aside their rural vacation pleasures and devote themselves to farm labor which for a time became something of a fashion among them.

During these years the growing army of men and women from all walks of life, who had joined up under the new Christian banner of Tolstoy, began to find their way to Yasnaya Polyana, and they too participated in farm labor, often, he remarked, with more fanaticism than common sense. In general and with some cause they were not liked by his wife who truculently nicknamed them the 'dark people.' She at first made an exception of one, perhaps because of his attractive appearance, wealth, and aristocratic bearing. This was V. G. Chertkov who had relinquished a promising military career in a Guards regiment when he experienced the call of religion. Abandoning all luxuries, he endeavored to live as simply and frugally as a peasant. Ultimately Chertkov became both religious guardian angel and evil genius of Tolstoy and played a significant role during the remainder of his life. A narrow Calvinistic proselytizing streak displeased Tolstoy and more than once he warned Chertkov that his own path to the truth was not necessarily the only one. And the excessive proprietary feeling that developed in Chertkov about everything connected with Tolstoy made him unhappy at times, as did also this disciple's reverence for the institution of property. In the course of years, the bond between them became very close. Tolstoy fell into the habit of depending on him a great deal and especially upon his business skills in arranging for the publication of his forbidden writings abroad. On the other hand, Chertkov soon lost his attraction for Tolstoy's wife as she grew familiar with his influence on her husband's affairs, and eventually she regarded him as a devil incarnate.

The 'dark people,' who competed with Tolstoy's family for his attention, increased the dissension between husband and wife that grew out of his religious conversion. She had little sympathy for his beliefs and still less for his efforts to practise them. His religious writings did not interest her, and besides she feared the reactions of the Church and government to them, and worried over the fact that, unlike his immensely popular fiction, they were unremunerative. Sonya's principal concern was in the future of her family and she naturally expected her husband to devote himself to the same end.

Tolstoy was not intentionally ungenerous over his family's failure to understand or sympathize with his religious mission, but he did hope that Sonya, if not the children, would attempt to share with him the new obligation he felt to society. As time passed he found himself more and more alone in the family. To the former sinner trying to be a saint, the household was anything but a holy man's hermitage. There seemed no way of adjusting his new world of Christ to his old world of family happiness. Though he avoided demanding that they live according to his views, their natural, noisy, thoughtless, expensive existence, especially in the city, pained him, whereas the children felt that it was not they who failed to understand him but their father who did not understand them.

With increasing frequency Tolstoy left their Moscow home, usually during the high living of holiday festivities, for Yasnaya Polyana to obtain peace, he said, and leisure to write. On one such occasion he indiscreetly wrote his new disciple Chertkov to query whether he should continue to stay in this 'insane, immoral house in which I am forced now to suffer every hour,' since what he really wanted to do was to live 'in a hut with working people, working together with them according to my strength, bartering my efforts, nourishing and clothing myself as they, and without shame boldly speaking to all the truth of Christ that I know.'[5]

The correspondence husband and wife usually maintained when he was away now became progressively acrimonious – she opposed to his every move threatening the security of herself and family, he determined to change his old way of life without thought of their material security. But memories of years of a long and happy marriage usually brought about compromises on both sides, for each suffered for the other in this struggle in which principles warred against love.

In the fall of 1884, a real crisis occurred, one of a number during the succeeding years. Sonya's nerves were understandably frayed; she would soon give birth to another child, Alexandra, the twelfth in twenty-two years of married life. A further factor was her insistence on publishing on her own a fifth edition of his works written before 1881, in which she tried to include *What I Believe*, but the censorship would not grant permission. The whole business infuriated him as a money-making project (it turned out to be very profitable). But the immediate *casus belli* was that during the preceding summer at Yasnaya Polyana Tolstoy had gained sympathy from his two older daughters, Tanya and Masha, for his religious and social views. Their mother, when she discovered it, was horrified. All along she had feared such influence and, convinced that it would undermine the foundations of their family life, was determined to prevent it. A violent quarrel arose in which each threatened to leave the house. Finally he departed to visit a friend, taking his daughter Tanya with him, and leaving behind a letter for his wife. It is an account of his spiritual development and of the conflict of views it had brought about in their relations. There could be no agreement or love between them, he wrote, as long as she failed to accept the new way of life that his conscience and intellect demanded of him. And he ended with the ominous warning: 'Between us there is a struggle to the death. Either God or no God.'[6]

The whole letter is a mixture of arrant didacticism and the anguished cry of a human soul perplexed in the extreme. The quarrel was eventually patched up, as were later ones in the same cause, not only because of the long habit of living together but also because these two people sincerely loved each other. There were other factors. Many have wondered why he did not turn his back on the family and his rich estate, as he clearly desired to do, and go off to live in a hut as an impoverished religious hermit. This would have squared him with his conscience which on this score never gave him any peace of mind. But more than once he explained, and there is no good reason to doubt his sincerity, that this way out was a temptation which he must resist, for he was convinced that he had to work out his salvation in the milieu where God had placed him. Not till the end, when he was near death, did he weaken, and then it made no difference.

## II

The impoverished, downtrodden, and forgotten were often the cause of differences between husband and wife. For Sonya the poor had always been there and her response was the conventional one of casual charity. For Tolstoy they were a universal problem which he felt he must share, prompted not only by religious principles, but also by an extremely sensitive conscience which acutely reacted to the sight of defenseless human suffering. In his wanderings among the Moscow slums shortly after the family moved to the city, he was appalled by crowds of ragged, shivering, hungary derelicts who thronged around him. He bought them hot drinks and passed out alms freely. Even the poor he visited in a charitable institution sickened him. Returning home after one such nerve-racking experience, he tells how he sat down to a five-course dinner served by two lackeys in dress clothes, white ties and gloves, and it suddenly came over him with a rush that the existence of tens of thousands of such destitute people in the Moscow slums was a crime, and that he in his luxury not only tolerated it but shared in it.

Friends with whom he discussed the matter suggested organized philanthropy. Though instinctively dubious of its practicality, he took advantage of the approaching decennial census (January 1882) to propose that census-takers conduct a canvas of the city's poor in the course of their official duties. On the basis of detailed information obtained, a list of the most worthy cases would be compiled along with relevant data necessary for proper guidance in distributing aid. In the meantime, in order to implement the plan, he intended to use his influence to organize a large charitable fund. He wrote a stirring newspaper article to arouse interest in the project and set about visiting wealthy friends for financial contributions.

Tolstoy secured a position as an organizer in the census and requested assignment to one of the worst sections of the city where Rzhanov House was situated, a series of cheap lodgings that had the reputation of being a place of extreme poverty and vice. The conditions overwhelmed him, and the more he worked among the poor during the census and dwelt on the ultimate causes of all this poverty, the more he lost heart in the efficacy of his grandiose philanthropic scheme. He retreated to Yasnaya Polyana to write an article about the reasons why he felt it necessary to abandon the project. The article went badly until he recalled an earlier talk he had had with his unusual peasant friend Syutayev, who had argued against Tolstoy's project because philanthropy was just a way of getting rid of an indigent person, not really helping him. Give him spiritual charity, he said, meaning that each should take a poor man into his house and work together with him. For Tolstoy the suggestion contained the grain of a new truth, and he put his article aside in order to give the matter more thought. When he resumed the article it began to expand into a long and quite remarkable book on social and economic problems – *What Then Must We Do?*

The work was finished, after several years of strenuous effort, at the beginning of 1886. It developed not only out of Tolstoy's direct experience with the Moscow poor, but also out of what might be called a 'crisis of civilization' at that time which was symbolized by the query he heard from all sides, 'What then must we do?' the question put to John the Baptist in the Gospel. For society then seemed sick, the way of life wrong and bad, and people despaired of the possibility of changing it for the better. One thinks of the 'crisis of civilization' today and the literature it is provoking.

The first part concerns the census work of Tolstoy and his co-workers in the Moscow slums with their added obligation to collect data on prospective recipients of philanthropic aid. Questionnaire-filling and note-taking were vigorously pursued. One is reminded of a somewhat similar effort by another great writer a few years later (1890) – Chekhov's census of thousands of convict colonists on Sakhalin Island, which also resulted in a book. Chekhov's takes the form of a sociological study, but the part of Tolstoy's book devoted to his census activities has the attraction of his most vivid fiction, although this is no reflection on the reality of its contents. Scabrous interiors and skid row derelicts come to life under his deft, realistic brush strokes. All the pathos of a fallen member of the gentry emerges from pointed questioning. He begins, writes Tolstoy, not only readily but enthusiastically to tell the story of his misfortunes, 'fixed in his mind like a prayer.' Or we perceive how a few compassionate words suddenly arouse a group of hardened prostitutes to a flicker of interest in the questioner.

In his account of these degraded people, he often introduces his own reactions to them and their problems. Thinking of asking a charitable lady to intercede on behalf of a girl of thirteen whose prostitute mother has placed her in a brothel, he brutally wonders how a lady, who takes her daughter to fashionable balls, while the other mother takes hers to a brothel, both with the same idea of serving the lust of men, can save the thirteen-year-old victim. Though he personally helped a few of these unfortunates, their very number left him with a feeling of guilt, for he saw himself in them. Most, he felt, he could not help because they were insincere, untruthful, and regarded him not as a man but as a means. Only later did he come to realize that he had been blinded by pride in imagining himself as a prospective benefactor and had failed to see that nothing he gave them would make much difference, that they must first change their view of life. By the time the census ended, he concluded that his philanthropic project was not only stupid but, in a sense, evil.

The whole experience compelled him to examine the relations between rich and poor, his own material and spiritual position in this symbiosis, and the economic and social significance of money in society. After a number of striking pages in which he compares and contrasts the life-style of the well-to-do and that of the poor, he senses that the barrier of wealth between them is what makes him and members of his class so self-conscious and ashamed in their personal efforts to help the poor. By extortion, violence, and various other ways, he writes, workers are deprived of the necessities of life while non-workers, of whom he is one, consume in superfluity fruits of the labor of those who toil. The few, the rich, get richer and the masses, the laborers, get poorer. The very possession of money, he decides, is evil and immoral. But when he seeks to discover what money really is, none of the experts' answers satisfies him. The power that some people have over others does not come from money, but from the fact that the laborer fails to receive the full value of his work. Money's chief significance, then, is not as an instrument of exchange, but as an instrument of violence.

From his preliminary investigation Tolstoy seems to believe that money is not only an evil, it deprives people of life's greatest blessing, labor. Man must not use other people's labor, either by owning land, or by accepting government employment, or through money. These considerations allow Tolstoy to see more clearly the causes of the failure of his project to help the poor in Moscow. The first is the crowding of people into towns and the consumption there of the wealth of villages. In the villages, he says, it is relatively easy to satisfy one's needs whereas in the city everything is the product of someone else's labor and has to be bought. The second cause is the separation of the rich from the poor. If a man refuses to exploit other people's labor, the wall separating him from the working people will disappear. The third is the shame based on the immorality of possessing money with which he wants to help others. In turn it evokes demands he's unable to satisfy and a consciousness of himself being in the wrong.

Throughout the book Tolstoy persists in the assumption that the well-born tend to avoid toil while consuming the labor of others, that they remove themselves from the common duty of humanity of taking part in the struggle for existence. If they responded truthfully, he maintains, they would have to admit that what activities they engage in are not for the benefit of the masses but for their own personal advantage. After a historical summary of theological and Hegelian theories of the past which had justified avoidance of toil among this class, he concentrates on the widely accepted contemporary justification offered by scientists, especially 'experimental, positivist, critical, and evolutionary scientists, and the artists who follow the same tendency.'

In this respect Tolstoy's main attack is directed against positivism, particularly the thought of Comte, Herbert Spencer, and Darwin, which compares humanity or human society to an organism. Such a comparison, he points out, enables them to claim that the division of activities in human societies is organic and hence necessary, and since many evils exist in human societies, these phenomena must not be regarded as abominable but as real facts confirming a general law, the law of the division of labor. Thus modern science, he writes, justifies a man's doing anything he pleases, even if it involves his making use of the toil of others, for everything is a functional activity of the human organism. The real cause of economic distress, Tolstoy asserts, is overproduction which results from people's strange conception of the division of labor. Those associated with the Church, government, science, and the arts produce nothing really useful to the masses, yet they demand, pleading the division of labor, to be fed and well-dressed. Such an understanding of the division of labor is dictated not by man's conscience but by modern science. The people through their reason and conscience decide whether the division of labor is fair. And it is so only when a man's special activity is so needed by others that they, asking him to serve them, willingly offer him support for what he does for them. Therefore, Tolstoy argues, it is a deception for modern science to try to convince people that things which should be decided by conscience and reason ought really to be decided by observation of external phenomena, a procedure that renders science incapable of understanding definitions of good and evil determined by the whole preceding life of humanity. In the course of his theorizing on the division of labor, he repeatedly insists that scientists, scholars, artists, etc., besides pursuing their own special interests, have an obligation to work with their hands in the universal struggle with nature.

Tolstoy admits that scientists and artists, even on their own basis of the division of labor which frees them from physical work, may be said to have squared accounts by virtue of their own 'striking, wonderfull, and extraordinary' successes. But, he points out, it is generally agreed that their achievements have not improved the condition of laborers and have even made them worse. A number of interesting but not altogether convincing examples of this are cited. Anyway, he adds, their activities are not basically intended to serve laborers, but rather the rich and idle, capitalists and government. Among the professions he considers, medicine in particular comes in for severe criticism, and besides, he says, peasants cannot afford the services of physicians.

This section of the book, concentrated mostly on science (in the comprehensive Russian meaning of the word which includes all the learned professions) and on art, is concluded with a series of generalizations on their contributions to the well-being of society. He believes that scientists and artists will best serve the people by living with them and, without making any special claims, by offering their science and

art which the people will accept as they see fit. The slowness of
humanity's forward movement in his day is blamed on the division of
labor among men of science and art, that is, their dependence on the
labor of others. He emphatically states here, contrary to what is
sometimes said of him, that art and science are essential, but he believes
that those who work in such fields have failed, with certain exceptions,
to make art and science 'the whole reasonable activity of the whole of
mankind.' The trouble is, he says, that they have no interest in the
highest science, in the wisdom of a Confucius, a Buddha, a Moses, a
Christ. It is necessary for each to ask: What does that Power which
produced and guides me demand of me and of every man? For too
many modern scientists think they can resolve everything without
listening to the voice of conscience and reason. As for art, its purpose
should always be to express man's vocation and welfare; it should serve
the teachings of life. And in addition, he remarks, the true scientist
and artist must fulfill his calling not for gain but with self-sacrifice,
and his productions must be intelligible to all whose welfare he has in
view.

In answer to the question what must be done in the social and economic crisis he sees all around him, Tolstoy finally offers his own
intensely personal solution, one that he urges on all the privileged, the
rich and educated, the scientists and artists. They must acknowledge the
falsehood of their lives and follow reason and conscience without
considering what they may lead to. One's feckless and often evil past
must be repented, and the pride which comes from education, refinement, and from imagining oneself an advanced man different from
other people and really their benefactor must be banished. Then one
will joyfully accept the necessity of taking care of all one's daily needs
and serving others to the extent of one's ability and their requirements.
By doing this one satisfies not only all physical needs but also one's
spiritual needs. No doubt as a kind of practical application of his
theorizing, Tolstoy next sets down the fullest account anywhere in
his writings of how he attempted to live his own daily life in keeping
with his new faith. He divides his day into what he regards as four
periods of natural activity: heavy labor, craftsmanship, mind and
imagination, and social intercourse. How he carries out these various
activities is carefully detailed.

Tolstoy frankly confronts in the book the anticipated charge of
readers that he is a ridiculous visionary. He refuses to give any ground,
for he sees in the activities prescribed by his theories an expression of

human dignity and man's obvious duty and obligation. Moreover, he declares, the necessity for all, who are able, to be involved in physical labor assumes another significance – that of a sermon and an activity preventing terrible calamities that threaten humanity. This dire threat is the old insoluble one of the exploitation by some of the labor of others, an exploitation expressed in the root of all evils – the ownership of property. It causes the suffering of those who possess it and of those deprived of it, the reproaches of conscience of those who misuse it, and conflict between those who have a great deal and those in want. Obtaining property guides all society's activity. And because of property, most of the world's terrible evils take place: war, executions, imprisonment, vice, murder, and people's ruin. If these evils, which Tolstoy particularized at some length, are not eliminated, he predicted the following consequences for Russia:

> A workers' revolution with horrors of destruction and murder threatens us. . . . The hatred and contempt of oppressed masses are growing and the physical and moral forces of the wealthy classes are weakening; the deception, on which everything depends, is wearing out, and the wealthy classes have nothing to console themselves with in this deadly peril . . . only one thing is left for those who do not wish to change their way of life, and that is to hope that 'things will last for my time' – after that let happen what may. That is what the blind crowd of the rich are doing; but the danger is ever growing and the terrible catastrophe draws nearer.[7]

Thirty-one years after this was written, the Bolshevik Revolution engulfed Russia.

Nevertheless, towards the end of *What Then Must We Do?*, Tolstoy announced with incorrigible optimism that society is standing on the brink of the kind of new life he has been writing about. What is essential in its promotion is a rapidly forming public opinion, and in this respect, he says, women are particularly important. This seems to be a cue to devote the final chapter to the subject of women and their functioning in the new life. The theme had been on his mind, perhaps because of recent quarrels with his wife over the 'new life,' for echoes of their differences reverberate, especially on the matter of childbearing which occupies much of the chapter.

After dismissing with scorn the craze among women in his own social circle for recent fashions in dress with which to entice men, and the thriving feminist movement the responsibility for which he blames in part on educated men who have infringed the law of real labor he turns to woman's primary duty, that of mother. He adamantly writes:

> Every woman, however she may dress herself and however she may call herself and however refined she may be, who refrains from childbirth without refraining from sexual relations is a whore. And however fallen a woman may be, if she intentionally devotes herself to bearing children, she performs the best and highest service in life – fulfills the will of God – and no one ranks above her. [8]

His strictures on a mother's duties in bringing up her children are obviously motivated by his wife's insistence that hers enjoy all the social amenities of the class into which they had been born, despite her husband's protests that this did not accord with the new way of life he had adopted. A mother's duty, he writes, is to rear her children in a spirit of self-sacrificing fulfillment of God's will. Such women, he concludes, 'reign over men and serve as a guiding star to mankind; such women form public opinion and prepare the coming generation; and therefore in their hands the highest power lies, the power to save men from the existing and threatening evils of our time. Yes, women, mothers, in your hands, more than in those of anyone else, lies the salvation of the world.' [9]

Reading this chapter must have been for his wife a very mixed blessing, one of much pain and much joy.

## III

The main message of *What Then Must We Do?*, an impassioned plea to all to share in the manual labor of the world, could hardly be expected to arouse much enthusiasm among either idlers or toilers. Yet it stirred up widespread interest, and in its day, and to a certain extent since, it has had an influence on the lives of many people. The reasons for this, apart from the fact that the book was written by an internationally famous author, are obvious. In the first place, however deficient in economic analysis the work may be, it provided the most startling dramatization, up to that time, of an age-old problem – the coexistence of rich and poor. In the treatment of it, Tolstoy's forceful attacks on contemporary institutions, social inequality, economic theory, and science and art could hardly fail to provoke a rash of reactions, mostly negative. Finally, the book's purely literary qualities are such that they add an extra increment of appeal and persuasiveness to an undisguisedly didactic content.

The emphasis on physical labor amounts to much more than a romantic idealization of it which is not unfamiliar among primarily mental workers. It had become an essential part of Tolstoy's religious faith and as such he justifies it through various quotations drawn from the Gospels. Furthermore, it should be realized that he does not call upon all mental workers to turn themselves exclusively into farmers or factory workers. In terms of his own conception of the theory of the division of labor, they would have time to pursue their professions to the extent that what they produced was needed by the people. What is never convincingly explained is how universal physical work, full or part-time, will solve the problem of poverty in our complex modern civilization, or even appreciably alleviate it, although this was the problem that started him on his investigation.

Tolstoy's argumentation, of course, is seriously limited by the fact that his frame of reference is restricted mostly to an agricultural country, Russia, whereas he thinks of his panacea as applicable to any society. He had some familiarity with Western Europe from his visits there. Though an intimate knowledge of the governmental structure, economy, and native social life of its countries would hardly have altered his fundamental theory, it might have qualified some of his harsher judgments in formulating it. Sharp condemnation of Russian upper-class life, to which he belonged, with at the same time a vaunting of the charms of simple peasant existence, suggests, unpleasantly, that his mind was made up: There would be no more cakes and ale. His conscience had led him to discover that the poor were inevitably second-class citizens, but the leveling process, implicit in his faith, could hardly resolve the inequities between rich and poor. Nor did his inclusion of himself among the 'priests of science and art' as 'the most worthless frauds' make this sweeping criticism any more palatable. In fact, an irritating irresponsibility characterizes some of his critical generalizations in fields of learning, such as 'what the difference is between the deductive and inductive methods, no one has ever been able to understand.'

Despite faults, Tolstoy's destructive criticism, his special strength, has an eerie prescient quality that tends to neutralize the dated aspects of his judgments and sustains our interest in *What Then Must We Do?* For at times it reads like the book of a latter-day prophet pronouncing not merely on the Russian crisis of the 1880s, the revolutionary consequence of which he so brilliantly foretold, but on the world crisis of our own time. If he could not anticipate the miraculous scientific, technological, and industrial advances of our computerized age, he saw clearly, on the basis of limited technical achievements of his own time, that they had infinite future capacity to harm or even to destroy man as well as to serve him. His criticism of technological progress in communications and industrialization grew out of his conviction that the future proliferation of such progress could cause irremediable ecological harm to nature. Though the 'problem of the city' did not exist then, he distrusted the city and deprecated the flight to it of growing numbers of people, a situation that has become a serious matter today in some nations. And his 'back to nature' position, urging city-dwellers to return to the country where they will lead a more civilized existence, has its counterpart in a similar growing movement today.

The parallels, however, go deeper. In the name of his new faith, Tolstoy rejected organized urban society because he believed that it was hypocritical, immoral, status-mad, money-mad, and pleasure-mad, that it was committed to aggression, violence, persecution of the defenseless, and so self-centered that it was willing to sacrifice everything that was good and honest and right in order to serve its own ends. There are large numbers of people, and not only the young, who feel very much the same about organized society in the crisis that exists today. And the remedy, interestingly enough, is pretty much the same – a recovery of moral and spiritual values, only theirs is guided by pragmatic considerations, Tolstoy's was determined empirically with a large infusion of absolutism in it. If he were alive today, he would have some sympathy with 'Consciousness III' in Charles A. Reich's *The Greening of America* and similar writings, but he would regard them as mere temporizing and not as an ultimate cure for the ills of mankind.

## IV

Once again Tolstoy became involved in a major social problem not unlike that among the impoverished of the Moscow slums. This was his participation in relief work during a severe famine that hit large areas of Russia in 1891. At first he resisted requests of a Tula government official to help, for his disillusioned efforts in philanthropy in Moscow had left him opposed to it on principle. Contacts with starving, disease-ridden peasants convinced him, and in October, accompanied by his two oldest daughters, he set up headquarters in the village of

Begichevka, Ryazan Province, one of the regions most severely affected.

Tolstoy undertook the work with that practical sense he possessed in abundance in organized efforts but which often deserted him in his theorizing. As a start lists of famine victims were quickly compiled, thirty supervised food kitchens in twenty villages were opened, and fifteen hundred people were fed two meals daily. Instead of peasant fare of large quantities of rye bread, variegated menus of wholesome dishes were offered with much smaller portions of bread. This was more nutritious, pleased the peasants, and, surprisingly, turned out to be cheaper.

As the winter came on, the famine spread. Tolstoy's two oldest sons, Sergei and Ilya, began to organize relief in the Tula Province and young Leo had gone to Samara to set up kitchens. Soon large sums of money were needed to buy stocks of food for distribution. The government, apparently fearful of advertising the situation at home and abroad, took the position that there was no famine and initially did very little to assist. Sonya, who at first quarreled with her husband for deserting their Moscow home again, finally became reconciled to famine relief as a charitable endeavor, particularly since now her children were deeply involved. She published an effective letter in the *Russian Gazette*, in which she described the serious condition of the sufferers and appealed for aid. It was reprinted in other newspapers and also appeared abroad. Soon she was deluged with money, provisions, and clothes. She bought huge amounts of food which she shipped to her husband and sons.

From the beginning Tolstoy had also realized the need for publicity and as early as September had submitted a magazine article, 'Letters on the Famine,' which the censor had refused to pass, apparently because of the government's conspiracy of silence on the subject at that time. Later he wrote another, 'A Fearful Problem,' which did get published in the *Russian Gazette* (November 6, 1891). In it he enlarged upon the need of government purchases of wheat abroad if sufficient amounts did not exist to tide the population over until the next harvest. The article alarmed the public, and the government at last took more vigorous steps to distribute food.

Reactionaries were also alarmed by the article and Tolstoy was violently attacked in the press where it was hinted that he had become the darling of revolutionaries and had political ambitions connected with a 'new liberal party.' Unconcerned, he directed Sonya to send abroad for publication, in translation, copies of his earlier article, 'Letters on the Famine,' which the censor had forbidden. When it finally appeared there, excerpts from the London *Daily Telegraph* version were retranslated into Russian in the *Moscow Gazette* and compared with the original article which, in the meantime, had been permitted publication in Russia in a much censored form. He was promptly denounced publicly as a propagandist abroad against his own country. The language of the original was forceful, but no more so than in his other recent controversial writings. Critics described as 'unbridled socialism' his charge that government officials had failed in attempts to aid in the famine because of their attitude towards peasants. He also dwelt on the anomaly of the rich feeding peasants with food they grew to feed the rich, writing:

> The common people are hungry because we are too full. .... All our palaces, all our theaters, museums, all this stuff, these riches of ours, we owe to the efforts to these same hungry people who make these things which are useless to them, simply because they are fed by this means, that is, they will always be obliged to do this kind of work to save themselves from the death by starvation that constantly hangs over their heads.[10]

Minister of the Interior, I. N. Durnovo, thought Tolstoy's article dangerous enough to report to Alexander III and suggested the possibility of action. News of the threat of her husband's arrest terrified Sonya, and rumor that the Minister had in mind to incarcerate Tolstoy in the dread dungeon of Suzdal Monastery, that graveyard of forgotten victims of the Church, was enough to send Granny into action, although this old friend was hardly on speaking terms then with her 'grandson' because of their differences on religion. Taking advantage of her closeness to the royal family, she obtained an interview with the Emperor. In her account of it, she writes that he told his Minister of the Interior: 'I ask you not to touch Tolstoy. I have no intention of making a martyr out of him and then earning for myself universal indignation. If he is at fault, then so much the worse for him.'[11]

Though this drama disturbed Tolstoy at Begichevka, mostly because of public recriminations following a letter, which his frightened wife had begged from him, repudiating portions of the translated text of the English version of his article, he went busily about his famine relief work as enormous contributions continued to pour in from Western Europe and the United States. His two objectives were to provide work for those capable of it so that the peasant economy in the region should not break down entirely, and through his kitchens to feed the starving young and old, the weak and sick. He achieved a large measure of success. Peasant horses, by special arrangement, were sent for feeding to areas not hit by the famine so that they would be available in good condition in the spring sowing for which seed was distributed. Wood for fuel was provided, flax for sacking and bast shoes, clothes and material for making them, separate kitchens were set up for very young children with special nutritious foods, a few schools were organized in the villages, and small gifts of money went to individuals for debts, funerals, and books. Besides overseeing the management of all this, Tolstoy had statistics collected of all peasants fed and those with further needs. He kept full accounts of income and disbursements, and letters on the famine from all over the world were answered. Besides this, he heard individual peasant requests, often as many as 125 a day. Many were heartrending and tore at his sensibilities – a muzhik would kneel before him and beg for aid, and Tolstoy, his eyes filled with tears, would also kneel and beseech this man, beaten by want, not to humble himself in this fashion.

By July 1892, when he was preparing to return to Yasnaya Polyana, his job done, he estimated for his final report that he had set up 246 kitchens, feeding 13,000 adults daily, and 124 for children, feeding 3,000 daily. Perhaps his greatest reward was the realization of a Christian ideal of which he had often dreamed – his wife's invaluable cooperation in all this charitable work. He wrote a friend: 'I have not been so close to my wife as now, and this is more important than anything else.'[12] Sonya, lonely without him in Moscow and weary with her own efforts, wrote him towards the end of the work: 'What a misfortune at my age to be attached to and to love a man such as you.'[13] And he replied: 'I know only one thing, that I love you with all my soul, and I want to see and calm you.'[14]

Tolstoy's widely publicized relief work added to the growing legend about him in Russia and abroad and brought many visitors, including some foreigners, to the headquarters at Begichevka to discuss methods of famine relief or just to talk with him. One day two nameless Americans arrived and pretended to be interested in his views. He conversed in English with them and to his disgust soon discovered that they were quite unconcerned about his views. They had made this long journey, he told a friend, simply to be able to say that they had talked with Tolstoy. 'It is just as though they had read about me in a Baedeker and had come to confirm it.'[15]

Back at Yasnaya Polyana preparing his report, Tolstoy recalled the months he had spent in feeding the hungry as among his happiest. A feeling of positive accomplishment pleased him, and his assistants testified to his high spirits as he directed their labors with enthusiasm. Yet in these cheerful moods the Satan of theory seemed ever behind his back as he wrote. Had he not condemned this kind of charity as something that corrodes and debases the moral nature of the poor? Had he not learned from his Moscow slum experiences that the more you give the poor, the less they will work? And he felt compelled to write friends and disciples that the aid he had provided in the famine may well have been harmful to the very peasants he had tried to help. He apologized for his weakness and rationalized that he had simply acted as a good man and a worthy servant of God. But he repeated his conviction that the only way famines could be ended was for the well-to-do to change their lives, draw nearer to the common people, and return what they had taken from them.

However, when it seemed that the famine might break out again the next year in the same Ryazan area, he felt it his duty to return. Since the threat of a recurrence did not turn out to be serious, he accepted a disciple's offer to take his place. In short, he could not deny his nature. The hungry had to be fed. Perhaps against his will, the dimension of brotherhood, of love of man, counted for more than the truth of theory, and it is wonderfully reflected in a passage in his famine report. He tells how a muzhik and his boy of fourteen appeared at his famine headquarters one frosty morning just as he was about to set off on a walk. Clothed in rags, wearing torn bast shoes, their faces emaciated, they began to beg. Impatiently questioning the man, Tolstoy guessed that he was a professional beggar type. He tried to push by him, but the man continued his desperate pleading:

'It's from hunger. Help us to a bite. . . . I've never begged, now God has brought me to it.'

'Well all right, we'll go soon and see,' I say and try to go past him, but my glance by chance falls on the boy. The youngster looks at me pitifully, his beautiful brown eyes filled with tears and hope, and a single tear rolled down his nose at that moment, and fell on the snow-trodden boarded floor of the vestibule. The boy's sweet, worn face, with his flaxen hair curling in a crown round his head, twitched with suppressed sobs. For me the words of his father are an old, customary annoyance. But for him, this recital of the harsh times he has

experienced with his father, a recital at just this solemn moment
when at last they have made their way to me and to help, unnerves
him, weakened as he is by hunger. To me, it is all wearisome,
wearisome, and I think only of how to get away quickly for my walk.

To me it is old, but to him terribly new.

Yes, it has wearied us. But they still want to eat, to live, to be
happy, to love, just as I see by the charming tear-filled eyes of this
boy fixed on me that he also desires all this too; good, unhappy lad
that he is, tortured by want and full of naïve self-pity.[16]

# 9

## Back to Art

After Tolstoy's spiritual struggle life in the household during the 1880s began to take on aspects of a religious revival. When Sonya was not complaining about swarms of 'dark people' who sought out her husband, she was lamenting his desertion of the imaginative writing she loved for the religious and social tracts on which he now spent most of his time. 'He is an artist,' she angrily told one of his disciples, 'and suddenly he becomes a shoemaker.'[1] Many of Tolstoy's close friends also regretted his forsaking the art that had made him Russia's foremost novelist. Turgenev, on his deathbed in 1883, pleaded with him in a well-known letter, to 'return to literary activity! That gift came to you from whence comes all the rest. . . . My friend, great writer of the Russian land, heed my request!'[2] To the novelist, P. D. Boborykin, who remonstrated with him for not employing his artistic powers, Tolstoy caustically replied: 'Why you know, that is just like the former admirer of some ancient French whore repeating to her: "Oh, how adorably you used to sing chansonettes and flip up your petticoats!"'[3]

There are indications in Tolstoy's diary and correspondence at this time that he wanted to abandon art entirely, as he had done in the case of other activities of the years before his religious conversion. But to discard art was impossible; it was too much a part of his being. Yet he quickly concluded that the aesthetic aims he formerly held were incompatible with his new spiritual beliefs and morality. As early as 1882 he tried to formulate in an article a theory of art which would be in accord with his altered views on life. He never finished it, apparently conscious that he had not thought the matter through, but he ruminated on the subject for a long time and fifteen years later it took the form of that extensive and amazing treatise, *What Is Art?*

Meanwhile, he began to think of art in terms of the simple folktales and legends he had written for his *ABC Book* and children's readers years ago, for he had already come to the conclusion that the themes and language of sophisticated literature were less effective, artistically, than those of the popular tales of uneducated folk. Moreover, some of the early stories for his readers had embodied Christian virtues which he now thought important in the new kind of art he was contemplating. *What Men Live By* (1882) was perhaps a trial flight in this new emphasis. Though he wrote it for children, Tolstoy believed, as did Chekhov later, that one should write for youngsters as one did for grown-ups, only better. This short story is a beautiful retelling of the old legend of the angel God sent to earth to teach men to live by love.

Even before his preoccupation with educational theory and teaching, Tolstoy had been concerned with the idea of making easily accessible to the poor artistic literature that was comprehensible, enlightening, and not devoid of moral content. The recent spread of elementary education in Russia with a consequent growth in the reading public now underscored this need. In 1884 he read a paper to a group interested in public education on the necessity of providing cheap editions of good literature for the masses. With the important aid of his chief disciple, Chertkov, an arrangement was made with a Moscow publisher to print and distribute booklets to be written by the best authors, illustrated by distinguished artists, and to be sold for the very inexpensive price of one and a half kopeks. These little books, that went under the trade name of Intermediary, had an immediate success; during the first four years some twelve million copies were sold.

Tolstoy maintained a continued interest in the venture and often recommended works for publication, usually foreign books which he thought reflected the right moral tone, such as Dickens's *Oliver Twist*, *Little Dorrit*, *Bleak House*, George Eliot's *Felix Holt*, and Kingsley's *Hypatia*. In fact, the initial popularity of Intermediary booklets owed a good deal to his own contributions, for Chertkov, mindful of the success of his earlier *What Men Live By*, kept urging him to write similar pieces. And during 1884–1885, he contributed no fewer than fifteen tales, as well as texts that described pictures, to Intermediary.

These brief stories, now favored by Tolstoy as the proper artistic medium for mass readers, were mostly based, as he said himself, on folktales, legends, and fables which describe marvelous things that never happened but are true because they reveal the truth of the kingdom of God. In the retelling he makes them entirely his own, catching the folk spirit in a narrative style of utter simplicity and clarity quite different from that of his earlier fiction. Some convey feelings of love of God, such as *Two Old Men* (1885), *Where Love Is, God Is* (1885), *The Repentant Sinner* (1886), and *The Three Hermits* (1886), where the moral is enlivened by a gentle humor. Others transmit the simplest feelings common to all men, especially those stories based on folktale motifs with their trappings of devils, supernatural happenings, and other-worldly plots, such as *Evil Allures, but God Endures* (1885), *Little Girls Wiser than Men* (1885), *Elias* (1885), *A Spark Neglected Burns the House* (1885), a tale of the causeless enmity of peasant neighbors, *The Story of Ivan the Fool* (1885), which contrasts the hero's dedication to hard work with the vain hopes of easy success of his shiftless brothers, *A Grain As Big As a Hen's Egg* (1886) on people who prefer to live on the labor of others, and *The Godson* (1886), which suggests that one must care more about others than about oneself. *How Much Land Does a Man Need?* (1886) is a little homily cast in attractive fictional form, in which a peasant with his traditional greed for land discovers only too late that all he needs is the six feet in which he is buried. Rarely does the instructive element obtrude or is the moral forced. In *The Imp and the Crust* (1886), for example, an amusing and charmingly told folktale about the devil who finally tricks the kind peasant into drunkenness, the message of temperance is never once overtly stated but is a conclusion the reader must draw for himself. Before the end of the 1880s Tolstoy seems to have lost interest in re-creating popular legends and folktales into short stories that would reflect, however indirectly, his religious and moral convictions, but the considerable group he did write contains some of his most memorable artistic gems.

## II

It was also in the latter half of the 1880s that Tolstoy returned to playwriting which he first attempted long before his religious conversion. For in 1864 he had written a five-act farce, *A Contaminated Family*, which satirized devotees of the radical movement then. He pokes fun at an 'emancipated woman' type who wears abbreviated skirts, dark glasses, short hair, smokes cigarettes, and mouths sententious phrases about the 'social web of prejudices' among the rich while living off her wealthy uncle. Ridiculed also is a radical student who imagines himself an advanced intellectual. Tolstoy was eager to have the play performed but his efforts came to nothing. He soon dismissed it as inadequate, although it has attractive qualities, and he never attempted to publish it.

Two years later he approached the same dramatic problem from a different point of view in *The Nihilist*, a three-act comedy which he dashed off in several days for the amusement of a large gathering of family and guests at Yasnaya Polyana where it was acted by the young people present. In it, several youths, including a student obsessed by nihilist ideas, visit a married couple. The conservative husband imagines the student has designs on his wife, but after some laughable scenes at the expense of the nihilist all is satisfactorily explained at the end.

Though comments by Tolstoy indicate that he seriously aspired to do something of significance in drama, he did not turn to the form again until twenty years later, and then he intended to make it serve the purpose of his new religious and social beliefs. In 1886 he wrote a light *jeu d'esprit*, *The First Distiller*. It is a clever dramatization of his short story *The Imp and the Crust*, in which the message of temperance is now underscored but with increased emphasis on the amusing give-and-take of the developing action. Sparse realistic dialogue sustains the fable of the Devil's success in ensnaring the rich and idle as well as his failure to beguile peasants who are protected from sin because of their devotion to hard work. Only by teaching them how to make and drink vodka does the Devil befuddle the better judgment of the peasants who then easily fall victim to him.

Of all Tolstoy's plays there can be no doubt that the grim tragedy, *The Power of Darkness* (1886), is his most celebrated and most enduring as literature, and though it bears traces of the new moral direction he gave his art, its total effect is achieved by an application of the brilliant realistic techniques of his earlier writing. It is based on a village crime involving adultery, murder, and infanticide, the details of which he became familiar with when the case came up for trial in Tula. The village wencher Nikita marries his mistress Anisya after the murder of her husband. Mired in the evil-begetting power of evil, which is reflected in the play's subtitle 'If a Claw Is Caught the Bird is Lost,' Nikita next seduces his stepdaughter Akulina, and later, with Anisya's help, he kills the illegitimate infant of this liaison. The now typical Tolstoyan moral message of atonement for evil appears in the drama's finale when the conscience-striken Nikita makes a public confession of his terrible crimes. Repentance at this point may seem contrived and unrealistic, but the action gains in dramatic impressiveness and convincingness for it is immediately followed by the startling declaration of Nikita's father, the old, religiously-minded Akim: 'God will forgive you, my own son! You have had no mercy on yourself. He will show mercy to you. God! God! It is He!'

Events are more often talked about in monologues than realized in action, which interferes with the fullness of characterization. In this respect as in others Tolstoy reveals a certain ineptness in playwriting compared to his superb mastery in the novel. Though his concern and intensity of feeling for the tragic weaknesses of the main protagonists compel belief in them, some of the secondary figures, especially the God-fearing Akim with his devotion to non-resistance to evil by force, are somewhat emblematic. On the other hand, Matronya, who stops at no sin to further the interests of her son Nikita, is a truly memorable creation of human wickedness. With his profound knowledge of peasant nature, which included a fine ear for their language, Tolstoy artfully reproduces their characteristic speech patterns in his dialogue. And though he now tended, in his non-literary writing, to favor peasant virtues in terms of his new faith, in *The Power of Darkness* he does not spare their vices.

Apart from the suspense involved in the conspiratorial plotting that leads up to the tragic denouement, the main dramatic tension in the play is concentrated in the mounting struggle between the two women, Anisya and Akulina, for the affection of Nikita and the premier position in the household. There are also several gripping scenes, such as that of the old peasant soldier, Mitrich, telling a bedtime story to little Nan, Anisya's daughter, while he suspects – and the audience knows – that at the same time Nikita's illegitimate infant is being murdered near by; or the striking scene where Mitrich tries to arouse Nikita to confess, which George Bernard Shaw comments on:

> I remember nothing in the whole range of drama that fascinated me more than the old soldier in your *Power of Darkness*. To me the scene where the two drunkards are wallowing in the straw, and the older rascal lifts the younger one above his cowardice and his selfishness, has an intensity of effect that no merely romantic scene could possibly attain.[4]

Besides Shaw, other distinguished writers abroad have had high praise for *The Power of Darkness*, such as Maeterlinck, Ibsen, and Zola, who was the first to have it performed in Western Europe. Tolstoy's efforts to have the play staged in Russia were unavailing. Although Emperor Alexander III, impressed by a private reading, suggested that it be performed, he withdrew support when he received a scathing denunciation of the play from Pobedonostsev, Procurator of the Holy Synod. Through an oversight of the censor, however, the play was allowed publication in 1887, an action that aroused the sovereign's ire. Not until the reign of Nicholas II was the play certified for the stage in 1895 in St Petersburg. An enthusiastic audience, aware of Tolstoy's triumph over censorship in this instance, acclaimed him and demanded that a congratulatory telegram be sent to the author. Shortly after, the play was performed at the distinguished Moscow Maly Theater with great success. At its conclusion, a crowd of excited students paraded to Tolstoy's house to pay tribute to him.

Pleasant circumstances presided over the last of Tolstoy's plays to appear during this period. Instead of moving to Moscow for the winter of 1889, the family remained at Yasnaya Polyana. The young people, on the lookout for entertainment, discovered in their father's papers the draft of a comedy in four acts. It amusingly treated the foibles of high society in a plot concerned with peasant distress over the lack of land. His children were delighted with it, particularly because they recognized prototypes of some of the large cast of characters, in friends, members of the family, and Yasnaya Polyana peasants. Though Tolstoy objected to their desire to perform it – staging a play, he said, was an amusement of the rich and idle – he quickly entered into the spirit of fun, directed rehearsals, laughed uproariously when humorous lines were effectively rendered, and frequently altered the dialogue to suit the personalities of the actors. *The Fruits of Enlightenment* was first performed in December 1889 to a gathering of family, guests, and servants. The great manor house of Yasnaya Polyana, which had become a centre for spiritual activity, had not experienced such gaiety for years.

The play's action is centred in the Zvezdintsevs' Moscow home, a wealthy gentry family caught up in a whirl of social events and waited on by a swarm of servants. The plot turns on a farcical situation in which at a spiritualism seance, then a popular fad in high society, the maid Tanya tricks her master into selling a large tract of his village land to a delegation of peasants who desperately need it for cultivation and grazing. The play allows Tolstoy ample opportunity to contrast the social parasitism and intellectual vulgarity of the Zvezdintsevs and their friends to the hardworking servants and peasants with their concern for daily bread.

Tolstoy, however, does not allow his moral bias to become a mere hobbyhorse. He never forgets that he is writing a comedy and not a social treatise. There is no meanness or bitterness in his satire. If the fecklessness and reprehensible behavior of the gentry come in for palpable hits, so do the oddities and foibles of servants and peasants. Nor does he fail to balance the faults of the gentry with their kindness. And the texture of the dialogue, spoken by a large and variegated cast, is unusually well adjusted to individual speakers with their idiosyncratic turns of expression and comic malapropisms. Except perhaps for the last act, the play's planning and smooth flow of scenes and action make it, technically speaking, his best theatrical achievement.

*The Fruits of Enlightenment* had its first public performance at Tula and then appeared in Moscow in 1891 under the direction of Stanislavsky, who was at that time just beginning his celebrated career. It was a huge success and has held the boards in Russia ever since, as has *The Power of Darkness,* although this tragedy is less frequently played.

## III

Different in theme and treatment from the short stories already mentioned in this period are several longer tales that recall the literary manner of Tolstoy's earlier fiction. But a major feature in them is the presence of a subjective moral element quite alien to his imaginative writing before his religious conversion. Nevertheless, the literary artist in Tolstoy seems to transcend the religious teacher in the best of these stories.

In 1884 he worked on *Memoirs of a Madman* which he unfortunately left unfinished. It is a powerfully fictionalized handling of a searing experience he underwent on a journey years before. In a tiny hut where he stayed for the night, the phantom of death confronted him with horrifying vividness. In retrospect he connects the experience with his new conviction that the life he led then was entirely irrational, fit only for a madman. One remembers Prince Andrei's haunting encounter with the phantom of death in *War and Peace* with significantly different results.

Death, as is well known, hounded Tolstoy's consciousness, and it is not surprising that during this same year (1884) he probably began the famous story *The Death of Ivan Ilych* which he planned as a surprise for his wife who was so chagrined over his desertion of artistic writing. It was not finished and published until 1886. Sonya was delighted and she and his literary friends regarded it as the first substantial piece of fiction he had produced since *Anna Karenina*.

On one level this compressed masterpiece in the short novel genre is an account of the life and death of Ivan Ilych, a most simple and ordinary life, remarks Tolstoy, and therefore most terrible. In his climb to success as a magistrate, he reveals no exceptional qualities unless it be that his conception of his duties as a judge compels him to eliminate all human considerations that might interfere with strict enforcement of the letter of the law. A prisoner in the dock was allowed no appeal to compassion; he was obliged to confine himself solely to the legal facts of his case. And Ivan Ilych manages his family and social life very much as he manages his courtroom – with self-aggrandizement and a vulgar sense of proprieties that contribute to his self-importance.

The other level of the story concerns Ivan Ilych's prolonged, incurable illness and shattering self-examination of his life as gradually the expectancy of death dawns upon him. He tries to justify his life which he had always thought a good one, but now he begins to wonder if he had been of use to anyone. In moments of illumination it occurs to him that he has been living a lie, a victim of self-deception. These moments of truth come to him when he observes the grief of his young son over his sufferings or experiences the patient, willing ministrations of his peasant servant Gerasim. Although there is some ambiguity about the ending, Tolstoy does not contrive a solution in accord with his new faith. Rather he appears to communicate a mystical experience of Ivan Ilych as death overtakes him. Like Prince Andrei, he discovers that death is an awakening in which he glimpses the spiritual destiny of man as a loving communion with people. He asks forgiveness of his family for his sins, and at last unafraid, he welcomes death.

It is little wonder that admirers of Tolstoy the novelist saw in *The Death of Ivan Ilych* a welcome harbinger of his return to the art of major fiction. The story fulfils his prescription mentioned in *War and Peace* that where there is no grandeur in art, there is no simplicity, no truth. The brilliant realistic effects of his early fiction reappear, but to these he adds a different strain, new in Russian literature up to that time – unsparing details on the physical horrors of sickness and death. As always, one is captivated by his use of artistic devices, such as the superb irony in the scene where the doctor treats his sick 'prisoner,' who pleads for information and human concern, the way Ivan Ilych treated prisoners before the bench; or the deft psychological touches revealing the mourners' insincerity which is suggested by their concentration on trivia during most solemn moments; and the hypocrisy of Ivan Ilych's wife and professional colleagues that masks their secret concern about the material gain that will accrue to them because of his death, while at the same time we know that he would have behaved in similar fashion if any of them had died.

## IV

Tolstoy's concern with the sexual problem began, as we have seen, in his early youth, but so did his concern with moral values in relation to women. If anything, growing maturity seems to have intensified his reaction to sex and contributed to extreme views on the sanctity of marriage which no doubt entered into the conviction that his own marriage was an essential solution of his sexual waywardness. A natural concomitant of all this, once he had adopted his new faith with one of the five commandments being 'do not lust,' was to declare for absolute sexual faithfulness of husband and wife. The problem would appear to have been solved for Tolstoy and he remained faithful to his wife, although he frankly admitted that at least once he was sorely tempted to sin. As might be expected, the problem, having become a matter of faith, persisted in a doctrinaire sense. It added to the domestic unhappiness of husband and wife and erupted quite positively in his artistic writing in what are referred to as his 'stories of sexual love.'

The first was *The Devil* which he wrote in 1889 and concealed from his wife, for it was inspired by his liaison, before his marriage, with the Yasnaya Polyana peasant Aksinya, passionate reference to which in his diary had aroused Sonya's jealousy. It was published posthumously in 1911. Irtenev in *The Devil*, like Tolstoy, has a serious love affair with Stepanida, a young married peasant woman in his village, but after his marriage his passion for her continues. In this respect, there is a further autobiographical basis for the action, for eight years after his marriage Tolstoy was strongly attracted by a peasant girl but managed to overcome his desire only by taking rather extreme measures. Irtenev in the story is not so fortunate. Tolstoy, dissatisfied with the first ending in which Irtenev commits suicide, wrote another in which the lover, convinced that Stepanida is a devil who has possessed him, murders her.

The psychological analysis of Irtenev's obsession is a masterly performance, and his failure to overcome his lustful desires, unlike Tolstoy in the incident mentioned above, may be regarded as a triumph of art over life. Since the story is pretty much concentrated on the fierce moral struggle of Irtenev, whose conscience is torn between the demands of an illicit passion and an apparently happy marriage with an adoring wife, the supporting characters are comparatively neglected. On the whole, the second conclusion that Tolstoy provides seems to satisfy better the artistic resolution of the action, for at the end Irtenev's mind has been quite warped by his futile battle with his conscience.

The most celebrated of Tolstoy's stories of sexual love is *The Kreutzer Sonata*. In 1887 a friend told him of hearing in a train an unfortunate stranger's account of his wife's betrayal. This suggested the theme for a story which Tolstoy began but soon put aside. He took it up again the next year, influenced by a new conception after hearing a performance of Beethoven's Kreutzer Sonata which produced a powerful impression on him as music often did. Draft after draft piled up, for the story had taken on a deep personal significance which he communicated to a friend:

> The contents of what I wrote were as new to me as to those who read them. In this connection an ideal remote from my activity was revealed to me so that at first I became horrified and did not believe it, but then I grew convinced, repented, and rejoiced in what was to me and others a happy impulse.[5]

The new ideal was absolute chastity, for both married and unmarried people, although only a few years before, in *What I Believe,* he had advocated marriage as the only normal and moral outlet for sexual satisfaction. Perhaps his own marital difficulties since acquiring his new faith had something to do with his altered views. At about this time he was reported as declaring: 'Man survives earthquakes, epidemics, terrible illnesses, and every kind of physical suffering, but always the most poignant tragedy was, is, and ever will be the tragedy of the bedroom.'[6] He sought support for his new conviction in the Gospels and found it in Matthew (19: 12): '. . . and there are eunuchs, which made themselves eunuchs for the kingdom of heaven's sake. He that is able to receive it, let him receive it.' And he plied his disciple Chertkov, whom only a few years earlier he had persuaded to marry for the good of his health and morals, with letters in which he defended his altered views. While arguing that sexual relations can have no physical or moral justification except to produce children, he goes on to insist, first repeating Matthew: '"He that is able to receive it, let him receive it," that is, let everyone aspire never to marry, but having married, let him live with his wife as brother and sister.'[7] And Tolstoy rejoiced to find that his views were similar to those in Alice B. Stockham's work *Tocology: A Book for Every Woman*. He wrote this representative of the Shaker movement in America of his admiration of their belief in celibacy and chastity, a doctrine based on the fact that Christ had not married, but he acknowledged his indebtedness to her ideas which, he said, were relevant not only to women, but to all mankind.

In *The Kreutzer Sonata* (1889) Pozdnyshev becomes the mouthpiece of these new convictions to Tolstoy. The hero acquires them in the course of his married life which had ended in the murder of his wife because he had jealously suspected her of betraying him with a musical friend. In his anguished dialogues and monologues on the train, he arraigns the whole practice of sex, among the married and unmarried, as something loathsome, contrived by modern society to debauch the innocent and rob mankind of its most precious spiritual values, and he does this in the belief that carnal love is selfish and that unselfish love requires no physical consummation. In Pozdnyshev's account of his pre-marital sexual indulgence, his courting the woman he married, their intimate life together, and the rearing of children, one repeatedly encounters known experiences of Tolstoy. Sex becomes the primary evil, and in his condemnation of accessories to it, he repeats the extreme caveats of Tolstoy, such as drink, dance, dress, and even certain effects of music, literature, and the theater. Nor will the hero make allowances for any mitigating circumstances of sincere intentions. When in one of the dialogues in *The Kreutzer Sonata* a lady indignantly declares to Pozdnyshev: 'But you are speaking of physical love! Don't you admit the existence of love founded on identity of ideals and on spiritual affinity?' he answers: 'Spiritual affinity! Identity of ideals! But in that case (excuse my rudeness) why do they go to bed together?'

Though it might be supposed that the work was doomed from the outset to turn into a boring didactic tract on celibacy and chastity, it is really an amazing example of Tolstoy's ability to explicate an extreme moral ideal through the medium of artistic narrative. Despite its abrasive and exaggerated argumentation, the tight structure, the psychological development of Pozdnyshev's thought and action that so convincingly drives him on to kill his wife, and the gripping account of the murder itself – all make for an absorbing story. Though contemporary critics were so shocked by its views that they ignored its artistic achievement, as fine a judge of literature as Chekhov, who as a physician found fault with Tolstoy's ignorance of certain medical matters treated in the work, declared of *The Kreutzer Sonata* that of all that was being written in Russia and abroad, 'it is hardly possible to find anything of equal power in the seriousness of its conception and the beauty of its execution. Apart from its artistic merits which in places are striking, one ought to be thankful for just one of the features, that it is extremely thought-provoking.'[8]

*The Kreutzer Sonata* aroused more popular controversy than any of Tolstoy's works during his lifetime. Though forbidden publication at first, this outspoken treatment of certain aspects of sex, the first such in Russia, shocked multitudes. A contemporary writes that 'reproduced in hundreds and thousands of copies, they [hectograph copies] passed from hand to hand, were translated into all languages, and were read everywhere with incredible passion. It seemed at times that the public, forgetting all its personal cares, lived only for the literature of Count Tolstoy. The most important political events rarely seized everyone with such force and completeness.'[9] Such was the demand that bookstores dared to sell these illegal hectograph copies at exorbitant prices. Finally, in 1891, Tolstoy's wife, after securing an interview with Alexander III with great difficulty, convinced him to permit her to print *The Kreutzer Sonata* in the thirteenth volume of her edition of her husband's works. She argued, either deliberately or ignorantly, that since the ideal behind the story is perfect chastity, it therefore preached that people could be pure only in matrimony, and she added that as part of an expensive edition which few could afford to buy, the story would receive little dissemination. Of course, to meet the demand, the publisher produced the thirteenth volume separately and in great quantity.

Tolstoy was deluged with letters. Some readers accused him of immorality, of advocating free love, and others understood the story as autobiographical, as though he had murdered his wife. He was denounced from the pulpit, threatened again with government persecution, and he heard that the book was forbidden to be sent through the mails in the United States. Becoming convinced that the real import of *The Kreutzer Sonata* was being distorted by critics, many of whom labored to point out the obvious, that if his position on absolute chastity were enforced, the world would come to an end ('I could do without it,'[10] he noted in his diary at this time), he felt it necessary to write an 'Afterword' (1890) to his story. There he affirms that he believes in some but not all the views of his hero, and he carefully explains that though absolute chastity for all is desirable, he regards it as an ideal, something unattainable in reality. Moreover, he reaffirms this stand in his Preface to *Christian Teaching* (1898) where he points out that striving after any degree of chastity among married and unmarried people was possible, would improve the lot of mankind, and was in conformity with Christ's teaching. In actuality, this was Tolstoy's position in a number of the more extreme pronouncements on his faith. They were ideals, attainable only in infinity, and if he had made the matter clearer in his writings and actions, he would have saved himself much criticism and even ridicule. Though the goal he set was often perfection, and he could be uncompromising about it as a goal, he never expected men, least of all himself, to achieve it. Striving for perfection was the end. Perhaps with the goal of absolute chastity in mind, he wrote in his diary at this time: 'We search for mind, powers, goodness, perfection in all this, but perfection is not given to man in anything....'[11]

The abuse he suffered over *The Kreutzer Sonata*, the Church's surveillance of him, and demands made on the government that he be punished may have contributed to his eventual revulsion to his story, for he wrote Chertkov: 'There was something nasty in *The Kreutzer Sonata*. It has become terribly revolting to me, every remembrance of it. There was something bad in the motives directing my writing of it, for it has evoked such wickedness.'[12] Certainly his own striving to practise his ideal of chastity greatly intensified unhappy relations with his wife. After twenty-seven years of married life, his suggestion that they sleep apart made her feel that the very fabric of their existence together had been torn to shreds. Nor could he abide by his resolution on chastity. Cynical critics, after the appearance of *The Kreutzer Sonata*, suggested that the author was getting old and that the grapes had turned sour. Yet when he was nearly seventy, he told his English biographer Aylmer Maude: 'I was a husband last night, but that is no reason for abandoning the struggle. God may grant me not to be so again.'[13] As for his wife, she bore him the last, her thirteenth, child, Vanya, during the year he began writing *The Kreutzer Sonata*. In her diary she wrote: 'He is killing me very systematically. . . . It would be terrible to become pregnant again, for all would learn of his shame and would repeat with malicious joy a joke just now invented in Moscow society: "There is the real 'Afterword' of *The Kreutzer Sonata*." '14 The family tragi-comedy had turned to pure tragedy.

The third and last tale on the subject of sex as a central motif is *Father Sergei*, which Tolstoy may have begun as early as 1889 or 1890, but apparently did not finish until 1898. Since it was published post-humously (1911), it lacks correction of a few small matters that he no doubt would have made in a final revision. It is a powerful story of an aristocratic officer, Prince Kasatsky, who abandons a brilliant career to become a monk, Father Sergei, when he learns that the beautiful woman he is engaged to has been the emperor's mistress. Without any sacrifice to special pleading, Tolstoy combines the theme of sex with spiritual regeneration. The secular pride that had motivated the hero's sudden renunciation of the world pursues him as a monk. Father Sergei falls victim to spiritual pride and as a holy man is still tempted by sexual desires. The point of the story is that he must learn through experience that he cannot live a spiritual life of his own as a religious recluse, that peace of mind comes only when man lives to serve God in the world. The prescription conforms to Tolstoy's desire to live an active life of faith in God.

Father Sergei's first temptation comes when an attractive loose woman, as a kind of lark, seeks him out in his monkish retreat to seduce him. In a desperate effort to subdue his lust for her, he chops off his finger, and the woman, terribly shaken by the experience, enters a nunnery. The action brings him fame in the region and in his spiritual pride he complies with designs of the monastery elders to set himself up as a miracle-worker. In this guise he succumbs to a feeble-minded girl whose parent brings her to him for treatment. Horrified by his sin, Father Sergei flees the monastery. In a dream an angel directs him to seek out a poor relative, a kind and selfless woman who rarely goes to church. In his brief stay with her he learns that in her self-sacrificing life she lives for God although she imagines that her mission is to help the poor and unfortunate. Only then does Father Sergei realize that he has been living for man on the pretext of living for God. He departs to take up the life of a humble pilgrim and to do good deeds. The reader is left with the impression that Father Sergei has vanquished his pride and perhaps even his faith in institutionalized religion, and that he has learned to attach less significance to the opinions of the world of men by becoming closer to the world of God.

The story, told with Tolstoy's careful attention to details and dramatic handling of scenes, is deeply moving. Though he may seem to interfere with the somewhat mystical experience of Father Sergei at the end, so penetrating has been the analysis of all factors shaping the character's being that his spiritual rebirth seems entirely natural and not at all surprising.

# 10

## The Kingdom of God
## Is Within You

I

By 1890 Tolstoy's new faith confronted him with another major decision. He had long been disturbed by the fact that he remained in possession of a wealthy estate although he had publicly declared the ownership of property to be an evil. Critics accused him in the press of being a 'pharisee,' and disciples who subscribed to his teaching of poverty wondered why he failed to divest himself of his property. His earnest desire was to give it all away, but conscience compelled him to recognize his family's claims and to resist the temptation to leave them for a penniless existence of his own. Though he had tried more than once to persuade his wife to accept, legally, full ownership of his estate, she adamantly refused.

The matter came to a head when Sonya, who managed the estate, rejected her husband's plea to pardon several peasants who had been arrested for stealing timber. Tolstoy was tormented by the thought that peasants would be sent to jail for taking from him what he regarded as necessary for their existence. Stormy scenes followed, and after many sleepless nights, he finally told her that he saw only one of two ways out for him: either to leave home or give all his land to the peasants. The upshot of the struggle was the usual compromise with his principles which never ceased to distress him: to rid himself of the property by dividing it among his wife and children just as though he had died, a decision that was legally arranged.

The settlement of ownership of land and buildings, however, did not involve the regular and very considerable income from the sale of Tolstoy's writings which was at Sonya's disposal. In his diary he mentions: 'Conversation with my wife, always about the same thing: to renounce the copyrights of my works. Again the same misunderstanding of me. "I'm obligated to the children. . . ." She does not understand, and the children do not understand, that in spending the money every rouble squandered by them out of profits of the books is my suffering and shame.'[1] He had earlier given her the right to publish on her own behalf any of his works written before his religious change in 1881 and he felt that he could not retract this permission. Their quarrels over the issue grew desperate. She warned that she would no longer live with him as his wife, and on several occasions threatened to commit suicide. Tolstoy remained resolute and pleaded with her to agree in a spirit of kindly understanding because, he said, a good deed is only good when it is done at some sacrifice. Sonya finally bowed to his desire. The announcement appeared in the press on September 16, 1891. Tolstoy gave permission to all who wished to do so to publish in Russia and abroad, in Russian and in translation, and also to perform on the stage, all his works written after 1881 and all future works. Although she agreed, Sonya never became reconciled to this step, complaining that he had deprived a numerous family of its rightful income.

## II

These domestic tribulations, like earlier ones growing out of his religious beliefs, were of Tolstoy's own making, and now they coincided with the beginning of another major work which was of exceptional importance as a further elaboration of his religious convictions. The focus of this long book, *The Kingdom of God Is Within You* (1893), is a treatment of non-resistance to evil by violence, an uncompromising affirmation of his belief in non-violence which he regarded as the keystone of his new faith. He had considered the subject previously in *What I Believe*, but now he undertook a comprehensive study of it in the context of government, society, the Church, patriotism, and war. His joyful discovery at this time of like-minded American predecessors and contemporaries, such as Thoreau, William Lloyd Garrison, Adin Ballou, and others, and the fact that his views had already begun to receive considerable support in the United States, no doubt influenced this formidable attempt to set down his thoughts on non-violence at greater length and more systematically.

The book first appeared in 1893 in a French translation in Paris and the next year in the original Russian in Berlin. Its publication, of course, was not permitted in Russia. In fact, when a friend, as a kind of test case, submitted the French version to the Russian censor of foreign books for clearance, he wrote Tolstoy that this official declared it to be 'the most harmful of all books that he had ever had an occasion to ban.'[2]

Tolstoy writes in the Preface of *The Kingdom of God Is Within You* that since the appearance of *What I Believe* in 1884 he has received many criticisms from abroad and a number in Russia where, he ironically remarks, the book has been forbidden. They have come from men of varying faiths or none at all and have been mostly directed to his statements on non-resistance to evil by violence. The criticisms and important historical events that have happened since, he says, have led him to fresh deductions and conclusions on the subject which he now proposes to consider in a new study.

At the beginning Tolstoy makes the point that although Christ's doctrine of non-resistance to evil or non-violence has been professed from earliest times to the present by a minority of men, its practice and writings about it have been strangely subjected to a kind of conspiracy of silence. Accordingly he devotes the early chapters to a succinct historical survey of attitudes towards the doctrine among various faiths and writers from the period of primitive Christianity to modern times, in which he dwells on Christians of the Middle Ages, Quakers, Mennonites, Russian sectarians, and others. Particular attention is paid to William Lloyd Garrison whose followers published in 1838 the amazing 'Declaration of Sentiments Adopted by the Peace Convention in Boston,' which Tolstoy quotes at length. It turns out to be a much more uncompromising statement on non-violence and civil disobedience than any Tolstoy ever made. The activities and writings of Adin Ballou also receive special notice, and it is in this connection that Tolstoy, with perhaps more good intentions than good judgment, argues the point on which so many of his critics have belabored him: his refusal to resist by violence any violence directed to him personally. What an immense amount of evil, he declares, results from people arrogating to themselves the right to prevent an evil which may occur but has not yet occurred. And he improbably asserts that ninety-nine per cent of the evil in the world, from the Inquisition to high-explosive bombs, executions, and the sufferings of tens of thousands of so-called political offenders, results from just such reasoning.

Further on Tolstoy complains that not a single critic of *What I Believe* understood that he was considering Christ's teaching as a philosophical, moral, and social doctrine; most of them had attacked

him in terms of their own conviction that Christ was the founder solely
of a religion of worship and personal salvation. And the clergy among
his critics, believing in the divinity of Christ and ignoring his most
explicit utterances, were caught up in the contradiction in which they
live. This leads them, contrary to Christ's teaching, to sanction violence, wars, and executions. And lay critics had regarded the substance
of *What I Believe* to be his theory of non-resistance by which they
understood that he forbade any kind of conflict against evil. Since they
believed that man was bound to defend by violence all who were
wronged or oppressed, therefore they condemned the teaching of non-
resistance to evil by violence as immoral. What Tolstoy is mostly
concerned with in the first three chapters of *The Kingdom of God Is
Within You* is in making explicit by the use of numerous examples
what had been implicit in his treatment of the formal practices of
various Christian churches in *What I Believe*. It amounts to a devastating
critique of what he claims is the mere lip service churches pay to the
exact teaching of Christ and especially to the clear meaning of the
statement on non-resistance to evil in the Sermon on the Mount.

In the important fourth chapter Tolstoy propounds as lucidly as he
ever did the moral and social implications of Christ's teaching as he
understood it. He rejects the familiar protest that this moral teaching
may be good in theory but impossible in practice. Nor will he accept
claims of those who believe that socialism or communism are more
efficacious remedies for the ills of the world, claims which he dis-
misses as 'simply an exaggeration and not worth talking about.'[3]
People who judge Christian teaching as they do social problems, says
Tolstoy, are mistaken, for they assume perfection is indicated and
they ask, as they do in the case of social laws: What would be the result
if everything were carried out? The assumption is wrong, he insists,
for Christ never envisaged that complete perfection is attainable but
that striving for it will constantly increase the good in man. However,
the ideal of complete, infinite perfection acts on men and moves them
to action. Tolstoy then elucidates the five commandments of the
Sermon on the Mount in terms of the ideal conception of each and the
level below which it is possible for man not to descend. In the case of
the fourth, he explains, the ideal is never to employ violence for any
purpose, and the level below which it is quite possible not to descend
is not to return evil for evil; the ideal of the fifth is to love our enemies
and those who hate us, and the level below which it is possible not to
go is to do no evil to our enemies. Here he is anxious to be clearly

understood, for his absolute pronouncements without any qualifications had confused and still confuse many. What he is saying in all this is that Christian teaching seems to make life impossible only when people mistake the indication of an ideal as the laying down of a rule.

Tolstoy also regards as mistaken all those, mostly the educated, who confuse aims of Christian teaching with their own theory that the only reasonable and good life is one of service to the whole of humanity. True Christian teaching, he declares, has nothing in common with those preachers of a universal brotherhood of man that is based on its advantageousness. Such love of humanity emerges from a social conception of life, a theoretical deduction from analogy, whereas true Christian teaching is concerned with the human soul.

Tolstoy regards the tendency to think that Christ's teaching can be accepted without changing one's form of life as the principal reason for the contradiction between life and Christian consciousness. He sees a crisis of conscience confronting humanity which has outgrown its governmental and social stage and is entering upon a new one. But in a spirit of optimism he writes: 'A time will come, and is already coming, when the Christian principles of equality (the brotherhood of man, the community of property, and non-resistance to evil by violence) will appear just as natural and simple as the principles of family, social, or national life do now.'[4]

A discussion of the economic plight of workers in modern times leads him back to his central theme of force or violence used by governments to maintain themselves in power and the masses in subject to an un-Christian life. Various aspects of governmental coercion are considered, especially military conscription and war. Chapters of the middle section of the book are largely concerned with this subject and the result is one of the most powerful denunciations of war ever written. He examines at length the causes of war and its colossal expenditures of treasure and life with their demoralizing effects on national economies. Much space is accorded attitudes towards war of rulers, statesmen, theologians, military men, scholars, writers, and just plain folk. Often he quotes from them, such as the moving threnody on the horrors of war of Guy de Maupassant which contrasts so jarringly with von Moltke's declaration: 'War is sacred, it is instituted by God, it is one of the divine laws of the world, it upholds in man all the great and noble sentiments – honor, self-sacrifice, virtue, and courage. It is war alone that saves men from falling into the grossest materialism.'[5] The conclusion Tolstoy reached is:

All talk of the possibility of establishing peace instead of everlasting war is pernicious sentimentality and chatter. . . . They lie and delude themselves and others in most refined ways to obscure and deaden their conscience. Instead of changing their way of life to correspond with consciousness, they try by all means to stifle and deaden consciousness. But the light shineth even in the darkness, and so it is beginning to shine at the present time.[6]

The treatment of compulsory military conscription is introduced by a series of observations on the power of the State to compel man to act contrary to his wishes or conscience. Tolstoy affirms that the basis of this power is physical violence and that all governmental demands, from tax payments to conscription, to which people appear to submit voluntarily, are effective only because of the State's power to threaten or to inflict punishment in one form or another. Nor will he accept the justification that State power also suppresses private violence which, he charges, always introduces fresh forms of violence into the lives of men and does this increasingly as it continues and grows stronger. He admits, however, that most people firmly believe that governments exist for their benefit and without them they would perish. On the other hand, people do not realize that the reason governments constantly increase their armies is not solely to defend themselves against external enemies, but also against their own op-pressed subjects from whom they have more and more to fear because of the growing spread of education. And this situation exists not only under despotic forms of government, but also in constitutional monarchies and republics, the only difference being that in the latter power is divided among a larger number of oppressors and is expressed less crudely.

Against this background of supreme State power which makes it all possible, Tolstoy considers universal military conscription as the cheapest way for governments to raise large armies and at the same time turn citizens into their own oppressors. It was an inevitable logical necessity, he says, a final expression of the contradiction inherent in the present social conception of life which began when violence became essential for its maintenance, and yet it destroys the very social order it is meant to support. In nothing, he writes, is the degree of contradic-tion in man's life so strikingly seen as in universal conscription, 'that last resource and final expression of violence.' An infinite pity for the plight of the conscript mingles with rage at the deceit, hypocrisy, and force that have condemned him to his fate. Through many pages of the book Tolstoy is at his most eloquent in stigmatizing the system, which he illuminates by brilliantly narrated scenes from his personal experiences, with its brutalizing effects in the recruiting stations in Russia. As a kind of symbol of the practice at its worse, he quotes from a newspaper account of 1891 (apparently supplying his own italics) of Kaiser Wilhelm's words to a detachment of new conscripts:

> Recruits! You have sworn fidelity to *me* before the altar and a minister of God. You are still too young to understand the full importance of what has been said here; but take care above all to obey the orders and instructions given you. You have sworn fidelity to *me*, lads of my Guard; that means you are now *my* soldiers, that you have *given yourselves to me, body and soul*. For you there is now one enemy – *my* enemy. In these days of socialistic sedition *it may come to pass that I command you to fire on your own kindred, your brothers, even your own fathers and mothers* – which God forbid – and even then it will be your duty to obey my orders without hesitation.[7]

Tolstoy envisages no future hope for the abolition or even the amelioration of universal military service in a modern civilization committed to the violence of war. The victim must submit, he says, for he has no principle for the sake of which he alone could resist violence, nor would those in authority ever allow him to unite with others. Moreover, in an order of society willing to accept the most humiliating degradation, there is no point in attempts to rebel by socialists and communists, who consider capitalist governments as an evil, or by anarchists who regard all governments as evil. If any of them triumphed, he warns,

> it would have to employ not only all the existing methods of violence, but also to devise new ones in order to bring its schemes into operation and maintain its power. Other men would be enslaved and forced to do other things, but the violence and oppression would be the same or even more cruel, since hatred of one another would be increased by the struggle. . . .[8]

It was Tolstoy's conviction that war, universal military conscription, and all other coercive governmental actions will end only with the gradual dissolution of the State, and the concluding chapters of *The Kingdom of God Is Within You* are dedicated to a serious and often deeply moving statement of how this may be brought about. A true

Christian, he asserts, is free from every human authority by virtue of the fact that he regards the divine law of love implanted in the soul of every man, of which Christ has made us conscious, as the sole guide of his life and of the life of others. The purpose of his life is to fulfill the law of God. In the pursuit of it he will endure suffering and violence and by so doing will not only free himself from external power, but the world also.

Without expressing undue hope in them, Tolstoy believed that he saw many signs of this kind of new Christian awakening, manifesting itself usually in refusals of individuals, as a matter of conscience, to commit acts of violence, to serve the government as conscripts, jurymen, and in civil positions, or to take oaths or pay taxes to support armies or armaments. Thousands of sectarians, defectors from Russian Orthodoxy, and many protesters abroad took these positions, and he cites numerous examples of such cases. The more than thirty volumes of correspondence in the ninety-volume Soviet edition of Tolstoy's complete works contain a vast number of letters in which he answers queries of Russians and foreigners who sought his advice on doctrinal matters or on problems connected with governmental coercion. It may be instructive to quote a few sentences from one as typical of his approach in coping with the latter kind of request. He answers a letter from a German youth who wants to know whether he should go to jail for refusing to be conscripted into the army when all he desires in life is to be allowed to teach in school instead of becoming a soldier. In the response, which was first published only in 1968, Tolstoy says in part:

> Moral acts are distinguished from all other acts by the fact that they operate independently of any predictable advantages to ourselves or to others. No matter how dangerous the situation may be of a man who finds himself in the power of robbers who demand that he take part in plundering, murder, and rape, a moral person cannot take part. Is not military service the same thing? Is one not required to agree to the deaths of all those one is commanded to kill?... Perhaps you will not feel strong enough to bear the consequences of your refusal and, knowing your weakness, will submit and become a soldier. I understand completely and I do not for a moment allow myself to blame you, knowing very well that in your place I might perhaps do the same thing. Only do not say that you did it because it was useful or because everyone does it. If you did it, know that you did wrong.[9]

Tolstoy contemplates in his book the possibility of the withering away of the State on spiritual grounds with much less assurance than Marx did in economic terms. One is unable to prove by abstract reasoning or experience, he declares, that the abolition of the State would involve social chaos or – as opponents of government maintain – that a time will arrive when men will become so reasonable that they do not wish to rob and murder and find that the continued existence of the State exercises only a harmful influence under the pretence of protecting people. Of the inevitablity of the change, Tolstoy is positive, but he mentions no definite time, which he vaguely indicates as being in the distant future; and, like Marx, he offers no blueprint of the form society will assume when governmental rule ceases. However, he regards the present age as actively transitional and places much emphasis on a growing 'Christianized public opinion' which, he believes, has already begun to have a restraining effect on the violence of the State and on people in general. He is confident that it will continue to do so until it transforms men and brings them into accord with Christian consciousness which is a driving force among the most advanced people. All the usual activities of the world will continue, he says, but the attitude towards them will be quite different. Men will be guided by something independent of all this. For a time is coming, he writes, 'when all institutions based on violence will disappear because it has become obvious to everyone that they are useless, and even wrong.'[10] It is within the doing of each man, he affirms, to bring to realization the prediction of the Gospels that a new form of life is coming to which humanity is approaching with increasing rapidity, when war will no longer be known and men will beat their swords and spears into pruning-hooks and ploughshares.

Much of the book's long Conclusion is given over to the impressive narration of a series of incidents drawn from Tolstoy's experiences, in which violence is inflicted on citizens for their opposition to what he considers unjust laws. In analyzing the state of mind of the perpetrators of the punishments, he discerns a hypnotic condition induced by their sense of obligation to the government but which nevertheless does not allow them to avoid the inner pain of conscience. Such men, too, he feels, could be responsive to the consciousness of Christian truth. He is much harsher on the 'do-gooders' of the world who believe they can cure the political, social, and economic ills of society by gradual ameliorative acts while protecting their own interests. They do evil by concealing the truth from themselves and represent the type of hypocrisy which Christ denounced.

The life of man and humanity in general, claims Tolstoy, is nothing but a continual movement from darkness to light, from a lower stage of truth to a higher. Truth not only points out the path of human life, but it also reveals the only path along which it can go. And man's freedom lies in having that choice. However, the Kingdom of God can only be reached by an effort to rise above external conditions and attain the acknowledgment and announcement of the truth. For, he concludes his book:

> The sole meaning of life lies in serving the world by promoting the establishment of the Kingdom of God. This service can be accomplished only by recognition and avowal of the truth by each separate individual. 'The Kingdom of God cometh not with outward show; neither shall they say, Lo here! or, lo there! for behold, the Kingdom of God is within you.'[11]

## III

This book, generally regarded as the finest of all Tolstoy's writings on his new faith, was also the one most widely praised and most fiercely attacked in his own day. No summary can do its complex reasoning full justice or convey the high seriousness and intense moral passion of its message to the world. Nowadays, when that message, however utopian it may seem, has an almost urgent relevancy, the work is almost entirely forgotten. In popular condemnation it has suffered much from critics – many give the impression of never having read the book through carefully – who single out for their barbs its central thesis of non-resistance to evil or non-violence as impossibly paradoxical or a quixotic mental aberration. The stock argument against Tolstoy's plea for non-violence was nearly always put as William Jennings Bryan formulated it on a visit to Yasnaya Polyana. What would you do, asked the Great Commoner, if you saw a bandit murdering or assaulting a child? And Tolstoy, as usual, offered his stock reply, that in his long lifetime he had never met anywhere the fantastic bandit who would murder or outrage a child before his eyes, whereas in war millions of brigands kill with complete license.[12] What Tolstoy's answer suggests is that it is very difficult to formulate a moral principle applicable in every case. In his book he was concerned with the whole vast subject of violence as it was exercised through the power of governments and affected the lives of the majority of citizens. In our own day Tolstoy's understanding of violence and its enormous significance, if not his proposed resolution of it, would probably be widely accepted, for he clearly recognized that violence is not a problem only of the criminal.

In his day the practice of non-resistance to evil by violence and other doctrines that were part of Tolstoy's faith could hardly have given him much hope for the future reformation of mankind. This was particularly true in the case of Tolstoyan colonies that quickly sprang up in the wake of interest in Russian populism and cooperative communes. Disciples began to organize agricultural colonies based on his principles in a number of rural communities at the end of the 1880s. In varying degrees their members were inspired to reject a society practising violence and exploitation and endeavored to live by the fruits of their labor and devote themselves to service to their fellow-men. The movement spread over Russia during the years, involving several thousand people, and also made its way abroad, especially in the United States, Britain, the Netherlands, and Bulgaria.

At first, Tolstoy manifested considerable interest in the colonists, helped them with advice on matters of doctrine, and interceded on behalf of those who fell afoul of the law for rejecting military conscription and in other conflicts. But he soon grew disillusioned with these communal efforts to realize in real life the teachings he expounded in his theoretical writings. To be sure, the colonists were often educated city people ignorant of agriculture and seemingly determined to apply his teachings in a narrow, literal sense. There are many accounts of hopeless quarrels which colonists got into among themselves but more often with canny peasants in the neighbourhood over enforcing with unimaginative rigidity Tolstoy's Christian anarchist principles, such as non-resistance to evil, the sin of owning property, and the injunction to love one's neighbor as oneself.[13] Though some of the Tolstoyan colonies continued as self-sufficient organizations until well into the Soviet period in Russia, eventually there and abroad they vanished like so many other utopian experiments in communal living.

Tolstoy's reaction to failure in this large experiment was in a sense consistent with a conviction he had expressed in *The Kingdom of God Is Within You,* namely, that the new religion had to be a lonely, individual experience. He was not deeply concerned that it was human nature violently to protect oneself against violence or deprivation of life's necessities, or that if moral and ethical principles failed to afford protection, then man would rebel against them as did many of the colonists. He was aware that his most devoted followers hoped to give the Tolstoyan movement a definite form by attracting masses to it and trying to persuade the master to leave his home, surround himself with disciples, and create a kind of moral Eden. However, he distrusted organized proselytizing. He wanted no church in his name, he told an American correspondent, and he spluttered to a friend that 'Tolstoyans are the most insupportable people.' Then he added: 'To stand aloof, to shut oneself up in a monastery, surrounded by such angels as oneself, amounts to creating a hothouse and those conditions in which it will be easy to be good oneself, but no one else will be warm. Live in the world and be good – that is what is needed.'[14] Towards the end of his life he pointed out that those belonging to the great society of God fulfill many Christian actions that are neither foreseen nor defined by Tolstoyan Societies, and he urged all who shared his faith to devote their time to ordering their own inner spiritual being rather than to promoting his beliefs.

In his sweeping condemnation of the violence, coercion, and abuses of State power in *The Kingdom of God Is Within You,* Tolstoy was again criticized by Europeans for not considering political, social, economic, technical, and humanitarian progress in Western countries. Though he had serious doubts about the efficacy of so-called modern progress in general, in this latest book, as already indicated, he sees no essential difference between Russia and the West in terms of the relevancy of his argument. Where he is plainly deficient is in opposing idealism to authority without ever seeming to realize that the ideal can easily slip into the absurd, nor did he ever entertain the possibility, as did Walt Whitman, whose poetry he admired, that authority may ultimately rest upon the common man. Yet in this kind of criticism there is a tendency to ignore two simple but fundamental aspects of the argument of *The Kingdom of God Is Within You*: that Tolstoy's panacea for the world's ills is religiously and not politically oriented, which is why he regards governments and property as regulated forms of violence for true Christians only; and though the application of every doctrine must inevitably be a compromise, its theory can allow for no compromise. In general, the substance of the book is directed towards one main purpose: to transform humanity by an inner, moral revolution, not through the seizure of power but by a rejection of it. It is his conviction that in the end this will remake society's institutions by elevating the individual to a higher Christian consciousness.


IV

In the years after *The Kingdom of God Is Within You,* Tolstoy continued to write about some of its themes, but he never again did anything as definitive on his religious thought as this book. Although no marked changes in Tolstoy's views are evident in later contributions, several of them reflect new emphases and nuances.

For example, in the extensive essay, *Christianity and Patriotism* (1894), he treats a subject he had hitherto scanted. His polemical powers were never better displayed than in this effort to illustrate how governments whip up national patriotism to support the bloody business of war. He begins with an often amusing account, based mostly on newspaper reports, of the contrived outpouring of patriotism and fraternal admiration that gripped Russia and France on the occasion of the exchange of their respective fleets to Toulon and Kronstadt in 1893, Then he shrewdly elaborates how all this enthusiasm has been deliberately and hypocritically manufactured by the two governments to enlist public support for a threatened war between France and Germany in which Russia's own purposes will be served. Almost cynically he projects what will happen when Russia publicly announces it will come in on the side of France:

> The bells will peal and long-haired men [priests] will dress themselves in gold-embroidered sacks and begin to pray on behalf of murder. The familiar, age-old, horrible business will recommence. The editors of newspapers will set to work to arouse hatred and murder under the guise of patriotism and will be delighted to double their sales. Manufacturers, merchants, and contractors for army-stores will hurry about joyfully in expectation of doubled profits. Officials of all sorts will busy themselves in the hope of being able to steal more than usual. Army commanders will bustle here and there, drawing double pay and rations and hoping to receive various trinkets, ribbons, crosses, stripes, and stars for murdering people. Idle ladies and gentlemen will fuss about, entering their names in advance for the Red Cross and getting ready to bandage those whom their husbands and brothers are setting out to kill – imagining that they will be doing a most Christian work thereby.[15]

In short, patriotism is indicted as a false sentiment and war as a catastrophe that has nothing in common with the real interests of the masses or the precepts of Christianity.

*Patriotism and Government* (1900) is a shorter essay, and in its debunking of the peaceful professions of great powers at the very time they are planning war, it is unusually abrasive. Tolstoy argues that congresses, conferences, and courts of arbitration will never deliver mankind from the increasing evils of growing armaments and war. In fact, he had already declared with striking prescience in *The Kingdom of God Is Within You*: 'It is often said that the invention of terrible instruments of destruction will put an end to war: war will destroy itself. That is not true.'[16] The only remedy, he insists in this essay, is to do away with governments which are the ultimate instruments of violence. And a step in this direction would be to convince people that the feeling of patriotism, which supports violence, is a bad feeling and is immoral. But it can be eradicated, he concludes, only when men accept Christ's teaching that it is wrong to kill. And he predicts that unless universal disarmament is achieved, more terrible wars are certain to come.

Tolstoy's final work on the subject of non-violence and Christian consciousness was a short book, *The Law of Love and the Law of Violence,* which he finished in 1908, two years before his death. The old man of eighty apologizes rather pathetically for turning once again to such matters, but aware, he says, of the one means of salvation for Christian humanity from its physical suffering and moral corruption, 'I, who am on the edge of the grave, cannot be silent.' He repeats with uncommon vigor his excoriation of war as the ultimate manifestation of violence, and he points out, with convincing documentation, that Christianity in the first four centuries of its existence categorically forbade its followers to engage in it, but that thereafter they have never ceased to murder in war while professing the very faith that condemns it. Surprisingly his old artistic skill emerges with extraordinary freshness in telling the story of the trial and conviction of a Russian for refusing to bear arms – lively characterization of the participants, expressive, realistic dialogue, and homely touches as when the priest who administers the oath is described as still under the influence of a quarrel with his wife on account of a carpet he had given away against her express wish.

Nor has anything altered much in the corrective for these evils that he had offered more than twenty-five years earlier in *What I Believe* - Christ's supreme law of love which obliges every man to listen to the dictates of his conscience and to refuse to serve governments, since all of them maintain themselves through coercion and violence. But in this little book, as in many of his other religious writings, Tolstoy, however much he may try, fails to resolve the central dilemma of his faith, which really did not exist for him although he knew it did for the majority of his readers. That is, on the basis of Christ's gospel of love, how can we live peacefully in this world of violence without requiring or enforcing laws or without meeting violence by violence? In short, can he be asking readers to surrender supinely to Stalins and Hitlers.

If Tolstoy's panacea is unconvincing, his statement of the ills of the world that prompted it has an oppressive immediacy for readers today. His arraignment sounds like a bill of complaints that a moral philosopher among statesmen at the United Nations Assembly might have offered only yesterday:

> All thinking people must admit that the present life of Christian nations will deteriorate more and more if we cannot make up our minds to modify it. The misery of the disinherited and the luxury of the rich increase each day; the struggle of all against all: revolutionaries against governments, governments against revolutionaries, oppressed nations against their oppressors, state against state, the West against the East – it is becoming ever more bitter.[17]

Or numerous writers and thinkers nowadays may find their dire forebodings on our technological age reflected in these words of Tolstoy in *The Law of Love and the Law of Violence*:

> ... each step that we may make today towards material progress not only fails to advance us towards the general well-being, but shows us, on the contrary, that all these technical improvements increase our miseries. Submarines, subterranean and aerial machines may be invented for transporting men with the rapidity of lightning; the means of communicating speech and human thought may be multiplied *ad infinitum;* but it would still remain a fact that the travellers who are so comfortably and rapidly transported, are neither willing nor able to commit anything but evil, and their thoughts and words can only incite men to further harm. As to the beautifully perfected armaments of destruction, which, while diminishing the risk of those who employ them, make carnage easier, they only give further proof of the impossibility of persevering in the direction we are going.[18]

# II

## *What Is Art?*

I

At the beginning of 1895 the harmonious relations of Tolstoy and his wife once again ended in a violent quarrel, this time over his decision to publish without remuneration a recently completed story, *Master and Man*. Ignoring their agreement, she demanded the manuscript for inclusion in the last volume of her edition of his works. Suddenly the domestic turmoil was muted by the death of seven-year-old Vanichka in February, their last child who had been born when Sonya was forty-four. From all accounts he was a most unusual youngster whose extraordinary sensitivity recalled the same quality in Tolstoy as a child. He told his wife: 'I somehow dreamed that Vanichka would continue after me the work of God.'[1] And he wrote a friend that the boy was endowed with more than ordinary gifts, one of those children God sends into this world too early, like the swallows who come too soon and are frozen.

Sonya's extreme grief filled him with anxiety and their life together again became warm and close. He watched over her tenderly and like a spiritual father sought to detect the slightest religious change. With hope, he noted in his diary: 'The pain of bereavement at once freed her from all that darkened her spirit. It was as if the doors had been rent asunder and laid bare that divine essence of love in our souls.'[2]

He considered taking Sonya abroad to allay her sorrow, but the thought that the government might prevent him from returning dissuaded him. Instead, since she found solace in her grief in a passion for music, various performances were arranged at Yasnaya Polyana during the summer of 1896. Much of this interest was connected with the distinguished pianist and composer S. I. Taneyev, a house guest. Her growing attachment for him disturbed Tolstoy and later became the source of serious disagreements between husband and wife.

Indeed, as the months wore on, Tolstoy's hope of a spiritual trans-formation in Sonya waned. He wrote a family friend: 'Of everything spiritually beautiful that revealed itself immediately after Vanichka's death and from the manifestation and growth of which I expected so much, there has remained only despondency and egotistical grief.'³ Yet sympathetic relations under the shadow of their mutual sorrow continued. When she asked him to remove passages in his diaries that were offensive to her, he went over them all and did so. Then he added an entry:

> She was an ideal wife in the pagan sense – in the sense of fidelity, domesticity, self-denial, family love – and in the very pagan in her lies the possibility of a Christian friend. I saw this after Vanichka's death. Will it develop in her? May the Lord help. The events now are joyful to me. She saw and will see the power of love – the power of her love over me.⁴

During this period, however, Tolstoy had little to be joyful about; government persecution of his disciples for refusing military service and distributing his illegal books and pamphlets intensified. Since these violations of the law were ultimately his responsibility, he wrote the authorities, why not arrest him? And either naïvely or ironically he pleads with them not to fear any imaginary national popularity or his social position:

> I not only do not think this, but I'm convinced that if the govern-ment acted resolutely against me, exiled, imprisoned, or even took sterner measures against me, it would not encounter any special difficulty, and public opinion would not only fail to be agitated by this, but the majority of people would thoroughly applaud such action and would say that it ought to have been done long ago.⁵

Tolstoy received no answer, but the Minister of Justice told one of his close friends, who relayed it to Tolstoy, that 'the government is unable to prosecute Leo Nikolayevich himself, but that prosecution of people who distribute his works serves as punishment for Leo Niko-layevich.'⁶

## II

Neither domestic tribulations, nor grief, nor guests were allowed to interfere with the master's long hours of work in his study. Like most dedicated, self-disciplined men, this refuge from social intercourse was more than a habit; it was essential to his peace of mind. Though as usual Tolstoy was busy at this time with extensive reading, notetaking, and several pieces of writing, what largely absorbed his attention was the project that had been in his thoughts for years – a treatise on aesthetics. Multiplying diary observations on the subject, especially in 1896, began to indicate that the project was at last coming to a head.

Though he had a measure of sovereign contempt for critics of the arts – the stupid who discuss the wise, he said – he had contributed a formidable amount of such criticism himself during his lifetime. On literature alone, the Soviet standard edition, not entirely complete, runs to more than 700 pages of formal essays and a multitude of random judgments on authors and their works, Russian and foreign, drawn from his diaries and letters.[7] The contents tend to be individualistic and arbitrary. Lofty praise of Pushkin or Gogol or Turgenev is suddenly deflated by withering comments on later encounters. With some exceptions, his evaluation of poetry lacks the penetration and authority he brings to the appreciation of fiction which evokes memorable and quite original judgments emerging from contemplation and practice of the art of the novel. Until his religious change, Tolstoy's criteria in appraising fiction were reasonably objective. Ruthless in criticizing his own art, he applied the same high standards to others. From his earliest concern with aesthetic theory, the subjects that interested him most were the purpose and content of art, their relation to life, the nature of realism, the significance of forms, technical skill, the function of language, and psychology in the creative process.

Tolstoy tells us that from the outset of his career he began to judge artistic productions in terms of three factors: the extent to which the contents of a work of art reveal a new side of life; how far the form is good, beautiful, and in accord with the contents; and, most important, to what extent is the relation of the artist to his subject sincere.[8] Many of his critical comments are elaborations of these points. It may be that the simple and inartistic are not good, he remarks, but what is artistic and not simple cannot be good. And the artist must see things not as he would like to, but as they really are. To reveal the truth of life, he believed, must be the principal objective of an artist in dealing with psychological analysis. 'In general, my heroes and heroines,' he told a friend, 'sometimes do things I don't want them to do; they do what should be done in real life, just as it happens in real life and not as I would like.'[9] Perhaps one reason why he preferred Dostoevsky's *The*

*House of the Dead*, a work based directly on the author's prison experiences, was because the characters thought and behaved according to life's logic, which did not appear to Tolstoy to be true of many imaginary characters in Dostoevsky's novels. Authors who sent books for his opinion always ran the risk of blunt, uncompromising criticism. To the questions of one such victim, he replied that he did not have talent and should discontinue his literary endeavors. And for good measure he added: 'A person should write only when he experiences within himself an entirely new and important subject which is clear to him but misunderstood by people, and only when the need to elucidate this subject gives you no peace of mind.'[10]

Tolstoy's keen interest in problems of art was not only evident in his early years, but during that time he occasionally fell into the critical posturing that suggested the radical position he was later to adopt in *What Is Art?* His struggle with religion in 1880, however, virtually compelled him, intellectually and spiritually, to write a treatise on art that would accord with his new religious and moral philosophy of life. For he had by then come to the conclusion that the art he and others served seduced people from the good and led them into evil.

Since he realized that the credibility of any system of aesthetics bore a sensible relation to its satisfactory explanation and justification of sincere works of art, Tolstoy wrestled long and hard with the project. During the course of some fifteen years, he read a small library on aesthetics, philosophy, and belles-lettres; studied music, painting, and sculpture; attended concerts, operas, exhibitions, and dramatic performances; and wrote eight separate articles and drafts and fragments of others, in which he pondered, defined, and redefined his position.[11] From these preliminary efforts it seems clear that his chief difficulty was in convincingly establishing his own moral and ethical principles as universal, immanent, organizing factors in the artistic process. There is evidence that his mounting opposition to the direction contemporary Russian and European art was taking spurred him on to finish the work. He spent a good deal in 1896 and most of the next year on the subject and finished it in December 1897. *What Is Art?* was published in Russia in 1898 but in a form so mutilated by editor and censor that Tolstoy repudiated it. What he declared to be the first complete and correct edition of *What Is Art?* was published in England in a translation by Aylmer Maude under Tolstoy's supervision.

III

In the first part of *What Is Art?* Tolstoy dubs as 'enchanted confusion' various definitions of theorists which centre on the concept of beauty. The trouble with them, he argues, is that they are concerned primarily with the pleasure art may give and not with the purpose it may serve in the life of man. It is at this point in the treatise that he puts forth his own definition:

> To evoke in oneself a feeling one has experienced and having evoked it in oneself then by means of movements, lines, colours, sounds or forms expressed in words, so to transmit that feeling that others experience the same feeling – this is the activity of art.
>
> Art is a human activity consisting in this, that one man consciously, by means of certain external signs, hands on to others feelings he has lived through, and that others are infected by these feelings and also experience them.
>
> Art is not, as the metaphysicians say, the manifestation of some mysterious Idea of beauty or God; it is not, as the aesthetic physiologists say, a game in which man lets off his excess of stored-up energy; it is not the expression of man's emotions by external signs; it is not the production of pleasing objects; and, above all, it is not pleasure; but it is a means of union among men joining them together in the same feelings, and indispensable for the life and progress towards well-being of individuals and of humanity.[12]

Tolstoy delays the application of his definition to good and bad art in order to engage in a brief historical survey of the field and the aesthetic theorizing that followed. Since beauty and goodness seemed to him to coincide in the deficient moral development of Greeks and Romans, he avoids any formal treatment of classical art. But he traces the gradual displacement of sincere, moral, and religious feeling expressed in early Christian art by concepts of beauty and pleasure which were derived from it in the Renaissance when art fell under the tutelage of the upper classes. This condition, he contends, has carried over into modern times and has been sanctioned by aestheticians. The survey prepares the way for a forthright attack on modern art which he regards as a creature of the ruling classes and on the evils of their cultural ideology whose main purpose is to afford pleasure. Though they represent hardly one per cent of the population, he asserts, they consider their art the only true and universal one, acclaimed by their aestheticians as the highest manifestation of the Idea, Beauty, God, and spiritual enjoyment, yet the other ninety-nine per cent, the workers, whose toil is often necessary for the production of much of this art, live and die generation after generation without knowing or understanding it. Nor will Tolstoy accept any of the usual rationalizations of the situation. Idealists who believe that modern industrial and social progress will eventually provide the masses leisure to enjoy this art do not realize, he says, that if the 'slaves of capitalism' are freed it will be impossible to produce such art. Similarly he rejects the argument that education will make it accessible to them, for the chief subjects of present-day art evoke only bewilderment or contempt in working men. If by chance something is understood, it would not elevate their souls. And anyway, if upper-class art is not accessible to everyone, then it is not the vital matter it is represented to be or it is not real art.

Tolstoy's quarrel with contemporary art, especially belles-lettres, is an outgrowth of his new religious and moral convictions. He accuses artists, in their unbelief, of concentrating on what affords the greatest enjoyment to a certain class of society while largely ignoring artistic activity that aims to transmit the highest feelings of humanity that flow from religious perception. That is, profound and varied religious subject-matter proper to art is scanted, loses its beauty of form, and becomes affected and obscure. It ceases to be natural or sincere and lapses into artificiality. So impoverished in subject-matter is upper-class art that Tolstoy feels able to reduce nearly all of it to the expression of three feelings: pride, weariness of life, and sexual desire which, he remarks, amounts to a veritable 'erotic mania.'

The new Decadent School of art bears the brunt of his attack. Though he singles out French writers because he believes them most imitated, Russian and Western European writers and artists in general are also arraigned. Poems and prose of Mallarmé, Baudelaire, and Verlaine are analyzed, but faults of other authors are listed, with illustrations from their works confined to a series of appendices. Music and painting, particularly Impressionists and Neo-Impressionists, are likewise discussed. The burden of his objections is that all this new art is variously dedicated to a cult of unintelligibility which feels it unnecessary to be comprehensible to the 'vulgar crowd.' It is a kind of premeditated obscurity, he declares, and even if some meaning can be discovered, it usually turns out to be filled with evil and base feelings. The whole lacks simplicity and sincerity and is penetrated with artificiality. It is impossible for such would-be artists to find anything new and important to say, and to freshen things up they invent new forms and pornographical details. A few recent fiction writers have a high-flown style and elevated feelings, he admits, but he cannot make out in their stories what is happening, to whom, and where.

Tolstoy agrees that simply because he cannot understand this art, which is more exclusive than the art he is accustomed to, it gives him no right to conclude that it is bad or unreal art. But the advantage which the art he acknowledges has over Decadent art is that it is comprehensible to a larger number of people. Nevertheless, he protests, a conviction has arisen that art may be art and still be incomprehensible, which means that it has become not a serious and important matter of life but a mere amusement. Perverted art may not please the majority of men, but good art always pleases every one. Great works of art, he adds, such as the *Iliad*, the *Odyssey*, and the Biblical stories of Joseph, Isaac, and Jacob, and folktales and legends, are great only because they are accessible and comprehensible to all. For if the aim of art is to infect people with emotions the artist has experienced, how can one talk about not understanding?

There is a growing commercialization in contemporary art, Tolstoy says, and in order to meet the demand real art is rapidly being replaced by a simulated or counterfeit art through borrowing, imitation, and other methods, and it satisfies people with perverted aesthetic tastes. Whole subjects or special features are borrowed from former works and reshaped with additions designed to convey the appearance of novelty. Among illustrations of this process, he writes of the most amazing one:

> A work founded on something borrowed, like Goethe's *Faust* for instance, may be very well executed and be full of mind and every beauty, but because it lacks the chief characteristic of a work of art – completeness, oneness, the inseparable unit of form and content expressing the feeling the artist has experienced – it cannot produce a really artistic impression.[13]

By imitation Tolstoy means several things: in literary art the effort to describe everything just as it is in life, even to the extent of copying real speech; in pictorial art the method which assimilates painting to photography and thus 'destroys the difference between them'; and in music the attempt to imitate by rhythm and sound those sounds which in real life accompany the thing it wishes to represent. Another kind of appeal to jaded tastes is the introduction of actions, often purely physical, that have a 'striking' or 'effective' impact on the outer senses. These devices, he says, are designed to afford pleasure and give a semblance of the feeling received from real art in terms of critical clichés of 'poetic,' 'realistic,' 'striking,' or 'interesting.' But none of these attributes, he declares, offers a standard of excellence in art or has anything in common with it. For example, in appraising a work according to its realism, we indicate that we are concerned with a counterfeit and not with art.

What Tolstoy is trying to demonstrate here is that borrowing, imitation, other devices, and even a measure of talent are necessary to produce counterfeits of art to satisfy the burgeoning market of the upper classes, but they must not be confused with real universal works of art. He writes:

> Many conditions must be fulfilled to enable a man to produce a real work of art. It is necessary that he should stand on the level of the highest life-conception of his time, that he should experience feeling and have desire and capacity to transmit it, and that he should moreover have a talent for some one of the forms of art. It is very seldom that all these conditions ... are combined.[14]

Along with counterfeit art he considers commercialism, professionalism, art criticism, and schools of art, all of which, Tolstoy maintains, weaken and eventually destroy art's most precious quality – its seriousness. He sees no point in efforts of critics to explain art, for if a work does not infect people, no interpretation can bring this about. And the professional schools of art he ridicules for trying to do the impossible – to teach men how to become artists. Critics are blamed for elevating many of the world's greatest artists to what he regards as undeserved esteem. The Greek tragic dramatists, Dante, Shakespeare, Milton, and Beethoven are only a few of the notable names in this devastatingly inclusive list. Perhaps one should also mention Wagner, for to him, or more specifically to his *Nibelungen Ring*, Tolstoy devotes a long analysis as a work of counterfeit art so gross, he says, as to be even absurd.

Tolstoy frankly states that what he has been saying about the perversion of art in contemporary society will hardly be accepted by anyone. Moreover, he also admits that counterfeit productions are often more effective and in subject more interesting than those of art, but he insists that the qualitative artistic difference between them is not detected by most members of the upper classes whose feelings have been atrophied by the kind of education they have received. Counterfeit art, he says, is always more ornate, while true art is modest. In the examples he cites to illustrate the difference, however, it is obvious that, in the works of real art he stresses, the simple feelings conveyed are such as would be more appealing to simple people than to the sophisticated.

In a key chapter of the treatise, the sixteenth, Tolstoy attempts, in terms of subject-matter, to identify good and bad art in relation to what he regards as its purpose: to further the movement of humanity towards perfection. There are only two kinds of good art tending to unite men: religious art transmitting feelings that flow from a perception of man's position in the world in relation to God and the brotherhood of man; universal art which transmits the simplest feelings of common life accessible to all, the art of the people. In literature, as modern examples of the first category of the highest art flowing from love of God and man, he mentions Schiller's *Die Räuber*, Hugo's *Les Pauvres Gens* and *Les Misérables*, Harriet Beecher Stowe's *Uncle Tom's Cabin*, George Eliot's *Adam Bede*, Dickens's *A Tale of Two Cities* and *A Christmas Carol*, and Dostoevsky's *The House of the Dead*. With reservations he mentions examples of good universal art, such as Cervantes' *Don Quixote*, Molière's comedies, Dickens's *David Copperfield* and *The Pickwick Papers*, and tales of Pushkin, Gogol, and Maupassant, for he believes their appeal is restricted compared to the truly universal appeal of ancient stories such as that of Joseph in the Bible.

Illustrations of the two categories in music, painting, and sculpture come with more difficulty, although he does mention a few little-known artists. All art which has no claim on the two categories, because it divides rather than unites people, he summarily condemns. This includes every representation of miracles in painting, not excepting Raphael's *Transfiguration,* and the later compositions of Beethoven, after his deafness, such as the Ninth Symphony. Though he realizes that these repudiations of many accepted masterpieces of art, very few of which he attempts to justify by analysis, will arouse widespread indignation, he persists in designating them as bad or counterfeit art on the basis of his conviction that they serve no useful purpose in the spiritual unification of mankind.

In the concluding chapters, Tolstoy recapitulates the sorry state of art, real and counterfeit, in contemporary European society. It infects people, he declares, with the worst feelings of superstition, patriotism, and sensualism; its concentration on sexual love tends to disseminate

183

vice widely. To be deprived of all art rather than continue the depraved variety would be better, a fantasy he supports by calling to witness Plato in *The Republic* and others in the past who revolted at the extreme social license of art.

But he goes on to strike an encouraging note. The religious ideal by which humanity lives is becoming more clearly recognized, and the material well-being of man is ever increasing. However few in number, the best works of art in his own time, he insists, transmit religious feelings that contribute to the union and brotherhood of man. Though the change is still distant, he predicts that the time will come when art for the lower and upper classes will disappear and be supplanted by one common universal art.

This art of the future will be created, not by a select few, but by gifted members of the whole people who feel so inclined and will be accessible to all. Complex techniques will give way to brevity, simplicity, and clarity. The professionalism of artists absorbed primarily in monetary gain, which Tolstoy regards as most detrimental to the production of sincere art, will be replaced in the future by artists whose chief delight will be the widest diffusion of their works without financial payment. And the universal subject-matter of this art will be infinitely richer, for it will appeal not to exclusive feelings of the few who have freed themselves from the kind of labor natural to human beings, but to all who experience feelings in living a life natural to mankind.

Tolstoy ends *What Is Art?* on an interesting note. He observes that science and art are closely bound together, and he connects what he considers the false development of contemporary scientific thought with what he deplores as the falseness of art. He accuses scientists of devising a theory of science for science's sake not unlike the theory of art for art's sake. The proper sphere of real science, he urges, is not the study of whatever happens to interest us, but the study of those questions of religion, morality, and social life whose solutions are essential for the well-being of man. The feelings transmitted by art, he maintains, grow out of the false preoccupation of experimental science, and he calls upon scientists to redirect their interests to the primacy and importance of religious, moral, and social problems. 'In our age,' he concludes, 'the common religious perception of men is the consciousness of the brotherhood of man – we know that the well-being of man lies in union with his fellow-men. True science should indicate the various methods of applying this consciousness to life. Art should transform this perception into feeling.'[15]

## IV

Tolstoy's pronouncement on the modesty of art bore little relevance to his study of the subject. Artists who visited his home left with frayed nerves after being catechized by him on *What Is Art?* If its public appearance aroused much attention, it was hardly that of a *succès d'estime,* for its sweeping condemnation of so many great works of art outraged readers. Nor did he understate his conviction in the book of the hostility his extreme views would encounter, for with the passage of time *What Is Art?* has been mostly forgotten as the effort of an author with a fissure in his brain who tolerated no intellectual compromises with his extreme ideas. Other faults, perhaps, have contributed to this fate. Apart from occasional brilliant passages, in none of Tolstoy's argumentative writings is there so much repetition, awkward language, and loose terminology, as though complete absorption in what he was saying for once distracted him from how he was saying it. Then, too, some of his value judgments, if not actually absurd, come close to being that, such as his positive assertion of the futility of criticism or interpretation of works of art, although here one must be careful to distinguish between the artistic process itself and its finished products, which he had been criticizing all his life. Nor does experience support his assurance that 'upper-class' art can never be understood or appreciated by the masses. At times, indeed, the contrary seems to be the case. And the claims he makes for 'infectiousness' of art in his two categories, religious and universal, seem fuzzy and even exaggerated, as though the degree of infectiousness were something that could be precisely measured.

*What Is Art?*, however, is a work that ought to be read from the vantage point of an understanding of Tolstoy's personal prejudices, intellectual arrogance, and moral absolutes. Then it becomes thoroughly stimulating and its indubitable contribution to aesthetic theory can be evaluated on its own terms. He never regarded himself as a professional aesthetician, remained dissatisfied with his treatise, for he always felt that something important and mysterious about art had evaded him, and he clearly undertook the project out of a feeling of pressing moral necessity as a piece of unfinished business on the agenda of his new faith. It was not so much hedging as conscience that prompted him to slip in a rare footnote, in which he confessed to being 'insufficiently informed in all branches of art' (apart from literature, his treatment of the other arts is often woefully inadequate). And he points out that he attaches 'no special importance' to his selection of illustrative examples of the best art, for as a member of the upper class, 'perverted by false training,' he may have mistaken for absolute merit impressions a work had produced on him as a youth. Then, with the supreme irony of incorruptible moral consistency, he adds here: 'I must moreover mention that I consign my own artistic productions to the category of bad art, excepting the story *God Sees the Truth but Waits*, which seeks a place in the first class, and *A Prisoner of the Caucasus*, which belongs to the second.'[16] Though his derogation of *War and Peace* and *Anna Karenina* as 'bad art' is often cited in refutation of his theory of artistic infectiousness, an understanding of the full implications of the theory tends to support the amazing integrity of his consistency. The trouble is that he makes no allowance for individual free choice in artistic preference.

Tolstoy was indebted to the literature of aesthetics that he studied for aspects of his theorizing and of his definition of art.[17] But original thinking is everywhere reflected in his treatise, especially in the formulation of the definition and in the moral and ethical emphasis on its application to art. He also makes a contribution in his treatment of that hoary lost cause of Beauty, the philosopher's stone as it were of aestheticians, which had bedevilled his predecessors in the field.

Striking parallels have been drawn between Tolstoy's art of the future described in *What Is Art?* and the art of Soviet Socialist Realism. The most obvious one is that both are concerned with the proposition that the main mission of art is to serve society and contribute to the universal brotherhood of man. But the means by which these aims are to be achieved have little in common. Though both, ideally, anticipate a future existence when the 'withering away of the state' will end for ever the interposition of government between the artist and his art, Tolstoy envisages its accomplishment through the growing ascendancy of spiritual and moral forces over the mind of man, whereas the Soviets attempt to bring it about, paradoxically, by the exercise of political power. Needless to say, Tolstoy abominated political power. Moreover, his definition of art, with its theory of infectiousness, has never been espoused by Soviet theorists of Socialist Realism.

If Tolstoy attacked the confusion of beauty and goodness in his treatise, he himself has been criticized for confusing the moral and the aesthetic. Though there is always a certain futility involved in trying to propound an aesthetic theory that is applicable to all art, there may also be a positive gain if its focus of application is relevant to excessive emphasis on a particular subject-matter of art in a given age. Tolstoy's overwhelming moral and ethical concentration on the relation of art to life was quite relevant at a time when the theme of sex and other pleasures had already begun to dominate in art until at the present day it appears that one half of society is busily engaged in entertaining the other half. One may justly deplore Tolstoy's attitude that there must be no more cakes and ale, but there is wisdom and also prophecy in his reminder in *What Is Art?*: 'Man's enjoyment has limits established by nature, but the movement forward of humanity which expresses itself in religious consciousness has no limits.'[18]

## V

The aesthetic principles of *What Is Art?* guided Tolstoy's subsequent literary criticism. During the period of deep contemplation on his treatise, he took time to fulfill a promise to a publisher to write a long *Introduction to the Works of Guy de Maupassant* (1894), for whose short stories he had earlier expressed great admiration. It is an impressive example of his analytical method of appraising fiction. By now, however, he had discovered, especially in Maupassant's novels, a cheap catering to popular demand for themes of sexual love, in which moral factors are generally ignored, and he deals with him as harshly as he did with the Decadents in his treatise on art. But with avidity Tolstoy seizes upon those places where Maupassant's artistic vision compels him to detect honest feelings in his wayward characters and to resolve their struggles between good and evil in a manner consistent with moral truth.

Tolstoy tended to prefer Maupassant to Chekhov as a short-story writer because the Frenchman distilled greater joy out of life, but Chekhov was his favorite among the young Russian writers of the time. And Chekhov responded, though not uncritically, with what amounted to virtual reverence for Tolstoy, and for a brief period was influenced in his thought and fiction by Tolstoy's religious and moral philosophy. If Tolstoy utterly failed to appreciate the innovating power of Chekhov's great plays, he was one of the first to recognize the original qualities of his stories and declared that he had initiated a new development in fiction. But in the spirit of *What Is Art?*, he preferred the early tales in which a single theme is directly handled with an emphasis on moral feeling. His favorite was *The Darling* about which he wrote a brief article (1905). Tolstoy saw in the story a satire on the 'new woman', a type which he disdained in real life, and he praises the unintentional art of Chekhov's humanity in not ridiculing his heroine. It seems clear that Chekhov is not satirizing the 'new woman' in *The Darling* and the poetical effect in the characterization of the heroine, which Tolstoy so much admired, is in no sense unintentional but a conscious achievement of Chekhov's rare art. In truth, at times Tolstoy failed to perceive Chekhov's tender understanding of his off-center characters, a fact so well exemplified in his comment on *Attack of Nerves,* whose hero, he said, ought to have slept with one of the prostitutes before experiencing the anguish of a guilty conscience.

The image-breaking spirit of *What Is Art?* dominated Tolstoy's last extensive critical study: *Shakespeare and the Drama* (1906). His disparagement of Shakespeare's art had been of long standing. Now, as an old man of seventy-eight, this supreme novelist set out to destroy the image of the supreme dramatist. With critical deliberateness, he singled out *King Lear* as a typical example of the plays and could find nothing in Shakespeare's treatment that would dignify it as great art – proportion, characterization, human relationships, situations, artistic refinement, language. The real motivation behind his hostility soon becomes apparent in terms of the dogma of *What Is Art?* All Shakespeare's devotees, Tolstoy declares, take the view that in drama no religious illumination is necessary in depicting passion and human characters, that objective art should treat occurrences independently of any evaluation of what is good or evil. But the real fault of Shakespeare as an artist, he says, is that he despises the common man and elevates the mighty, rejects not only religious but also humanitarian efforts to alter the existing order of society, has no clear understanding of the relations between man and God, and creates without any sincerity.

Of course, Tolstoy was not alone in believing that Shakespeare was neither thinker nor philosopher, but critical irrelevance to evaluate his position as a great creative artist never seems to have occurred to him. Nor does Tolstoy reveal any awareness of the formidable technical obstacles which Shakespearian English and the *mores* of the Elizabethan period placed in the way of a Russian realistic novelist of the nineteenth century who elected to make a study of Shakespeare's plays. However indefensible is the main thesis of *Shakespeare and the Drama*, it repays reading for the same reason that, in a much larger sense, *What Is Art?* does. The distinguished literary scholar G. Wilson Knight puts it

quite cogently in his study, *Shakespeare and Tolstoy*, in which he describes Tolstoy's writings on art as:

> a massive collection of some of the most masculine, incisive, and
> important criticism; all, whether we agree or disagree, of so rock-like
> an integrity and simplicity that its effect is invariably tonic and
> invigorating, and often points us directly, as in this essay on
> Shakespeare, to facts before unobserved, yet both obvious and
> extremely significant.[19]

# 12

## *Resurrection*

During his preoccupation with *What Is Art?* and after its publication, Tolstoy, with varying success, endeavored to conform to its aesthetic theory in his imaginative writings. The major test was the last of his great full-length novels, *Resurrection* (1899), but certain circumstances, and perhaps his fixed artistic habits of work in this genre, contrived to make the task a difficult one. He conceived the novel at least ten years before finishing his treatise on art. It was inspired by an incident in real life which had been told to him by his friend A. F. Koni, an eminent jurist. A man had asked his legal assistance on behalf of a woman who had been sent to prison. As an orphan of sixteen she had been taken into the home of relatives of his and lived there virtually in the position of a servant. On a visit to his relatives, he seduced her and then deserted her in a pregnant condition. Thrown out by her benefactors, she at first vainly tried to earn an honest living but was finally driven to prostitution. Arrested on the charge of stealing money from one of her drunken 'guests' in a brothel, she was brought to trial, and by chance her seducer served on the jury that convicted her. His conscience awakened by the injustice of his behavior, he obtained permission to marry her, but shortly after her sentence ended she died of typhus.

Deeply moved by the account, Tolstoy decided to make use of it in fiction and appears to have begun the novel as early as 1889. The years that followed were extremely busy ones for him, and though he returned to *Resurrection* on various occasions, it is possible that he would never have finished the novel if it had not been for a crisis situation that arose in the affairs of the Dukhobors, a peasant sect. Practising a form of Christian communism not far removed from Tolstoy's own beliefs, they were harshly persecuted by the government, especially for their refusal to bear arms. Tolstoy and his disciples rallied to their cause in the only effective way possible in Russia – by stirring up sympathy for their plight abroad. Interested people finally decided that the practical solution was emigration. The Canadian government offered to accept twelve thousand Dukhobors, who were skilled peasant farmers, and the Russian government agreed to let them go. As an international figure, Tolstoy publicly supported the project, and to help finance the emigration he offered to donate the proceeds of the sale of several hitherto unpublished literary works, although this would mean violating the free public assignment of copyrights of all his writings since his religious change. At first he contemplated submitting three substantial stories, but he ultimately settled upon the longest, *Resurrection,* as the one calculated to earn the largest sum of money. Guiltily he wrote his disciple Chertkov that the work would not conform to his present ideas about art, especially in form, but that perhaps some good would be done, for the end in view was aid for a persecuted and deeply religious people.

Having sold the Russian rights for a handsome advance of 12,000 roubles to the publisher A. F. Marx in whose periodical *Niva* it was to appear first in serial form, Tolstoy, in 1898, plunged into the immense task of completing *Resurrection* which called for revising and rewriting the considerable amount of manuscript he had accumulated during the past ten years. The task was often made onerous by the pressure of having to read proof in order to meet the frequent deadlines of serial publication while creating fresh copy. He told his wife that never since *War and Peace* had he been so seized with the creative urge. During the writing he read books on prostitution, consulted experts on legal procedure, visited jails and talked with convicts. In the maze of discarded material, which prints up to almost as many pages as the finished novel, are revealed uncertainties about the beginning and ending, altered motivation, shifts of emphasis, rejected scenes and incidents, changes in plot line, relentless working over psychological niceties and the external appearance of characters – there are as many as twenty variants of the description of the heroine, Katya Maslova. Not a few of the complications, as the drafts and diary entries indicate, were caused by his struggle between the felt need to write in terms of the moral mission he stressed in *What Is Art?* and his natural tendency to fall into the posture of the emancipated artist he had been in *War and Peace* and *Anna Karenina.* The result of his ambivalence was a compromise to the artistic detriment of *Resurrection.*

Censorship was another vexatious factor. Tolstoy expressed amazement that the novel was allowed to appear at all because of his severe attacks on both government and Church, but his manuscript was freely cut by the censor and also by editors trying to anticipate the censor. It is estimated that only 25 of 129 chapters in the book entirely escaped changes or deletions.[1] Though Tolstoy sometimes protested, more often he ignored the mangling of his text as though anxious not to endanger its publication because of his promised aid to the persecuted Dukhobors. Finally, on December 18, 1899, he wrote in his diary: 'Completed *Resurrection*. Not good, uncorrected, but it is done and I am no longer interested.'[2]

Before Russian serial publication was completed, the international fame of this first full-length novel from Tolstoy in twenty years was assured. Indeed, it enjoyed a larger sale abroad than any of his previous works. Although arrangements had been made for first-publication rights in England, France, Germany, and the United States, numerous pirated editions began to appear abroad and often in execrable translations, which were usually justified by his earlier public repudiation of copyright privileges. The situation caused Tolstoy much embarrassment and also reopened the old quarrel over publishing matters with his wife who taunted him with breaking his promise in this instance by selling *Resurrection* for a huge sum and yet depriving his children and grandchildren of the necessities of life (hardly the case) in order to give money to the Dukhobors whom she could in no sense love more than her own family. He was ultimately happy to revert to his rule of not accepting money for his writings while stubbornly refusing to realize that the rule itself was the cause of his difficulties.

## II

Like his two earlier masterpieces of fiction, *Resurrection* is a long complex narrative filled with the stuff of life, and if anything it contains a more pervasive autobiographical content. Koni's story which originally suggested the novel's theme appears also to have stirred Tolstoy's guilty conscience in connection with a similar incident in his own life. He told his Russian biographer about 'a crime' which, he said, 'I committed with the maid Gasha in my aunt's house. She was a virgin. I seduced her, and she was dismissed and came to grief.'[3] His wife, while confirming her husband's story, indicates that he exaggerated its unhappy consequences. Much other material from Tolstoy's life is drawn upon and some of the characters are modeled on real people, such as Toporov, an unflattering portrait of K. P. Pobedonostsev, Procurator of the Holy Synod.

Moreover, *Resurrection* is in many respects the story of Tolstoy's spiritual biography, for the novel's hero, Nekhlyudov, not only reflects his characteristic traits, but also becomes the mouthpiece of his creator's moral and religious views. The period of the hero's youthful idealism, which is submerged in the debauchery of life in the army and high society, bears obvious parallels to Tolstoy's experiences. After his attack of conscience at the trial of the prostitute Katya Maslova, whom as a pure girl he had seduced ten years before, Nekhlyudov's moral crisis and search for the meaning of life begin. His spiritual awakening is patterned on Tolstoy's and he reaches much the same convictions.

Only in the novel's first part do we enjoy the wonderful creative exhilaration of the uncommitted artist in the earlier fiction. The incommunicable poetry of youthful dreams envelops the scene of the Easter service in the village church where the young hero and heroine, after giving the customary salutation 'Christ is risen,' exchange the traditional kiss but with the carefree rapture of mingled exaltation and dawning love for each other. And throughout the novel are remarkable scenes and characterizations in the style of the 'saturated realism' of *War and Peace* and *Anna Karenina* which reveal that the seventy-year-old author had lost none of his artistic powers: the famous trial scene in which judges and jurymen are perfectly limned in short, quick strokes; the advocate Fanarin who epitomizes the cynical irrelevance of justice in courts of law; the subtly differentiated women inmates of Katya's cell and the striking description of the brutal march of convicts to Siberia; and the scenes and figures of high society in Moscow and Petersburg – the Korchagin family whose daughter hopes to marry Nekhlyudov, the Vice-Governor Maslenikov adept at manipulating the duties of his office to indulge in social climbing, and the pompous general's attractive wife Mariette whose sly suggestions of a liaison strike Nekhlyudov as much less honest than the approach of a street-walker.

In the second and third parts of *Resurrection,* however, Tolstoy often ignores his former conception of the novel which should enable people to 'weep and laugh over it and fall in love with the life in it.' At times, in fact, *Resurrection* becomes a blatant purpose novel in which the depiction of life is overwhelmed by special pleading as the author's views obtrude, although he endeavors to disguise this with a measure of objectivity. Institutions and aspects of contemporary society are directly attacked: government, property, the law, the administration of justice, the Church, bureaucracy, capital punishment, class differences, social snobbery, and sexual morality. Occasionally there are lapses of taste, such as his blasphemously satiric account of an Orthodox church service. And in the maligned group of revolutionary intelligentsia he portrayed, he seems to have missed their real historical significance. But in general polemical positions are argued with consummate skill in which satire, irony, and paradox are effectively employed. For much of this sweeping indictment, as well as the moral correctives he offers, parallel arguments, even to exact duplication of language, may be found in Tolstoy's controversial books and articles.

To what extent the attack on Russian society may be regarded as fictionally necessary in order to justify the spiritual and moral resurrection of the hero is a matter of opinion. In the early chapters, Nekhlyudov's portrayal wins our sympathy. As a member of the gentry, he possesses some of the engaging qualities of Prince Andrei and Vronsky in the earlier novels, and the passing love affair with the pretty but lowly Katya Maslova was a conventional fling for a young man of his class. Nor does his determination to marry her after the trial seem alien to his nature, for he has convinced himself that he is the cause of her degradation. It is in the subsequent radical transformation of his spiritual, moral, and intellectual personality that he progressively ceases to remain believable. Tolstoy's similar transformation is understandable in terms of his known previous life experience and the extraordinary spiritual and intellectual qualities of his genius. This kind of motivation is lacking in Nekhlyudov's portrayal up to the time of his spiritual awakening. Tolstoy's failure to see this is the novel's most serious fault. In effect, he sacrificed the artist's essential freedom to choose to an adamant didactic purpose. Nekhluydov is turned into an intellectual Tolstoyan, more acted upon than active, an image quite irreconcilable with the earlier logic of his developing personality.

Some of Tolstoy's uncertainty in the hero's later delineation may be indicated by the fact that in one of the drafts he has Nekhlyudov marry Katya who helps him in his religious activities, clearly a lame and impotent conclusion. In handling this situation in the final version, the truth of the artist prevails over that of the moralist. Nekhlyudov follows Katya to her prison in Siberia and his patient care of her finally works a moral change and her first pure love for him is restored, although the change is somewhat unconvincing, for Tolstoy strangely enough offers no detailed motivation for it. But this is supplied in her final decision not to marry him. She perceives that his wish is prompted by a self-sacrificing desire to atone for his sin against her. Love, she reasons, must come from the heart, purged of all self-interest and sentimentality, and this he will achieve only through turmoil and suffering in finding his way to his new faith in which she will only be a hindrance. The compromise she settles on is marriage to a fellow-prisoner who loves her with an entirely platonic love. Sex is the inevitable victim of the higher synthesis of the Tolstoyan life of the spirit.

Nekhlyudov goes on his way pursuing his intense search for the meaning of life. He abides by the Biblical injunction to judge not that you be not judged, and he condemns the violence of government and the hypocrisy of the Church. Like Tolstoy, he finds the meaning of life in the Sermon on the Mount. 'From that night,' the novel concludes, 'there began for Nekhlyudov an entirely new life, not because he had entered into new conditions of life, but because everything he did after that night had a new and quite different meaning for him. How this new period of his life will end, time alone will prove.'[4] This hint of an intended sequel is supported by an entry in Tolstoy's diary: 'I want terribly to write an artistic, not a dramatic, but an epic continuation of *Resurrection*: the peasant life of Nekhlyudov.'[5] Was this a confession of artistic failure, by his lofty standards, in the novel? If he had ever lived to write an 'artistic' sequel, the hero, in his reformed existence, would have played the part of a peasant – his creator's suppressed dream – and perhaps a successful Tolstoyan peasant, which would have been unique either in fiction or in life.

Tolstoy made no claims for *Resurrection* as a novel exemplifying the aesthetic criteria of *What Is Art?* He was fully aware that in form and narrative manner, if not always in content, his novel was in the tradition of *War and Peace* and *Anna Karenina*. Ironically enough, when there are superb scenes and characterizations in *Resurrection* that seem to fulfill the main principle of art, as defined in his treatise, of infecting readers with the author's feelings, it is because he has reverted to the artistic manner of his great novels of the past. But this infectiousness vanishes when he tries to impose on his work that aura of the 'best art' – an evocation of feelings of brotherly love and of the common purpose of all humanity. Despite some magnificent accomplishments in *Resurrection*, it is manifestly inferior to *War and Peace* and *Anna Karenina*. There is an unpleasant harshness and lack of human sympathy in it, an absence of the rich fullness and unfailing optimism of life so prevalent in the earlier works. Rather, in his determination to preach, life is presented as something preordained, from which the challenging human mystery of the search for it has quite vanished.

## III

In the remaining years of his life Tolstoy undertook no further literary projects of the dimensions of *Resurrection*. But inspiration never ceased to work upon his imagination, and during this last period he contributed short novels, short stories, and plays, several of which belong to the corpus of his enduring art. More so than *Resurrection,* a few of them better reflect the spirit if not the letter of what he had in mind when he wrote *What Is Art?*

*Walk in the Light While There Is Light,* a short novel begun earlier but published in 1893, is unique in his fiction both in content and its undisguised effort to teach directly the dogmas of his religious faith. It is even credited with influencing disciples to set up communes where they could live according to the beliefs and practices of the early Christians described in the story. The story is preceded by an Introduction in which Tolstoy discusses with a group representing his own social class, as he must often have done with his own family, the relative merits of continuing to live as they do or abandoning their present genteel life in order to exist like peasants by hard labor, in service to others, and thus come closer to God. He then projects this motif into the era of the Roman Emperor Trajan where the debate is carried on by the young Christian Pamphilius and his pagan friend Julius, the son of a rich man. The prolonged argument between the attractions and superiority of the pagan way of life and that of Pamphilius in his persecuted Christian community where all live according to the teachings of Christ is presented with surprising objectivity and Tolstoy's usual dialectical skill. Later, he told his English biographer Aylmer Maude who asked his opinion of the tale: 'I never hear it mentioned without feeling ashamed of myself. It is thoroughly inartistic. In the story Christian and pagan are sharply contrasted. The Christians are all good and the pagans all bad, whereas in real life they would have shaded off into one another as in the case with our own sectarian and Orthodox peasants.'[6] The condemnation is an example of his invariable frankness about the artistic merits of his own writings as well as those of others.

He also asserted that he was unhappy about a certain lack of content in *Master and Man* (1895) and had a good word to say only about its artistic form, but in this work he created one of his most universally admired short novels. Tolstoy was right to praise its form, since it is impossible to imagine a more artistic way of narrating this story. Its style, which falls between the richly adorned language of the major novels and the bare, purged prose of his post-conversion moral tales, is perfectly calculated to convey the meaning of the simple content of *Master and Man* whose two main characters are the merchant Vasily and his peasant worker Nikita. The contrast between master and man is the paradigm of their fate – Vasily's grasping ambition to accumulate and the endless toil and service of Nikita who is regularly cheated by his master. In his relentless desire to anticipate competitors in a sale, the merchant orders his peasant to drive him a long distance in a fierce blizzard. They become hopelessly lost. Nikita wraps himself in his threadbare coat and fatalistically gives himself over to the will of God. The merchant, warmly dressed and still bent on outsmarting his competitors, mounts the unharnessed horse and pushes on alone. But in the darkness and swirling snow he travels in a circle and returns to the sleigh. Slowly freezing, Nikita asks that the money owing him be given to his son and then begs his master's forgiveness. The merchant experiences an inner feeling of spiritual illumination. He lies on his freezing worker, wraps the folds of his huge fur coat about them both, and as he feels warmth return to Nikita's body he rejoices with his whole being over this discovery of the ecstasy of brotherly love.

The story has been interpreted variously by critics, ranging from an emphasis on homosexuality to a symbolic reflection of Christ's passion.[7] But there is no good reason to go beyond what appears to be the explicit intention of Tolstoy's text: that the merchant undergoes a mystical experience which prompts him to try to save the life of his worker, not unlike the mystical experiences, in different circumstances, which occur in *The Death of Ivan Ilych* and *Father Sergei*. The master's triumph of selflessness over death through spiritual conviction is more artistically truthful and universal in its appeal than the intellectual conviction that brings about Nekhlyudov's conversion in *Resurrection*.

The most significant and extensive of these later short novels, a work of superb art yet one strangely neglected nowadays, is *Hadji Murat*. Tolstoy worked over it during 1896–1904 and accumulated some ten drafts, but it was not published until 1911, after his death, and without benefit of final revision. It was meticulously planned, one might almost say orchestrated, from beginning to end. From the beautifully evocative introduction, in which he describes how once when picking wild

flowers he came across a thistle, its lovely red flower dirtied and wounded by the plough but still clinging to life and symbolically recalling
the fate of the strong, fierce Caucasian hero Hadji Murat who also
tenaciously clung to life, Tolstoy moves through carefully meshed
chapters which produce with stunning effect a panoramic view of
Russia and the Caucasus, and then to the end of the story where he
returns to the image of the thistle.

For material he drew upon memories of his youthful experiences in
the Caucasus and diary notes, but with his infinite care for the correct-
ness of details he read widely in the ethnography of the region, the
history of its wars, and sought out local colour in published memoirs
and collected letters of people who had lived there. He was particularly
diligent in checking on every aspect of the appearance, traits, and
activities of the hero whose story he was telling. In the 1850s Hadji
Murat led warriors under Shamil in the native struggle to prevent the
Russians from conquering the Caucasus. Having broken with Shamil,
he deserts and offers to lead his followers against their enemy if the
Russians buy the freedom of his family held as hostages by Shamil.
Disappointed in promised Russian assistance, he and several of his
followers escape, are run down, and after the most heroic resistance
against a numerous force, they are killed in battle.

When Tolstoy was in the Caucasus, as a youthful soldier, he had
written his brother about Hadji Murat, praising his bravery but also
criticizing him for doing a 'mean action' in deserting to the Russians.
The outstanding characterization of him in the story, however, reflects
Tolstoy's abiding conviction that man is never all good or all bad, that
his nature, as indicated in a brilliant passage in *Resurrection*, is like a
river, infinitely variable, and that the artist must search out all his
qualities. Tolstoy does this in the case of Hadji Murat, presenting him
as a combination of the virtues and faults of his harsh environment, a
man of nature with admirable presence and dignity but also shrewd
and treacherous. In the portrait, as in others in the tale which is essentially one of action, there is little call for Tolstoy's characteristic dwelling
on psychological complexities, although a moiety of this appears in the
hero's confrontation with Russian aristocrats and governmental and
military officials for whose civilized artificiality he has only contempt.

The intricate design of the story provides considerable scope for
shifting back and forth from the Caucasus to European Russia, in
the course of which Tolstoy draws contrasting genre pictures of
Caucasian provincial Russian society, war in that region, peasant

existence, and high society in Petersburg. There is more than a touch of Tolstoy's early Caucasian army tales in his poignant narrative of the death of a simple peasant soldier during a Chechen attack. With his typical realism he describes the soldier's hardworking peasant mother, when informed of the tragedy, as weeping 'for as long as she can spare the time,' and his wife, already pregnant by a local shopman, as indifferent to her husband's death. But it is the older Tolstoy who, when Hadji Murat's terms are presented to Nicholas I, amusingly but mercilessly satirizes the Tsar and court life in general.

As sheer exciting narrative perfectly paced and told with studied simplicity and a minimum of literary adornment in style, Tolstoy never surpassed *Hadji Murat*. Though he was somewhat ashamed of working on a story of vengeance and violence, it is perhaps his finest example of the fiction he praised in *What Is Art?* as 'good universal art,' the category which, next to the highest form of 'good universal religious' literature, possessed simple feelings that were accessible to all.

Unlike nearly all this later fiction, *Hadji Murat* belongs to what might be called 'undirected literature'; much of the rest is directed by some edifying purpose connected with Tolstoy's religious or moral views. This is unashamedly so in the last of the short novels, *The False Coupon* (finished 1905, published posthumously, 1911), which accounts for its critical neglect and its rare appearances in standard English translations of Tolstoy's fiction. Yet in terms of both form and content it warrants notice. The plot turns on the counterfeiting of a banknote which motivates a series of evils related to good actions that in the end bring salvation to all concerned, usually through the medium of Tolstoyan moral principles.

The construction is unusual. Since the plot calls for a number of characters, their varied activities are tied together in a kind of building-block structure, a device that offers little opportunity for characterization in depth. Only the main character, the peasant Stepan, is reasonably well portrayed, and his murders are described with macabre realism, especially that of Mariya who lives by the golden rule and dies with pity for her slayer. Stepan, haunted by her image, has a mystical experience that leads him to give himself up to the police and confess. In prison he is reformed under the influence of an obvious Tolstoyan and his future activities alter the lives of other evildoers in the story.

Though the conversions of the sinners are hardly believable, Tolstoy's exposure of the crassness, meanness, cupidity, and criminal tendencies of many types belonging to various levels of society is realistic enough. These vigorous satirical onslaughts on social evils recall Tolstoy's denunciatory powers in a similar cause in *Resurrection*. In fact, one suspects that this was the principal reason for writing *The False Coupon*, along with an opportunity to play God in a situation that fairly reeks with the evil-begetting power of evil. Still one marvels at this old man of seventy-seven, contemplating, at about the time he was writing *The False Coupon*, the revival of a literary project of some forty years ago – his huge novel on the Decembrists! '*Ars longa, vita brevis*,' he sadly jotted down in his diary. 'Sometimes I am sorry. There is so much I wish to say.'[8]

## IV

In these later years Tolstoy almost abandoned the true short story which had played an important role in his early literary career. His affinity for the genre lacked that complete dedication to its exacting demands that Chekhov possessed to such an extraordinary degree. Tolstoy's performance in it was somewhat like that of his great rivals in the novel, Turgenev and Dostoevsky – occasional and sometimes memorable. The three short stories in this last period that call for comment were influenced in some measure by his moral and spiritual beliefs.

The inspiration for *After the Ball* (1904) was a love affair in Tolstoy's Kazan University days. With amazing freshness he recreates from memory the atmosphere, dress, manners, and behavior of the ingenuous provincial society he frequented there sixty years before. But the pleasing illusion of the past vanishes at the end of this short story. Returning home after the ball, young Ivan Vasilyevich, his thoughts filled with love for his beautiful partner of the evening, encounters by chance the grim spectacle of an army deserter being forced to run through the ranks of his fellow-soldiers who club him to death. The commanding officer present is the father of the hero's beloved. His passion for his daughter suddenly disintegrates and he mentally vows never to enter any form of government service.

The didactic message in *The Posthumous Notes of the Elder Fyodor Kuzmich* (1905) is conveyed more indirectly. In this instance Tolstoy apparently intended to write a long narrative, but he broke it off after a promising beginning and never returned to it. Even in its present truncated state, it may be regarded as an acceptable short story. Again he returns to memories of the past for his theme, specifically to the widespread notion that Alexander I falsified his death in 1825 and secretly made his way to Siberia in disguise to lead the life of a repentant, holy hermit. Unlike Tolstoy's historical portrayal of the Emperor in *War and Peace*, the emphasis is now on the utterly transformed Fyodor Kuzmich, the mysterious holy man who had forsaken a glittering worldly existence in order to live a life of poverty and humility in the pursuit of good deeds. The analogy to Tolstoy's own hopes and aspirations in the final years of his life is clear.

Apparently the last of Tolstoy's short stories, a piece of only a few pages, is *Alyosha* (1905). It contains a moral, like many of the brief tales he wrote for Intermediary years before, but the moral is, as it were, the reader's choice, lost in what can only be described as an effort of pure art. 'Alyosha the pot,' a kindly, simple peasant drudge, stumbles on the secret of human happiness through uncomplaining, self-sacrificing service to others. The story is a masterpiece in miniature and completely fulfills Tolstoy's prescription of 'universal art.'

## V

Of the plays during this last period,[9] *The Live Corpse* (1900) was never subjected to final revision and was first published, posthumously, in 1911. Like *The Power of Darkness*, it was based on a court case told to Tolstoy by a Moscow judge. A husband, addicted to liquor and aware that his wife had long been in love with another man, simulates suicide by drowning in order that she may marry her lover. She does, but through an indiscretion of her former husband the story comes out and all three are arrested and convicted.

Tolstoy turned the bare account of the court case into a powerful psychological drama. Perhaps influenced by the recently developed revolving stage, he required six acts, twelve scenes, and more than thirty speaking characters. In these respects, however, he had revealed in his playwriting years before a tendency to flaunt ordinary theatrical conventions. Despite its length and the human complications he introduced, *The Live Corpse* is expertly constructed and the dialogue, especially of the three principal characters, is highly natural, realistic, and most artistically adjusted to their different personalities.

Critics tend to regard the play as another example of Tolstoy employing an art form as a vehicle for exploiting his personal moral views, in this case his conviction of the harm that the law, an arm of the government as an organized instrument of coercion, causes by interfering in people's private lives. There may be some of this in *The Live*

*Corpse*, but if so it seems to be entirely sublimated in his concern for the central psychological problem of the tragedy. The resolution of it is really not that of the law but of the husband, who had finally come to realize that his wife, who had been in love with the other man before her marriage and yet could not confess it even to herself, ought to be freed to marry him. Divorce was extremely difficult in Russia and the husband – so he tells us – lacked the courage to commit suicide. But after the discovery of his simulated suicide and the arrest of all three of them, he finds the courage to shoot himself in order that his wife may continue to live in marital bliss with his rival.

In short, *The Live Corpse* is quite free of dogmatic moralizing, and the unhappy husband is one of Tolstoy's most successful characterizations in drama. The play also reflects a mellowness and deep sympathy for erring humanity, qualities rather uncommon in the literary works of his last years. *The Live Corpse* was first produced in 1911 by Stanislavsky's Moscow Art Theater and has held the boards ever since in Russia as a moving and deeply disturbing play.

Tolstoy appears to have conceived his last full-length play, *The Light Shineth in Darkness*, as early as the 1880s. He worked on it off and on for years, finished the fourth act in 1902, and then left only notes on the fifth and concluding act. Since it was a frankly autobiographical play, which – he wrote a friend – would contain all that was close to his heart, it was perhaps ordained that it would remain incomplete in his own lifetime. It is an important source of information for an understanding of the domestic struggle of Tolstoy's later years.

Although he allowed himself some measure of creative inventiveness in character and plot, the main action is concentrated on the growing domestic tragedy after his spiritual conversion – the struggle between him (as Saryntsev) and his wife and children, relatives and friends, who intentionally or unintentionally prevented him from living according to his religious convictions. The play fully supports the abundant evidence we have of his efforts to convince family and friends of his real spiritual need to abandon his present life and live by the teaching of his new faith. Saryntsev expresses the hope that they will join him in this endeavor, but only if their conscience moves them to do so. In the contentious dialogues that take place, the main Tolstoyan views are argued, and the remarkable fact is that he puts in the mouths of his opposition arguments that are often devastating answers to his views. To take one example, the real tension of the play is centered in the clash of wills between Saryntsev and his wife and the principal issue is his desire to give away the property from which the family derives its income. She replies to his arguments that she cannot agree to beggar her numerous children, and she wonders why this particular form of Christianity requires that he ruin the whole family.

The total picture of Saryntsev, of his views and actions, is anything but a flattering one. Everything he touches he seems to blight. In the end his wife and children are estranged from him; a young priest he converts rejects his 'Tolstoyism' and returns to the Church; another convert, Boris, engaged to his favorite daughter, rejects conscription into the army and dies under punishment, whereupon the daughter marries a socialite whom her father detests; and in the notes from the unwritten fifth act, the grief-stricken mother of Boris shoots Saryntsev.

No doubt, a certain self-consciousness may have prevented Tolstoy from creating a many-sided portrayal of himself in Saryntsev. In one respect the loss is perhaps a gain. Chekhov's dictum that art does not lie is perfectly exemplified in the characterization. Only a truly great writer would employ the sincerity of art to depict himself so unmercifully. Whatever human sympathy is lost in the dramatization of his spiritual struggle, Tolstoy revealed in the play with crucifying realism its harmful effects on all those he loved.

Judging from the notes to guide him in writing the last act, it apparently was not his intention in the completed play to demonstrate the futility of his beliefs in solving the ills of the world. Rather, he intended to show at the end that, whatever may be society's opposition to his search for truth, the search was necessary and its findings, if sincerely acted upon, would benefit mankind. This intention seems also to be implied in the play's title, that is, darkness, which does not comprehend the light, will one day vanish and then all will see the light. Some such view also appears to have been in George Bernard Shaw's mind, for he argued that though the play revealed the disastrousness of its creator's anarchistic doctrine, Tolstoy did not really pronounce a verdict against himself. 'It must be assumed,' Shaw writes, 'that if everyone refused compliance, the necessities of the case would compel social reconstruction on honest and peaceful lines . . . he is a Social Solvent, revealing to us as a master of tragi-comic drama, the misery and absurdity of the idle proud life for which we sacrifice our own honor and the happiness of our neighbors.'[10]

# 13

## Government – War – Revolution – Land Question – Death

### I

The last ten years of Tolstoy's life were crowded with concerns of government and revolution and marked by personal triumph and failure. Alexander III's death in 1894 elicited regrets, but this did not oblige him, he said, to change his opinion about the deplorable deeds of his reign. If his followers had suffered under the late Tsar, Tolstoy had given his government, as well as the Church, cause for alarm. In reporting to the monarch about a Tolstoyan who had created turmoil in a whole community, Pobedonostsev added:

> It is impossible to conceal from oneself that in the last few years the intellectual stimulation under the influence of the works of Count Tolstoy has greatly strengthened and threatens to spread strange, perverted notions about faith, the Church, government, and society. The direction is entirely negative, alien, not only to the Church, but to the national spirit. A kind of insanity has taken possession of people's minds.[1]

One of the last acts of Alexander III's government had been to prohibit Russian journalists from quoting anything in the foreign press about Tolstoy's life or works.

The manifesto of the new Tsar Nicholas II upon his accession to the throne bluntly reaffirmed the reactionary traditions of autocratic rule. It disappointed Russian hopes for a constitution or the prospect at least of many needed reforms. 'What insanity and baseness,' Tolstoy entered in his diary after reading the statement. Repressive measures intensified and Tolstoyans, not without provocation, became special targets of administrative persecution. Disciples' houses were searched for illegal literature; children were sometimes taken away from their parents to keep them religiously 'undefiled'; and young men, rejecting army conscription, were imprisoned or put into disciplinary battalions. Tolstoy wrote letters to victims, visited them in prison, and provided material aid. On occasion he protested to government officials, and in severe cases of punishment he published articles abroad to bring pressure on the government.

Nor did he hesitate to conduct frontal assaults on the repressive regime of Nicholas II. When a petition against a new anti-Semitic law was organized, he allowed his name to be used and wrote a prominent figure that the Jews 'have suffered so much and still suffer from the heathenish ignorance of so-called Christians.'[2] Then horrified by the bloody Kishinev pogrom, he joined the public protest of a group of distinguished scholars. Aware that the massacre was fomented by reactionary police authorities to divert people's attention from revolutionary activities, he replied to a cabled request from the *North American Newspaper* for a statement: 'The fault is that of the government, in the first place for excluding Hebrews, as a separate caste, from the Common Law, and in the second place for forcefully inspiring Russian people to substitute idolatry for Christianity.'[3] And he gladly contributed three stories to a literary collection edited by Sholom Aleikhem to aid pogrom victims.

When the courts reintroduced the old punishment of flogging peasants, Tolstoy wrote a scathing denunciation in an article, *Shame!*, in which he pointed out with bitter irony the 'legal' distinction between peasants and the upper classes invented by the authorities. He also sympathized with the student strike of 1899 over the brutal measures Cossacks used to break up a meeting. After talking with a student delegation that visited him, he drafted an article on their behalf which Chertkov put into shape and published abroad. The Molokans, a peaceful religious sect sharing some of his views, appealed to him for help because the authorities deprived them of their children in order to bring them up under Russian Orthodoxy. Outraged, Tolstoy wrote Nicholas II to plead for his intercession. Since no answer was received, he vainly tried to get an article in the Russian press on the matter, nor would distinguished friends take up so dangerous a cause at his request. Curiously enough, only after his daughter Tanya succeeded in obtaining an audience with Pobedonostsev on the subject was this lamentable situation corrected.

It was an effort on behalf of another sect already mentioned, the Dukhobors, that caused the government to deal Tolstoy its severest blow up to this time. The particularly harsh persecutions of this sect in 1896 shocked Tolstoy and his followers. Three of the most important disciples, Chertkov, P. I. Birykov, and I. M. Tregubov, vital in the propagation of Tolstoy's beliefs and the publication of his forbidden works, decided to write an appeal, entitled 'Help!', to which Tolstoy added an epilogue. Copies were sent to leading citizens, government officials, and the Tsar. The three disciples were promptly arrested and exiled for five years, Chertkov to England and the others elsewhere. As usual, Tolstoy went unpunished except indirectly, but he was deeply saddened at not being included among these disciples who were suffused by an exalted feeling of martyrdom. He continued to remain a modern Christ without a cross to bear.

When he went to Petersburg to bid the exiles farewell, he was shadowed everywhere by secret police whose dutiful reports on his appearance, dress, the people he met, conversations, and all his activities have subsequently been recovered from the archives. The government knew its real enemy and kept him under close surveillance if not under lock and key. Yasnaya Polyana enjoyed a kind of extraterritoriality all its own. In fact, the war between Tolstoy and the government and Church had long been a matter of general Russian and even international interest. Whatever the issues involved, there was something magnificent in this old bearded figure standing almost alone against the organized forces of a reactionary Church and State. At this time his was the only powerful voice that dared to speak aloud and fearlessly for the cause of justice in a vast country controlled by an autocratic despotism. Causes to fight were now being laid at his door in abundance by persecuted individuals and organizations, and if he could see the justice of them in terms of his religious convictions, he rarely refused aid. It was being widely repeated that Russia now had two tsars, Nicholas II and Leo Tolstoy.

Shortly after his excommunication in 1901 (see pp. 119–20), which so much enhanced his national popularity, Tolstoy addressed to Nicholas II *An Appeal to the Tsar and His Officials*. Alarmed by the Minister of the Interior's recent order to the police to disperse crowds promptly and fire at them if they failed to break up, he warned that the time would come when soldiers and police would refuse to commit the crime of fratricide. Thousands of people were being unjustly punished by a despotic regime, he said, when what was needed was to seek out the causes of social discontent and remove them. He then formulated four demands of the people: to grant peasants equal rights with all other citizens; to repeal special enactments that permit the Common Law to be disregarded; to remove barriers to education; and to abolish all limitations on religious freedom. After itemizing various abuses perpetrated by government and Church, he ended by pointing out that crimes would be committed on both sides if the government were concerned solely with suppressing disturbances without remedying their causes. No reply was received and no attempt was made to follow his advice. Clearly foreseeing the possibility of bloody revolt, Tolstoy had wisely put aside his own maximum program of Christian anarchism to suggest to a government, that he felt had no right to exist at all, the minimum terms that might prevent its total destruction. Ultimately he proved to be right.

While convalescing in 1902 from a serious illness on the southern shore of the Crimea, Tolstoy took advantage of a visit from Grand Duke Nikolai Mikhailovich to ask him to deliver a letter to his cousin the Tsar. Feeling that he might die soon, Tolstoy experienced a powerful urge to warn Nicholas II once again of the tragedy that awaited him and the country if he continued on his present course. Autocracy, he pointed out in the letter, was an outmoded form of government, and it, and the Church allied with it, were being upheld by the exercise of every kind of violence. Then listing coercive acts of his regime and the reforms demanded by the people, he pleaded with the monarch, once more in a spirit of compromise with his own religious convictions on the futility of government, to remedy these oppressive conditions before it was too late. And again failing to receive an answer, Tolstoy told a friend that there were only two ways out of the menacing situation, either by revolution or by the autocracy's realization that it must not oppose the law of progress but lead the people in the direction that humanity was moving. Since he was convinced of the inevitability of revolution, he ordered that his two recent appeals to the Tsar be published abroad in the hope that their message would somehow lessen the impending catastrophe.

## II

Actually, the rising tide of revolution was only temporarily diverted by the senseless Russo–Japanese War which the Tsar's government contrived. Tolstoy was appalled. The merits of the issues did not concern him, except as they substantiated his belief in the moral bankruptcy of governments and the conspiracy of their rulers to send thousands to destruction for the sake of a bit of land, national honor, or the capture of world markets. Though his attitude towards war was common knowledge, the foreign press hounded him to commit himself on a struggle that engaged his own country. To one cable from America as to whether he favored Russia or Japan, he replied with his usual courage: 'I am neither for Russia nor Japan, but for the working people of both countries who have been deceived by their governments and forced to go to war against their own good, their conscience and their religion.'[4]

Despite his previous writings about war, his convictions obliged him to state his position on the present conflict, and his many followers expected it of him. In 1904 appeared his pamphlet *Bethink Yourselves!* which was quickly translated into various European languages. If he had nothing new to add to the subject, quotations from distinguished writers and thinkers on the crime of war lent a suggestion of universal authority to his own position. With polemical skill he supported arguments by introducing direct evidence from Russian conscientious objectors, and the whole gained in effectiveness and eloquence from the fact that he had an immediate and peculiarly pointless and widely unpopular conflict to illuminate his moral judgments at every turn.

In *Bethink Yourselves!* it required fortitude at this tense time to oppose his country's so-called patriotic war and to condemn the Tsar and his commander-in-chief for sending thousands of peasant-soldiers to futile slaughter. Although some criticism of the pamphlet appeared in the British press, especially in *The Times,* for the most part reaction abroad reflected that of the *Daily News:* 'Yesterday Tolstoy released one of those great messages to humanity which leads us back to the first fundamental truth and at the same time impresses us with its surprising simplicity.'[5] Its influence in Russia is hard to estimate. Censorship forbade mention of the pamphlet in the press, but copies were smuggled into the country from abroad. Though some patriotic letters attacked him for betraying his country, and priests warned their congregations against the devil-inspired antiwar views of Tolstoy, the bulk of his mail and the swelling number of conscientious objectors indicate that his past and present agitation on the subject contributed to widespread discontent over the war.

It is interesting that successive Russian defeats in battle deeply distressed Tolstoy, and he frankly confessed in his diary:

This is patriotism. I was brought up on it and am not free from it, just as I am not free from personal egoism, from a family and even an aristocratic egoism, and from patriotism. All these egoisms live in me, but also in me is a consciousness of a divine law, and this consciousness holds these egoisms in check so that I am free not to serve them. And little by little these egoisms become atrophied.[6]

He also made the striking prediction in his diary that when non-Christian nations, whose highest ideals are love for the fatherland and heroism in war, catch up in technological skills, then Christian nations will never be a match for them in armed conflict.

Tolstoy saw no hope of eliminating war through international agreement on disarmament. When Swedish intellectuals had sought his aid in persuading the pending Hague Conference of 1899 on disarmament to consider a proposal on behalf of conscientious objectors to serving in wars on religious grounds, on the theory that its adoption would eventually lead to the end of large armies, he replied sympathetically but insisted that it was 'entirely irrelevant' because modern governments would never abolish conscription since it was an essential part of their very power structure. And to the *New York World*, which asked his reaction to the Hague Conference, he wrote:

My answer to your question is that peace can never be achieved by conferences or be decided by people who not only jabber, but who themselves go to war. This question was decided 1900 years ago in the teaching of Christ as it was understood by him and not as it has been perverted by churches. All conferences can be summed up in a single dictum: All people are sons of God and brothers, and therefore they ought to love and not kill each other. Forgive my sharpness, but all these conferences invoke in me a strong feeling of disgust over the hypocrisy that is so obvious in them.[7]

In fact, the question of disarmament which had originally inspired the Hague Conference of nations got nowhere, and scarcely before it had ended one of the participators, Britain, was engaged in the Boer War.

Because he also appraised its purpose as hopeless, Tolstoy declined an invitation to attend the Tenth International Peace Congress at Paris in 1900. But nine years later he did accept a request to speak at the International Peace Congress at Stockholm. However, it was postponed because of a Swedish workers' strike, although it was freely rumored at the time that the real reason was Tolstoy's acceptance of the invitation, for the committee had merely wished to use his name for publicity purposes and had been convinced that the old and ailing celebrity would never undertake such a journey.

## III

As the unpopular Russo–Japanese War drew to an end, a revolutionary outbreak was much on Tolstoy's mind. Social agitation that had been building up during 1904 culminated in 'Bloody Sunday' (January 9, 1905). That day Petersburg workers, who had gathered before the Winter Palace to petition Nicholas II for reforms, were fired on by troops and hundreds were killed or wounded. The event turned widespread protest into the 1905 Revolution, which brought about a temporary alliance of the two parties on the left, the Social Democrats and Social Revolutionaries, and the organization of workers into a decisive force under their direction.

Tolstoy's position in the movement was an anomalous one. As Russia's greatest public figure, a national symbol of fearless opposition to a reactionary government and Church, and completely identified with the cause of the oppressed masses, he was besieged by revolutionists, who had long been encouraged by his forbidden writings and outspoken protests against the State, to join them openly in their struggle for reforms. In doing this they somehow failed to understand that his 'revolt' was a religious and not a political one, and they tended to lose sight of that balance wheel of his whole system of thought, his uncompromising devotion to non-violence. For him, the only revolutionary thing in the world was truth.

Foreign correspondents rushed to Yasnaya Polyana for interviews on 'Bloody Sunday' and Tolstoy talked to them on God and immortality. But in his diary he deplored the violence before the Winter Palace, fulminated against agitators who aroused destructive instincts in workers, described the Tsar as a pitiful, insignificant, and even mean person, and declared that the revolution was in full swing and would result in killings on both sides. Yet he refused to throw his tremendous influence, publicly, on the side of any of the contending parties. When liberals, the Constitutional Democrats, asked him to head a petition to the Tsar to form a constitutional government, he declined. In fact, several years before he had written an epistolary article, *A Letter to Liberals* (1896), in answer to a request to assist their cause. He agreed that, unlike the violent methods of the revolutionists, theirs aimed to gain constitutional rights peacefully, bit by bit. But he recalled a statement attributed to Alexander II, with which he obviously agreed, that the Tsar did not fear liberals because he knew that they could all be bought – if not with money, then with honors. And the few who stood their ground, Tolstoy added, were suppressed by the government.

On the other hand, he also rejected a plea from leftists that he write an open letter to soldiers not to shoot down their revolutionary brothers. Because of the violence of their means and what he considered the ultimate futility of their ends, Tolstoy was even more unalterably opposed to the revolutionists, whether socialists or communists. He had attacked their programs years before in such works as *What Then Must We Do?* and *The Kingdom of God Is Within You*. Yet on his seventy-fifth birthday, Moscow Social Revolutionaries sent him greetings, praising him as 'the great humanist, the herald of universal brotherhood,' and they expressed their 'profound and warm thanks for all you have done for the triumph of socialism.'[8] To a group of their young radical friends who visited him, however, he explained the difference: 'I'm not at all a revolutionist in the sense in which you understand this word. My political convictions are a consequence of and part of my religious convictions, which you probably do not know, and if you know them, you do not share them.'[9] With other revolutionary youths whom he spoke to at about this time he was more severe:

> But has any one of you worked with peasants in the field or with laborers in a factory? Do you know what the peasant thinks and wants? I mean the real peasant in bast shoes and shit. This is not the peasant you read about in books. I'm sure that you do not know. Why, then, do you dare to speak and write in their name? To encourage them to strikes and to murders? Who among you has sat in prison? Then what kind of revolutionists are you?[10]

No, he was not for the government and not for the revolutionists, he told them, he was for the people.

In the end both liberals and revolutionists turned against Tolstoy. Whatever appreciation they may have had for his ideological consistency, they knew that the doctrine of moral self-perfecting was positively quixotic in a time of grave revolutionary crisis. Yet he had expressed in various ways in his early writings what he more succinctly said in diary notes for an unfinished article he had contemplated on the evils of the existing social order as recently as 1898. There is no point in the poor man's trying to convince the rich man to share with him, he declared in his notes, for the latter sees that the poor man wants exactly what the rich have. And he added:

> Socialists will never destroy poverty and the injustice of the inequality of capacities. The strongest and more intelligent will always make use of the weaker and more stupid. Justice and equality in the good things of life will never be achieved by anything less than Christianity, i.e., by negating oneself and recognizing the meaning of one's life in service to others.[11]

Then turning to Marx in another passage, he commented: 'Even if that should happen which Marx predicted, then the only thing that will happen is that despotism will be passed on. Now the capitalists are ruling, but then the directors of the working class will rule.' Economic ideals, he continued, are not ideals, and the mistake of Marxists and the whole materialistic school is in believing that economics is at the root of all problems, whereas the life of humanity is moved by the growth of consciousness and religion. Marx is in error 'in the supposition that capital will pass from the hands of private people into the hands of the government, and from the government, representing the people, into the hands of the workers.'[12]

In *The Kingdom of God Is Within You*, Tolstoy had earlier taken an unequivocal stand against the violence of revolution as a way out of the tyranny of autocratic or capitalist rule. He even argued there that the one sphere of human life on which present governmental power does not encroach, the domestic sphere, 'thanks to the efforts of communists and socialists, is being gradually encroached upon, so that labor and recreation, housing, dress, and food will all (if the hopes of the reformers are fulfilled) gradually be prescribed and allotted by governments.'[13]

'Socialism is unconscious Christianity,'[14] he remarked in his notebook, and he admitted that some of his aims, including the withering away of the State, could be equated with those of Marxian communism. But for him the ideal could be realized only by man's moral self-perfecting and not by an organized communist movement of revolutionary action. At the same time he made another pregnant observation: 'Only that revolution which is impossible to stop is a fruiful revolution,'[15] by which he meant a process of constant change through peaceful means in man's existence from something worse to something better. And he followed this up by an unusual statement to a close friend:

The present movement in Russia is a world movement, the importance of which is little understood. . . . Our revolutionists do not at all
know the people, and do not understand this movement. They might
help it, but they only hamper it. In the Russian people, it seems to me,
and do not think I am biased, there is more of the Christian spirit
than in other peoples.[16]

That is, he believed the Russian revolutionists did not thoroughly
understand the masses and their real needs and that their leaders would
seize power by violence which they would retain by force and revert
to the very oppression of the people that they had set out to destroy.
When a temporizing revolutionist tried to prove to him that there
were good and bad motives for violence and confronted him with
the proposition: 'Is there not a difference between the killing
that a revolutionist does and that which a policeman does?' Tolstoy
characteristically replied: 'There is as much difference as between
cat-shit and dog-shit. But I don't like the smell of either one or the
other.'[17]

Lenin's appraisal of Tolstoy's relation to the 1905 Revolution is,
from a Marxian point of view, almost generous and has naturally
become the *locus classicus* for all Soviet pronouncements on the subject.
As a leader of the Bolshevik faction of the Social Democrats, he was
much concerned with events at that time, and among his several articles
devoted to Tolstoy the most important is *Leo Tolstoy as a Mirror of the
Russian Revolution*. He paid a lofty tribute to him as a literary artist
and praised his relentless criticism of capitalist exploitation, governmental violence, and the sufferings of oppressed workers. But Lenin
condemned his doctrine of non-resistance to evil by force, and his
'advocacy of one of the most corrupt things existing in the world, that
is, religion – an attempt to replace the official state clergy with priests
by moral conviction, that is, cultivating a clericalism of the most
refined and hence most loathsome kind.' This criticism is a plain dis-
tortion of Tolstoy's religious philosophy and practice. There is more
point in Lenin's accusation that Tolstoy identified himself with the
moods, hopes, and aspirations of the peasantry, and that his contradictory views were a veritable mirror of the contradictory conditions
surrounding the historical activities of the peasantry which in turn
accounted for their failure as a class in the 1905 Revolution. Unable to
realize that the old order could be destroyed only by a class-conscious
socialist proletariat, Lenin declares, 'Tolstoyan non-resistance to evil

[was] the most serious cause of the defeat of the first revolutionary movement.'[18]

## IV

The spread of revolutionary activity soon forced concessions from the alarmed government of Nicholas II in the form of promises of civil liberties and an elected Duma or parliament with limited powers. Though far less than the demands of radical parties which tried to continue the struggle, these governmental measures won support from educated liberals and the masses and some degree of order was restored in the country.

Though inwardly pleased by the end of revolutionary violence, Tolstoy brusquely dismissed the Duma as alien to the real interests of the people. His fears were quickly realized for the Tsar soon dissolved it and in retaliation some of its disgruntled members issued an appeal to the people to refuse to pay taxes or submit to military conscription, a 'Tolstoyan' policy which he realized was motivated by political rather than religious or moral considerations. The Second Duma also had a short existence, dissolved on the charge of a leftist plot on the Tsar's life. But the Third Duma, which secured a conservative majority under the unbending Prime Minister P. A. Stolypin, who ruthlessly countered any remaining revolutionary activity in the country, provided a government more to the liking of Nicholas II.

These developments did not surprise Tolstoy, for he realized how difficult it was for man to change his pattern of thought. People could not contemplate a truly new idea such as the possibility that they could live without a government anymore than they could imagine at one time that they could live without slaves. And he saw no change in a Duma that had no real power. Instead of replacing a bad old idea with a good new one, the revolution had ended by sugar-coating the old conception of government with fine promises. As he had suspected all along, the reformers represented a graver danger than the defenders of tsarist bureaucracy. It seemed to him that both sides in the struggle justified the killing of each other for the sake of power by the same argument – they killed for the common good. Those fine slogans of revolutionists – 'freedom of the people,' 'democracy,' and 'constitution' – he recognized as masks to conceal their own eagerness for power, and he guessed that the future consequences would be the struggle of all against all, the substitution of hatred for love, and the destruction of national morality.

The anarchistic bent of his thought, of course, predisposed him to reject even the middle way of liberal proponents of some form of representative government in place of autocracy. His reaction was, why change one form of violence for another? In his article *On the Social Movement in Russia* (1905), he turned on those who believed they could achieve a kind of Utopia, by substituting constitutional government for despotic rule, by picturing the failings and lack of real freedom in parliamentary governments in the Western world. And he put this position much more strongly and at greater length in another article the next year, *The Significance of the Russian Revolution*. Convinced that backward Russian autocracy would sooner or later give way before progressive world forces, he devotes much of the article to a destructive criticism of the democratic conception of government in Western Europe and America. Democracy, he insists, will turn out to be more ruinous than Russian autocracy. Part of his argument is based on what he considers the fallacy of concentrating upon industry and trade in the democracies at the expense of agriculture which makes these nations more and more dependent on outside sources for their chief means of subsistence. Stick to the land, he advises Russians, and avoid the industrial civilization of the West. Better still, he urges, follow his doctrine of non-resistance to evil by force and bring to an end coercive government. On this theme he attempts to meet practical objections for the last time in his writings. After again explaining the nature of non-violence in the kind of future society he envisages, he asks the incredulous: Will all advantages of civilization, industry, and science have to be abandoned if the nation becomes one primarily of agriculturalists? No, for all advantages really essential for people will be retained. If government is done away with, will there be no organization to take care of the common needs of any community? Nothing more, he replies, than would be necessary to take care of the community needs of a Russian village. By freeing themselves from the law of man, they are not to expect a Utopia. In life under the law of God, he writes, people will not be

> some new kind of being – virtuous angels. People will remain exactly as they are now, with all their attributes, weaknesses, and passions; they will even sin, perhaps quarrel, commit adultery, walk off with property, and even murder, but all these things will be

exceptions and not the rule as now. Their life will be entirely different by virtue of the one fact that they will not accept organized violence as a good and necessary condition of life; they will not be brought up on the evil deeds of governments that are represented as good deeds.[19]

The emphasis here on agriculture, which involved the land question, was a fixed idea in Tolstoy's vision of Russia's destiny. The proletarianizing of Russian peasants in imitation of the West, which revolutionists spoke of, was repulsive to him. It is a feeling which in our own day and with a different emphasis seems to have occurred to George Lukács who, reviving a dormant element in Marx's thought, charged that Stalinist Russia's tremendous drive to industrialize had resulted in alienating man by depersonalizing all his relations with others. These fears are reflected in Tolstoy's enthusiasm for Henry George's unusual plan for the nationalization of land, tied to a single land tax, which would make it possible for peasants to cultivate as much acreage as their needs required. First attracted by *Progress and Poverty*, Tolstoy read other works of George, began to comment on him in his writings as early as 1884, and devoted articles to his ideas. He also advocated his plan for the abolition of private property in land and the single tax to all who would listen and corresponded with George whose visit to Yasnaya Polyana was prevented only by the American's death. There were weaknesses in his theorizing which Tolstoy felt did not go far enough, but he regarded the plan as a practical answer to the festering sore in the economic body of Russia – the land hunger of the peasantry. Though he thought of George's nostrum as at best a compromise and regretted that the tax would be collected by a government based on violence, he was willing to accept these disadvantages because the greater good of the greater number would be served.

Before the 1905 Revolution, Tolstoy made vain attempts to urge a consideration of Henry George's plan on Nicholas II. After the Revolution, when the agrarian problem was a central issue in the Duma and with the Prime Minister, Tolstoy wrote Stolypin to interest him in George's plan for nationalization of the land and the single tax as a possible way out of the country's difficulty. Only after a second letter did the Prime Minister send him a coldly polite refusal to consider Tolstoy's solution because the feeling of private property was an 'innate instinct' in people, and also because he was developing his own solution of the agrarian problem by establishing a class of small private landowners among the peasantry. Tolstoy promptly replied to express his dismay. Stolypin's proposal, he said, would destroy the village commune, the ancient basis of peasant life, and would increase the element of violence rooted in private property in land.

In general, the turbulent events of the 1905 Revolution and of the few years immediately following seem to have undermined what appeal Tolstoy's religious faith had for the Russian people. His message of peace was lost in a time of pervasive violence. Even some of his disciples quietly entered the ranks of radicals. Politics he loathed and hence had little appreciation of the importance of the rising middle class and proletariat, and the temper of the new generation of youth who read revolutionary pamphlets saddened him. The gulf that separated him from these forces was a wide one, yet they were the forces that in a few short years would destroy the governmental structure he deplored by a violent revolution instead of by his law of God, humility, and love. The unbridgeable polarization represented by this gulf is vividly reflected in an exchange of letters he had with a revolutionist exiled to Siberia. The man accused Tolstoy of being badly acquainted with the working class whose enemies, he declared, must be wiped out 'even though the whole world be bathed in blood. In short, kill until not a single one of the wretches remains, not even pitying their little children.' Appalled by this apostle of violence, Tolstoy wrote him of the futility of his convictions and supported his arguments by sending a selection of his printed pamphlets. The reply came: 'It is difficult, Leo Nikolayevich, to remake me. This socialism is my faith and my god. Of course, you profess almost the same thing, but you use the tactic of "love" and we use the tactic of "violence" as you express it.'[20]

The 'tactic of love,' however, won at least a moral victory over the 'tactic of violence.' In the summer of 1908 Tolstoy read a brief newspaper notice of the execution by hanging of twenty peasants (it later turned out that the number was twelve) for an attack on a landowner's home in the Elizavetgrad district. In a state of anguish he quickly wrote his famous article, *I Cannot Be Silent*. Revolutionary crimes are terrible, he asserted, but they do not compare with the criminality and stupidity of the government's legalized violence. The delusion is the same on both sides, for the excuse is 'that an evil deed committed for the benefit of many ceases to be immoral, and that therefore, without offending against the moral law, one may lie, rob, and kill whenever this tends to the realization of that supposed good condition for the many which we imagine that we know and can foresee, and which we wish to establish.' Since the government, he continued, claimed that all these executions were done for the general welfare of the Russian people, then as one of the people he insisted that he could not escape the feeling that he was an unconscious participator in these terrible deeds.

> And being conscious of this, I can no longer endure it, but must free myself from this intolerable position! It is impossible to live so! I, at any rate, cannot and will not live so. That is why I write this and will circulate it by all means in my power both in Russia and abroad – that one of two things may happen: either that these inhuman deeds may be stopped, or that my connection with them may be snapped and I put in prison, where I may be clearly conscious that these horrors are not committed on my behalf; or still better (so good that I dare not even dream of such happiness) that they may put on me, as on those twelve or twenty peasants, a shroud and a cap and may push me also off a bench, so that by my own weight I may tighten the well-soaped noose around my old throat.[21]

The immediacy of the theme and the emotional intensity and high seriousness with which he handled it contributed to the enormous success of *I Cannot Be Silent*. It created an uproar, appeared in translation in hundreds of newspapers and periodicals abroad, and in illegal form was known throughout Russia. A stream of letters poured into Yasnaya Polyana, the sentiments of most of which were reflected in one from a humble Moscow correspondent: 'You have removed a stone from our hearts, as it were, for you seem to speak as a symbol of faith and we repeat your words in our hearts, because we are unable to speak so and can only feel.'[22]

V

During these final years of intense activity on the national and international scene, Tolstoy was also absorbed with the lives of countless people and with family affairs, often unhappily so. The family's daily existence had become almost more public than private. Endless Russian and foreign visitors besieged the Moscow home and Yasnaya Polyana. Sometimes large delegations appeared and swarms of schoolchildren accompanied by teachers. As he grew old and feeble with age he became unusually gentle and tender. Yet he felt it his duty to meet and talk with as many of the visitors as possible. Occasionally silly questions would provoke his anger, which he nearly always regretted, but then, as he remarked once, the spirit of God lives in everything, and so does the spirit of stupidity. Floods of mail from all over the world kept him and secretaries everlastingly busy, and requests for financial aid became so overwhelming that he finally had to announce in the press his inability to fulfill them.

When in 1901 he was ordered south by physicians during a period of severe illness, government authorities took the precaution to alert police officials all along the railroad route to prevent demonstrations at the stations, but they took place anyway, huge crowds at the stopovers cheering him and wishing him health. And Pobedonostsev instructed priests at his destination at Gaspra to be prepared to attempt to persuade him, should the illness prove fatal, to return to the bosom of the Church – a vain effort.

Such evidence of national esteem stood in sharp contrast to sad developments in the Tolstoy household during these last few years of life. The psychologically sick passion of his wife for the younger composer and pianist, S. I. Taneyev, which years later she identified with the onset of her critical period, ran its lengthy, tormenting course until 1904. At that point the musician, who was never anything more than a passive receptacle for her ardent feelings, terminated the relationship. Though Tolstoy fully understood the reasons for her platonic pursuit, it continually exasperated him and led to frequent stormy scenes.

The fundamental cause of this aggravation, as well as of all their serious difficulties, was the profound irreconcilability of their way of life which had begun with his religious conversion and greatly increased at the end of his life. Sonya, of course, never really altered her mode of living, except in her rooted opposition to his radical change, whereas he had some tolerance for those who could not agree with him but none for anyone who tried to turn him from the new path he sincerely believed to be the truth, the law of God. Their many years of married love held them together but in manifold and curious ways intensified the dissension.

Tensions in the household became intolerable when Chertkov was allowed to return to Russia from exile in 1905 and for a time settled in a dwelling very close to Yasnaya Polyana. There, with autocratic piousness, he presided over a large entourage of Tolstoyans busily engaged in compiling a huge 'Vault' of the thoughts and sayings of the master. This chief disciple had a vested spiritual interest in Tolstoy and in everything connected with him. He had devoted the best years of his life in this service, and had no intention of allowing anyone, not even the master's wife, to deprive him of his premier position. With their complete identity of religious purpose, Chertkov had full access to Tolstoy's manuscripts, even to his 'secret diary' which he kept hidden from his wife. Now master and disciple met almost daily, which infuriated Sonya and she finally denied Chertkov her house.

Soon Tolstoy was caught in the middle of a bitter struggle between his wife and a man she hated but one whom he regarded as his closest friend, the designated editor of his huge literary heritage, and the continuator of his teaching after his death. Something resembling conspiratorial activity poisoned the atmosphere of the entire household. It involved nearly all members of the family and several intimate friends, secretarial aides, and Chertkov and a few other principal disciples. At issue were hidden diaries, the whereabouts of unpublished manuscripts, and ultimately future control, after Tolstoy's death, of his valuable literary works for which his wife had already been offered a million roubles for the publishing rights at a time when he was secretly planning a will that would bequeath his whole literary property to the public.

In these circumstances bedlam reigned in the household as Sonya believed that she was being deceived and also feared that Chertkov intended to slander her in the press after Tolstoy's death with information he had from her husband's diaries. In a family where there had never been any secrets between husband and wife, confidences were no longer possible because of her sick, unrestrained outbursts of rage and morbid suspicions. The children took sides in the struggle, three sons, with their property rights in mind, supporting their mother, and the two remaining daughters their father. But the aged and feeble Tolstoy became the victim of all as he tried, in the spirit of his doctrine of love, to mediate between the contending parties. There were violent quarrels almost daily, with Sonya demanding that Chertkov return manuscripts in his possession or that Tolstoy tell her whether he was concealing a will from her. She shadowed him on his walks, hoping to catch him in a rendezvous with Chertkov, searched his study for hidden papers at night when she thought he was asleep, and constantly begged him for information he was unable to supply. Confessing that she was insanely jealous of Chertkov, she finally accused Tolstoy of homosexual relations with him, and even demanded that her old husband resume intimate relations with her. She repeatedly threatened suicide and on several occasions actually attempted it. So hopeless did her situation become that doctors had to be summoned, and the neuro-pathist diagnosed a 'paranoial and hysterical' condition and recommen-ded treatment and separation from her husband for a period. But she refused to leave and persecution of Tolstoy continued.

Several months later this old man of eighty-two awoke in the middle of the night and heard his wife again rummaging around in his study. This time an unrestrainable aversion and indignation seized him. He got up later, wrote her a letter of explanation, aroused his physician and youngest daughter, Alexandra, and together they drove to the nearest railroad station. In his letter Tolstoy had written that his posi-tion in the house had become unbearable and that he was doing what old men of his age commonly do – leaving this worldly life in order to live out his last few days in peace and solitude.

Several days later on the train Tolstoy was taken with a severe chill and his doctor insisted they get off at the next stop, Astapovo, and he persuaded the stationmaster to provide the sick man a bed in his tiny house at the side of the tracks. Tolstoy had been recognized on the train and quickly all of Russia and soon the world knew of his flight from home and his illness. Doctors, correspondents, the family, in-cluding his wife, Chertkov and other disciples, and close friends arrived at little Astapovo. His dreams of years – the peace and solitude of the holy hermit in the desert – had vanished. He lingered on for almost a week. Only when the doctors knew he was dying was his wife allowed to enter the sickroom. She kissed his forehead, sank to her knees, and murmured: 'Forgive me!'[23] Almost the last words he was heard to utter before he died on November 7, 1910, were: 'To seek, always to seek.'[24] Throughout the cities and towns of Russia crowds had been waiting before the news centres, patiently following the bulletins from Astapovo. Then the flash came: 'Tolstoy is dead!' A hush fell over the people. All took off their hats. Some wept softly.

Tolstoy was buried, as he had ordered, without benefit of priests or religious rites, in the spot he had selected in the Yasnaya Polyana woods where his brother Nikolai, when they were at play as children, had supposedly hidden the mysterious little green stick. On it was written the magic message which, when known to mankind, would bring about a Golden Age on earth. Then all human misery and evil would vanish, and all men would be happy and love one another.

# 14

## International Recognition

### I

To appraise, however briefly, the international fame and influence of Tolstoy, who in his own day was described as the conscience of the world, is a challenging task. A Soviet scholar has devoted a large book to the subject, *The World Significance of L. N. Tolstoy*,[1] and specialized studies of his influence in various countries have appeared. Though he never left Russia during the last fifty years of his life, circumstances that went beyond the widespread popularity of his works contributed to his international renown – his fame as a religious reformer, the establishment of Tolstoyan colonies abroad as well as societies to study his writings, and endless foreign visitors who were often influenced by him, corresponded with him, and published their impressions of him in their own countries. Moreover, he was himself, by inclination and interest, an internationalist. A large number of books in his personal library of 14,000 volumes were foreign, most of them French, German, and English, languages which he read with ease (3,600 alone were in English). And he was fairly conversant with the press of these countries.

Before the 1880s, however, very few translations of Tolstoy's many literary productions had been published in Western Europe and the United States. For that matter, there was then hardly any awareness of the existence of Russian literature abroad, with the exception of the novels of Turgenev who was early translated, spent much time in the West, and was regarded there by 1870 as a celebrated European man of letters. At this juncture two significant events took place. A powerful reaction against the popularity of the scientific naturalism of Zola and his followers set in, and the French critic Eugène-Melchior de Vogüé, who had spent several years in diplomatic service in Russia, published his *Le Roman russe* (1886). The Introduction to his treatments of

Turgenev, Dostoevsky, and Tolstoy, which advocated an approach to realism that emphasized religious, moral, and spiritual values, was at once regarded as a literary manifesto by those opposed to scientific naturalism. De Vogüé's book soon became celebrated throughout Europe and America, not only because it effectively introduced the West to the whole subject of the Russian novel, but also because it offered a serious challenge to naturalism by espousing a realism in literature more in keeping with the spirit of the age, which demanded a concentration on 'real life' while responding to problems of the human soul.

One remarkable result of this development was the sudden discovery of Russian literature, especially fiction, in most of the countries of the West. Translations multiplied at a rapid rate and Tolstoy was the principal beneficiary. In 1887 alone thirty-one translations of his artistic works, which had been published in Russia before 1880, appeared for the first time in Europe.[2] The effect was that of a popular discovery some thirty years after he had achieved literary fame in Russia, and this process of frequent translations of his fiction continued for decades.

With the multiplication of translations in this enthusiasm for Russian literature came a wealth of critical studies, especially in major countries. Here again Tolstoy was a favorite subject and in general the bulk of his fiction was highly appreciated. In England, for example, Matthew Arnold led the way with his authoritative article in the December 1887 issue of the *Fortnightly Review*, in which in the course of comparing *Anna Karenina* to *Madame Bovary* he rates Tolstoy's novel distinctly higher in human qualities. It is 'the novel of Russia,' he writes, 'which now has the vogue, and deserves to have it,' and he adds that 'if fresh literary productions maintain this vogue and enhance it, we shall all be learning Russian.'[3]

Some British critics and novelists, like French admirers of Flaubert's impeccable sense of form, tended to regard Tolstoy's major novels as peculiarly formless and artless, chaotic outpourings, so to speak, of a super-reporter of life. One thinks of criticisms of George Saintsbury, Edmund Gosse, Andrew Lang, Henry James, and George Moore, who seemed to be overwhelmed by the scale of Tolstoy's huge canvases, and in some cases not a little shocked by the un-Victorian improprieties of his realism. This early impression of a kind of literary untidiness has carried over to otherwise fine appreciations of early twentieth-century critics, such as E. M. Forster and Percy Lubbock, both of whom, however, in the words of Lubbock, regarded Tolstoy as the 'supreme genius among novelists.' Eventually British critics recognized that these long novels, which dealt with the fullness of life while exposing its pretences and hypocrisies, had significantly added to the whole conception of fiction in our time. Though imitation of such masterpieces was as unthinkable as imitation of Tolstoy's amazing life, their sense of form, and their characters, scenes, artistic devices and psychological realism had an effect, as the writings of Shaw, D. H. Lawrence, Galsworthy, Bennett, and others testify.

Much the same could be said of the history of Tolstoy's literary works in France, Germany, and America. If anything, excitement over the discovery of Russian literature in America was greater and less restrained than in England. Translations, at least of Tolstoy, were more numerous – from 1884 to 1890 thirty-four titles of his works appeared –[4] and according to one comment, 'rival translations of his books were competing for sale in Boston as they compete in Paris.'[5] A contributor to *Harper's Bazaar* wrote: 'Nobody could possibly have foreseen a period when . . . the foremost novelist of the New World should place Tolstoï at the head of all writers of fiction, living or dead.'[6]

II

Perhaps more important than his purely literary influence as a gauge of Tolstoy's impact in the West was that of his controversial writings. Many of these works, all of which were written after 1880, appeared abroad first, because of Russian censorship, and sometimes even before translations of *War and Peace*, *Anna Karenina*, and other artistic productions. This deluge of translations on such a variety of literary and non-literary subjects over a few years contributed to the sudden fame and even positive awe in which Tolstoy was held abroad. Though Tolstoyism had adherents in a number of countries, its religious and moral doctrines seemed more congenial to the intellectual traditions of Britain and America to whose writers and thinkers Tolstoy was indebted, and who understood more readily than other foreigners the degree to which his religious and moral experience was really a natural and further development of his art. The English Tolstoyan movement, centered in the Colony at Purleigh and the publishing firm set up to handle his writings, encountered many difficulties created by its own members. But the appearance in translation during the 1880s and

1890s of such works as *Confession, What I Believe, What Then Must We Do?, The Kingdom of God Is Within You,* and *What Is Art?* strongly appealed to the British temper of non-conformity, as well as to opponents of the growing movement of rationalism and scientism at that time. On such matters as moral law derived from reason, the brotherhood of man, war, and the writer's relation to society, not a few correspondences may be observed between Tolstoy's thinking and that of Carlyle, Ruskin, Shaw, and H. G. Wells, to mention only a few prominent names. With interest British social reformers savored in him the essence of Rousseau's conviction that nature created man as a good and happy being but society made him depraved and miserable. And they admired Tolstoy's iconoclasm and his challenge to conventional religion and oppressive institutions of government and society. Without any wholesale acceptance of his controversial writings, they acclaimed what pleased them. Havelock Ellis in *The New Spirit,* a book that furthered Tolstoy's reception in Britian, approvingly declared that Tolstoy 'had nothing but contempt for "faith," which he regards as a kind of lunacy'; and G. K. Chesterton insisted that Tolstoy's Christianity was 'one of the most thrilling and dramatic incidents in our modern civilization.'[7] In fact, Gilbert Phelps, the principal investigator of the part played by the Russian novel in English fiction, has made out a strong case for the influence of Tolstoy's controversial works on the philosophical thought of writers of the novel of ideas. It was Tolstoy the thinker who stirred their moral conscience and captivated them by his unconventional attacks on the whole structure of modern society. And his influence, as Mr Phelps demonstrates, may be traced in the fiction and even the plays of Hardy, Gissing, George Moore, Galsworthy, H. G. Wells, D. H. Lawrence, Shaw, and Virginia Woolf.[8]

So rich is the material that a substantial book could be written on Tolstoy's acceptance and influence in the United States.[9] The ground had been prepared there for his welcome by such writers and thinkers as Emerson, Thoreau, William Lloyd Garrison, Adin Ballou, Henry George, and a host of others who had established a congenial climate of religious, social, and political dissent to which in some measure Tolstoy was indebted. In fact, in 1901 he addressed a brief message to Americans to urge them to heed these voices of protest in their past. And the long tradition of American utopian communities paved the way for experimentation in Tolstoyan colonies. As indicated, the sudden popularity of his fiction in America had been connected with de Vogüé's book on the Russian novel, which had been promptly translated there, but the influence of the great novels, as in England, was more ideational and philosophic than artistic and was clearly joined with the concurrent popularity of the controversial works.

William Dean Howells, who wrote directly about Tolstoy,[10] was one of the first in the United States to broadcast his significance, and like many contemporaries in the West, he refused to separate Tolstoy the artist from the thinker. Disturbed by the growing amoralism and materialism of the time, Howells's fiction was likewise inspired by Tolstoy's spiritual and moral struggle. He fully agreed that the writer must stand on the highest conception of art which in turn should be accessible to all and unite them in a community of feeling contributing to the forward progress of the brotherhood of man. In his fiction, especially in his utopian novels, *A Traveller from Altruria* and *Through the Eye of a Needle*, Howells's preoccupation with evils of the existing social order, the erosion of equality and justice, and the special virtues of hard work was clearly influenced by Tolstoy's teaching.[11] And later, in a general way, American novelists of ideas drew upon Tolstoy's ideals in their concern with the underlying malaise of the age.

During the last twenty years of the nineteenth century and the first decade of the next, this same excitement about Tolstoy's art and his moral and spiritual teaching, existed also in countries of the Southern and Western Slavs, in Italy, Scandinavia, Germany, and France. For example, the standard work on the subject in France is based on a massive bibliography of books and articles. Among them are absorbing published accounts of a number of distinguished French scholars, men of letters, intellectual pacifists, and journalists who visited Tolstoy. The conclusions reached in the study do not essentially differ from those already mentioned in connection with the popularity and influence of Tolstoy's writings in England and America.[12] French readers identified themselves with the heroes and heroines of Tolstoy's novels and reacted with delight to the brilliant originality of his psychological realism so different from the prevailing naturalism of their own fiction. Though older members of the élite sharply criticized the impracticality of his views in the controversial works, many French intellectuals were profoundly impressed by Tolstoy's theories and his efforts to practise them. They discovered with interest his advocacy of the creation of art for the masses and the need to make individual conscience the moral basis of a community among men. In general, French enthusiasts regarded him as a world symbol of individual liberty, and such leading writers of the time as Paul Bourget, Paul Margueritte, Edouard Rod, and Romain Rolland were much influenced by his thinking. Thaïs S. Lindstrom, the author of the exhaustive study *Tolstoï en France (1886–1910)*, points out that the French recognized in him 'une grande universalité.' She concludes that after the publication of *Resurrection* and during the years of political tumult that followed the social abuses of the Empire, 'Tolstoy's activities, in centering upon the burning actuality of the times, greatly enhanced his moral importance; this crystallized around the problem which preoccupied the West at the end of the century: the problem of the *survival of the human personality* in a society becoming more and more that of the materialist and statist.'[13]

## III

Since Tolstoy's death in 1910, the relevance of both his art and his message appears to have been obscured in a world in which events have moved so fast and so far beyond even his prophetic imaginings. Nevertheless, the intellectual accomplishments of no great nineteenth-century mind are more pertinent to realities of life today, although the uncompromising nature of his views tends to discourage any sympathy for them or reprints of the major works in which they were expressed.

Editions of Tolstoy's collected works appeared in Western countries in the early years of the twentieth century, but these are far from being complete, are often textually inaccurate, and are now mostly out of print. There is a real need for new foreign editions in translation based on the nearly definitive Soviet edition in ninety volumes, including the correspondence and diaries, which was finished in 1958. It is eminently scholarly, textually quite accurate, unexpurgated, and is surely one of the finest efforts of editing on behalf of the works of a great author. The universal attraction of his fiction continues, for almost every year in countries around the globe appear revisions of old translations of the novels or new versions, as well as anthologies of his shorter stories. Yet this persistent interest in his art does not appear to have any noticeable influence on recent developments of fiction in the West, so much of which Tolstoy, if he were alive, would categorize as 'counterfeit art' in keeping with his views in *What Is Art?* By and large our novelists today stand in awe of this great artist who loved life more than the abstract meaning of life. They are ready to challenge all the famous champions of European realism, as Hemingway put it, but not Tolstoy.

On the other hand, there has been a recent small renaissance of interest in the West in Tolstoy's life and artistic methods manifested in a steadily growing number of substantial biographical works and various critical studies that have contributed fresh and important insights on the development of his creative art.

Tolstoy's position in the Soviet Union, which came into existence only a few years after his death, has naturally been quite different from that in the West. The literary artist and the religious and moral thinker are kept strictly apart in published criticism. As we have seen, so completely did Tolstoy dominate the scene in tsarist Russia during the latter part of his life that it is almost irrelevant to speak of his literary influences then, although many such instances could be pointed out as in the case of Chekhov, Leskov, etc. He was so much larger than literature in the minds of the people. Chekhov, who spoke of Tolstoy's faith as that closest to his heart, echoed the feelings of most of his literary colleagues when he declared, upon hearing the news of his serious illness, that as long as Tolstoy lived and retained his immense authority,

> it is easy and agreeable to be a writer; even the realization that one has done nothing is not so dreadful, since Tolstoy will do enough for all. His accomplishment is a justification of the hopes and expectations built upon literature . . . bad tase in literature, any vulgarity – whether it be insolent or tearful – all coarse, irritating vanities will be kept at a distance, deep in the shadows. His moral authority alone is capable of maintaining the so-called literary moods and trends at a certain high level. Without him writers would be a shepherdless flock or a hopeless mess . . .[14]

Soviet reverence for Tolstoy the literary artist is no less unbounded, but the religious thinker who predicted the inevitable failure of revolutionary seizure of power by violence is either ignored or explained away by Marxian dialectical reasoning. Apart from the huge definitive edition, various small editions of selected works and numerous single items of fiction have been published, all of which total millions of copies. Up to 1969, for example, the centenary of the appearance of *War and Peace*, it is estimated that 200 editions of this novel, totalling 15 million copies, have appeared in the Soviet Union. Scholars have also produced a staggering number of biographical and critical studies on Tolstoy and his works. His Moscow home and Yasnaya Polyana have been established as State museums, and it is said that as many as

5,000 persons a day from all over Russia visit the latter estate to pay their respects to the great author. And no major Tolstoy anniversary arrives without a widespread national celebration accompanied by many more publications of works by him or about him, exhibitions, readings, lectures, and gala events which are often attended by top Party and government leaders.

The totalitarian state, as Orwell put it, exerts its maximum pressure on the individual at the point where literature and politics cross. That point was reached in the Soviet Union in the early years after 1917 when a dictatorial regime became fearful of the uncontrolled and thrilling experimentation of Soviet writers under the impetus of a revolutionary break with the past. A politically radical regime, instinctively conservative in things literary, paradoxically forced a return to classical nineteenth-century Russian realism for models in treating themes in fiction that were largely concerned with the struggle between the old and the new. In these circumstances Tolstoy's influence was most significant and stimulated a considerable group of novelists to draw upon his artistic form, language, and psychological approach in telling their stories of revolutionary heroes and heroines.

A few of these writers have turned out to be among the most notable in Soviet literature. In his most popular work, *The Nineteen* (1927), the able Alexander Fadayev confessed that he found himself unconsciously imitating Tolstoy, even in his choice of words and the rhythm of his sentences. In this novel and others, he plainly makes use of Tolstoy's device of the 'inner monologue.'

There are also clear Tolstoyan touches in the characterizations of Startsov in *Cities and Years* (1924) and Karev in *The Brothers* (1928) of Konstantin Fedin, one of the most highly regarded of Soviet writers. And in his fine postwar trilogy, Fedin reveals himself as fairly drenched in Tolstoy's fiction and ideas. It is not too much to say that this work was probably inspired by *War and Peace*. It covers the years shortly before Tolstoy's death and the action continues through the Revolution and the Civil War. Tolstoy is the idol of the thoroughly interesting Pastukhov and to a lesser degree of the future hero of the trilogy, Izvekhov, in the first volume *Early Joys* (1945). Tolstoy is much discussed as the active symbol of the past whose ideas influenced early revolutionists. But in the second and third volumes, *No Ordinary Summer* (1948) and *The Fire* (1962) (published in the UK as *The Conflagration*, 1969), he is made to serve a Soviet Marxian end, for his theory of history in *War and Peace* is transformed into an argument to persuade man to direct and fulfil the events of history by intelligently participating in them.

More intricately connected with *War and Peace* is Mikhail Sholokhov's huge novel *The Silent Don* (1928–1940) (published in the UK in two parts, as *And Quiet Flows the Don*, 1934, and *The Don Flows Home to Sea*, 1940), which has long since been regarded as a Soviet classic. In truth, it is difficult to conceive of the existence of this epic story of the struggle of Cossack people through war, revolution, and civil war without the example of Tolstoy's masterpiece. Sholokhov admits that of all the influences on him, he owed most to Tolstoy. *The Silent Don* is full of structural and stylistic echoes of *War and Peace*, and like Tolstoy he fills his vast canvas with a group of families and their interrelationships in love, social and political activities, and bitter, bloody combat. But in all this he is more a chronicler than an analyst of events, for he fails to identify himself with his characters as does Tolstoy. He is not a reflective artist; action is not a proving ground for the ideas of his men and women as it so often is in Tolstoy's fiction. And though Tolstoy's influence is apparent in Sholokhov's beautiful poetic descriptions of nature, the raw naturalism of his handling of scenes of human misery and tragedy goes well beyond the master's realism.

Boris Pasternak's remarkable novel *Doctor Zhivago* (1957) has sometimes been mistakenly compared to *War and Peace*. Tolstoy's massive shadow looms in the background and there are passages in which his ideas enter into the argumentation of the work, but his influence on it is mostly a negative one. Pasternak tells us in *Doctor Zhivago* that he prefers the artistic modesty of Pushkin or Chekhov to the pretentious concern of Dostoevsky and Tolstoy with universal questions of life and death. Nevertheless, these ultimate questions are there in his novel but without the probling analyzes to which Tolstoy subjects them in seeking answers. If Pasternak attempts answers, they are confined to the extraordinary sheaf of poems at the end of the work which only serve to compound wonderment and delight over the mystery of his poetic art. In the novel Pasternak also informs us that he agrees with Tolstoy's theory in *War and Peace* that rulers, statesmen, and generals do not set history in motion, but the idea, he says, is not carried out to its logical conclusion. With perhaps Lenin in mind, he insists that fanatical revolutionists do have an effect on events if only as instruments of destiny. Here the difference between the two authors lay in the fact that for Pasternak the mind's full awareness of purpose in directed action gives validity to what happens, whereas Tolstoy tended to condemn self-conscious activity as unfruitful. One thing Tolstoy and Pasternak seemed agreed on, namely, that whatever trials their characters endured, life was fundamentally a joyous, optimistic experience.

This radiant spiritual optimism is likewise the Tolstoyan hallmark of the Soviet Union's greatest living writer, Alexander Solzhenitsyn. It is interesting that all three notable Soviet novelists who have created in the spirit of Tolstoy have received the Nobel Prize in literature (Pasternak, under harsh official Party pressure, refused it). And two of them, Pasternak and Solzhenitsyn, owe much of their international fame to books published abroad after being banned in their own country, a misfortune also frequently visited upon Tolstoy.

There is one unique and striking similarity between Tolstoy and Solzhenitsyn. Like his great predecessor in the nineteenth century, Solzhenitsyn has become a symbol among Soviet writers of courageous and uncompromising protest against violations of the natural rights of man by an authoritarian regime. Apart from this spiritual affinity, Tolstoy's artistic – and to some extent his ideological – heritage has deeply influenced Solzhenitsyn's fiction, a fact that has been repeatedly demonstrated by specialists in the works of both authors. But the influence has been completely assimilated and in no sense reflects on the originality of Solzhenitsyn's writings.

The flavour of Tolstoy's style permeates Solzhenitsyn's earlier writing; some of his artistic devices reappear, as well as occasional incidents, such as the famous one of Prince Andrei's contemplation of the oak tree; and there are a few similarities in character delineations. For example, there are distant resemblances between Platon Karatayev in *War and Peace* and a series of peasants or lowly persons vaguely seeking certain values in an alien world. Such are Ivan and Alyosha in *One Day in the Life of Ivan Denisovich* (1962), Uncle Kordubailo in *An Occurrence at Krechetova Station* (1963), Matryona in *Matryona's House* (1963), Spiridon in *The First Circle* (1968), and Kostoglotov in *Cancer Ward* (1968). Like Karatayev, all these humble people seem to have a deeper understanding of the meaning of life's sufferings than do sophisticated characters.

But in a more important sense, the main preoccupation of many of Tolstoy's leading characters, a moral struggle with conscience in the face of problems of good and evil, is a dominant theme in Solzhenit-syn's fiction. Instead of the conscience-stricken nobleman involved in a clash of contradictory moral values over the treatment of his serfs or solving his relations with high society, it is the conscience-stricken communist bureaucrat undergoing a moral awakening or the intellectual political prisoner who must decide to cooperate fully with the State and be allowed to live, or oppose its exactions and risk his life. Some of the lowlier convicts, like Ivan Denisovich, who think that the only safe place to be in Russia is in prison, as Tolstoy once expressed it in his day, comply with the regulations without surrendering their moral values entirely and continue to exist. But Solzhenitsyn, as Tolstoy in the case of characters who have only one conscience to live, creates the remarkable political prisoner Nerzhin in *The First Circle*, who refuses to cooperate. Proudly he tells his fellow-convict: 'Let them admit first that it is not right to put people in prison for their way of thinking, and then *we* will decide whether *we* will forgive *them*.' Nerzhin embodies the moral of the novel that political prisoners, so long as they are able to reject cooperation with their jailers, are the really free people, whereas Stalin and his bureaucrats, imprisoned in their self-created fantasies of power, live constantly in the fear of losing it, and of death.

Tolstoy's name is evoked a number of times in *The First Circle*. The Socialist Realist, thinking of Tolstoy's search for truth in his fiction, admits that every Soviet writer secretly measures himself for 'Tolstoy's shirt,' and inwardly he laments that 'He tried for months not to look into Tolstoy, because the insistent Tolstoyan style kept taking him over.' Solzhenitsyn's destructive criticism of the evils of Soviet government and the oppression of its minions reminds one of Tolstoy's excoriation of tsarist Russia in *Resurrection*.

It has been observed by critics that the extensive discussion of Tolstoy's well-known short story *What Men Live By* in *Cancer Ward* has suggested the central *leitmotiv* of the novel. There can be no doubt of its significance for the matrix of the story, but it must also have been associated in Solzhenitsyn's mind with still another famous work of Tolstoy, *The Death of Ivan Ilych*. For in some respects, *Cancer Ward* is an elaborated version of Tolstoy's account of the judge's death by cancer. However, there is necessarily a great difference in emphasis in Solzhenitsyn's novel of disease and death, for the values that are ordinarily transformed by the reality of death are precisely Soviet values, which have been so distorted by daily experience that for many of the characters life itself seems like a long disease for which death is the only cure. Their attitude to death varies from that of a simple peasant woman who, like the peasant-worker in Tolstoy's *Master and Man*, fatalistically ascribes all to the will of God, to that of another character who, after reading Tolstoy's tale, asks 'What do men live by?' Solzhenitsyn's originality emerges, not unlike Tolstoy's, from his moral contemplation of the human circumstances that agitate the outlook of these sufferers. In the case of the principal cancer victim, the highly placed Soviet bureaucrat Rusanov, he fiercely clings to life, unable to imagine the futile termination of all his career successes, an attitude in stark contrast to that of Tolstoy's Ivan Ilych who in the end calmly accepts death as the spiritual fulfillment of life. Yet other sufferers in *Cancer Ward*, like Ivan Ilych and the merchant in *Master and Man*, learn that man does not live by his own devices and find in death a source of self-revelation, an awakening, a Tolstoyan mystical touch that raises the novel from the realistic plane to the level of enduring art.

Recent facts reveal that Solzhenitsyn has for years been planning a long novel conceived in the spirit of Tolstoy's *War and Peace*. If the first part, *August 1914* (1971), is any indication, it will not only become his masterpiece, but it will be the real Soviet 'War and Peace', a work emancipated from the ideological restraints of a Marxian view of history which had impeded the artistic freedom of Sholokhov in *The Silent Don*. In this first part, which concerns eleven days in the catastrophic offensive of the Russian Army in East Prussia in World War I, the author avoids formulating a theory of history and war, but he does draw on some of Tolstoy's ideas, such as the irrationality of history in terms of 'great men' who supposedly make it, and on Tolstoy's belief in the futility of war. Again very much as Tolstoy, he maintains a fine balance between the impact of war on the lives of his characters and on the life of the nation, for he clearly intends to show in the sequel how the war ultimately led to the 1917 Revolution. And there is a Tolstoyan flavor in the description of battle scenes and in the psychological probing of the thoughts and actions of characters. But in introducing modernistic techniques of structure and realism and in a new revelation of imaginative powers, Solzhenitsyn diverges not only from Tolstoy's practices, but also from those of his own previous fiction. Nevertheless, Truth, as with Tolstoy, remains the hero of all that he writes, the moral necessity to strip life of its lies, as he suggests at the end of *August 1914*: 'Falsehood did not come into the world with us, and it will not end with us.'

## IV

Though Tolstoy's world reputation has not been tarnished much by time, the popular image of him today reflects more sharply than it did in the later years of his life the distinction between literary artist and religious and social reformer. In 1960, at international commemorations of the fiftieth year of his death, at programs in the West, especially at the most elaborate one at Venice where many distinguished European intellectuals and writers gathered to honor his memory, the emphasis was definitely on Tolstoy the author of immortal novels. It seemed ironical that his philosophy of life, which had been derived primarily from the teachings of Christianity and had formerly stirred the conscience of millions, should be largely ignored as of no particular consequence precisely by the Christian West.

On the other hand, at a similar gathering at New Delhi, Tolstoy the thinker and religious philosopher predominated in various addresses in which Nehru played a leading role. This aspect of Tolstoy's activities seems to be favored in the Far East. He took a particular interest in its people and his controversial works are known there. Though he criticized the Japanese, whose imitation of Western civilization, he predicted, would eventually bring about their undoing, in his lengthy *Letter to a Chinese* (1906), in which he recommended his own panacea of civil disobedience and non-violence in the spirit of their revered religious teachers Confucius, Buddha, and Lao-tse, he further declared: 'In our time a great revolution in the life of humanity will be accomplished, and in this revolution China ought to play a tremendous role at the head of eastern peoples.'[15]

Certain features of Tolstoyism are still alive in India today. Initial interest in it may be credited to the late Mohandas Gandhi, who corresponded with Tolstoy in 1909 and 1910, read some of his controversial works – 'Tolstoy's *The Kingdom of God Is Within You*,' he wrote in his autobiography, 'overwhelmed me'[16] – and more than once paid tribute to him in his writings as his teacher. Gandhi was influenced by the doctrine of non-resistance to evil by violence, but he applied it successfully in his mass movement against colonialism with a practical direction alien to Tolstoy's interpretation. And his acceptance of the need for organized government, a reformed variety of it to be sure, was contrary to Tolstoy's conviction of its uselessness. After Indian independence, there was perhaps more pure Tolstoyism in the agricultural movement of Gandhi's disciple, Vinoba Bhave. Despite the residue today of a commingled Tolstoyism, Gandhianism, and socialism among some prominent Indian intellectuals, the new State has committed itself to the familiar policy of the violence of war when circumstances appear to dictate it, which Tolstoy would of course denounce as the inevitable consequence of compromise with his doctrine of universal love and non-violence.

Tolstoy had few illusions about the influence of his controversial writings during his lifetime and was even less sanguine about their future fate. At the age of seventy-nine he wrote in his diary: 'I know that these simple and clear truths about life which I now write will undoubtedly be defined by learned readers of the future as mysticism or even by some other title, thus enabling them, while not understanding these truths, to remain in their calm, self-satisfied ignorance.'[17]

Tolstoy overstated the future situation, for his controversial writings are very little read today. Either time has passed him by or the extremism of his advocacy prevents modern minds from perceiving the underlying relevance of his wisdom to their problems. For violence, the focus of his whole system of thought, has now become the insistent, omnipresent concern of mankind at a time when even many intellectuals, of whom Sartre is by no means the least, praise bloody combat with police and reactionaries and revolutionary terrorism as honorable means by which to effect political and social change. Since Tolstoy's death we have witnessed such incredible slaughter in two world wars, numerous little ones, revolutions, and racial and political genocide that Tolstoy's gloomy forebodings of future escalating violence now seem woefully understated. And one result of all this is the menacing ideological polarization of governments which has pushed world armament expenditures to over two hundred billion dollars annually. Tolstoy's lonely crusade against this ultimate form of violence now sounds like a pitiful small voice crying unheeded in a living world bent on universal thermonuclear destruction.

Then, too, in the years since his death, have come all the miracles of science and technology which have so benefited man and now threaten the elimination of his essential life resources. Though Tolstoy foresaw the possible evils of such 'progress,' his prediction of its consequences seems almost feckless today: 'When the life of people is immoral, and their relations are not based on love, but on egoism, then all technical improvements, the increase of man's power over nature, steam, electricity, the telegraph, every machine, gunpowder, and dynamite produce the impression of dangerous toys placed in the hands of children.'[18] Yet the statement does underscore his conviction, as well as that of many thoughtful people now, that the tendency to replace moral progress by technical progress is one of the calamities of modern life.

What is discouraging is that so many major problems of civilization which acutely disturbed Tolstoy in the 1890s are the same problems that agitate minds today, only now they are vaster in scope and much more terrifyingly imminent. It is as though he had told us, in Santayana's words, that those who do not learn from history are condemned to relive it. If his controversial writings have any contribution to make to us, it is one that grew out of the liberal dissent of the nineteenth century of which he was really a most original and radical part. Many elements of that message are now being carried to peoples of the world by innumerable 'Tolstoyan surrogates' as it were, who question the violence of war, coercion, and hypocrisy of all forms of organized government, the materialism and lack of spiritual and moral values of society, the huge economic disparity between rich and poor, the oppression of the many by the few, the existence of hunger in a world of plenty, the evils of industrialization, the massive flight of people from the country to the city, racial and religious persecution, the under-privileged position of women, the failure of the Church to adjust itself to the needs of society, the debacle of education that does not orient its students to life's demands, the development of coterie art instead of art for the people and the excessive commercialization and lack of sincerity and freedom in the arts, and the thoughtless and greedy despoliation of nature by modern science and technology. These and many other problems have been argued in Tolstoy's controversial works and are nowadays frequently discussed in his accents in print and from the platform: thousands of Buddhists and Taoists in Vietnam prisons who prefer suffering and death in their devotion to peace and non-violence; ever-growing numbers of conscientious objectors who refuse to serve in wars; a ringing plea in a conference of the World Council of Churches for strict adherence to the teaching of Christ on non-violence because every citizen's first obligation is to honor God and his con-science; expressions of the 'theology of peace' movement in the Catholic Church, which parallel widespread philosophical and political beliefs among laymen, that oppose the power of the State to coerce because it is more likely to turn to violence than is the relatively powerless private citizen; and numerous statements in the Western world of the moral and spiritual revolt of youth who seem willing to forsake personal comfort as a standard of truth in their campaigns against the hypocrisy of governments and the abuses of materialistic society more interested in acquisitiveness than in human betterment and the brotherhood of man.

These few examples, and very many more could be cited, are merely Tolstoyan straws in the polluted winds of the perilous world in which we live. If he were alive, Tolstoy would regard them as evidence of that new consciousness which he predicted would eventually take possession of the minds of all men and lead them to accept moral responsibility for their actions under the influence of belief in the universal law of love. For optimism about his faith never deserted him. 'No, the world is not a joke,' he once said, 'and not a value of trials or a transition to a better, everlasting world, but this world here is one of the eternal worlds that is beautiful, joyous, which we can and must make more beautiful and more joyous for those living with us and for those who will live after us.'[19]

# Notes

Unless otherwise stated all citations from Tolstoy's writings are from *Polnoye sobraniye sochinenii* [*Complete Collected Works*], 90 vols, ed. V. G. Chertkov *et al.*, Moscow, 1928–1958.

Chapter 1    Childhood, Boyhood, and Youth

1   *Recollections, Tolstoy Centenary Edition,* 21 vols, translated by Louise and Aylmer Maude, London, 1929–1937, xxi, 20. Hereafter cited as Maude Edition.
2   *Ibid.,* 3.
3   N. N. Apostolov, *Zhivoi Tolstoi (The Living Tolstoy),* Moscow, 1928, p. 18.
4   'Vospominaniya' *(Recollections),* P. I. Biryukov, *Biografiya L. N. Tolstogo, (Biography of L. N. Tolstoy),* 3rd edition, Moscow, 1923, i, 38.
5   N. N. Gusev, *Zhizn L. N. Tolstogo (Life of L. N. Tolstoy),* Moscow, 1927, i, 90.
6   P. I. Biryukov, *Biografiya L. N. Tolstogo (Biography of L. N. Tolstoy), op. cit.,* i, p. xviii.
7   N. N. Gusev, *Zhizn L. N. Tolstogo (Life of L. N. Tolstoy), op. cit.,* i, 106.
8   *Dnevnik (Diary)* (March 17, 1847), xlvi, 15.
9   V. N. Nazarev, 'Zhizn i lyudi bylogo vremeni,' *Istoricheski vestnik,* 'Life and People of Former Days' *(Historical Herald),* No. 11, St Petersburg, 1890, pp. 438–440.
10  A. B. Goldenveizer, *Vblizi Tolstogo (Companion of Tolstoy),* Moscow, 1922, i, 134.
11  *Dnevnik (Diary)* (April 17, 1847), xlvi, 31.
12  *Ibid.* (June 16, 1847), xlvi, 32–33.
13  *Pisma (Letters)* (January 10, 1850), lix, 54.

Chapter 2    The Caucasus

1   In a Letter, February 3, 1904 (N. N. Gusev, *Zhizn L. N. Tolstogo (Life of L. N. Tolstoy)), op. cit.,* i, 164.
2   *Dnevnik (Diary)* (December 8, 1850), xlvi, 39.
3   *Ibid.* (January 18, 1851), xlvi, 45.

# Notes

4  *Ibid.* (November 2, 1853), xlvi, 191.
5  *Pisma (Letters)* (December 23, 1851), lix, 130.
6  *Dnevnik (Diary)* (July 3, 1851), xlvi, 64–65.
7  *Ibid.* (May 30, 1852), xlvi, 119.
8  *Ibid.* (March 27, 1852), xlvi, 101.
9  *Ibid.* (May 22, 1852), xlvi, 118.
10  *Pisma (Letters)* (July 3, 1852), lix, 193–194.
11  *Dnevnik (Diary)* (August 29, 1852), xlvi, 140.
12  *Otechestvennyie zapiski (Notes of the Fatherland)*, 1852, x, 85.
13  See the excellent study: R. F. Christian, *Tolstoy, A Critical Introduction*, London, 1969, pp. 28–29.
14  *Dnevnik (Diary)* (December 1, 1853), xlvi, 206.
15  *Ibid.* (December 11, 1852), xlvi, 152.
16  *Ibid.* (December 18, 1853), xlvi, 214.
17  *Ibid.* (September 22, 1852), xlvi, 142.
18  *Ibid.* (August 3, 1852), xlvi, 137.
19  *Ibid.* (December 27, 1852), xlvi, 154.
20  *Ibid.* (June 11–12, 1851), xlvi, 61–62.
21  *Ibid.* (March 29, 1852), xlvi, 102.
22  *Ibid.* (June 29, 1852), xlvi, 128–129.
23  *Ibid.* (November 14, 1852), xlvi, 149.
24  *Ibid.* (August 28, 1852), xlvi, 140.

## Chapter 3  War, Travel, and Self-Definition

1  *Zapiski ob otritsatelnykh storonakh russkogo soldati i ofitsera (Report on the Negative Aspects of the Russian Soldier and Officer)*, iv, 285–290.
2  'Literaturnye prilozheniya' (*'Literary Supplements'*), *Niva*, No. 2, St Petersburg, February 1898, pp. 342–343.
3  *Dnevnik (Diary)* (October 10, 1855), xlvii, 64.
4  *Ibid.* (July 25, 1855), xlvii, 54.
5  *Ibid.* (March 4, 1855), xlvii, 37–38.
6  I. S. Turgenev, *Sobranie sochineni v dvenadtsati tomakh (Collected Works in Twelve Volumes)*, Moscow, 1958, xii, 197.
7  *Perepiska L. N. Tolstogo s gr. A. A. Tolstoi (Correspondence of L. N. Tolstoy with Countess A. A. Tolstoy)*, St Petersburg, 1911, p. 3.
8  *Dnevnik (Diary)* (June 9, 1856), xlvii, 80.
9  *Ibid.* (July 13, 1856), xlvii, 86.
10  *Ibid.* (October 1, 1856), xlvii, 93.
11  *Zapisnyie knizhki (Notebooks)* (October 25, 1856), xlvii, 199.
12  *Pisma L. N. Tolstogo (Letters of L. N. Tolstoy)*, ed. P. A. Sergeyenko, Moscow, 1910–1911, i, 58.
13  'L. N. Tolstoi i V. P. Botkin. Perepiska,' *Pamyatniki tvorchestva i zhizni*

*L. N. Tolstogo* ['L. N. Tolstoy and V. P. Botkin. Correspondence,' *Memories of the Works and Life of L. N. Tolstoy*], ed. V. I. Sreznevski, Moscow, 1923, iv, 20–23.

14 *Dnevnik (Diary)* (May 5, 1857), xlvii, 126.
15 *Ibid.* (May 15, 1857), xlvii, 127.
16 *Putevyie zapiski po Shveitsarii (Travel Notes on Switzerland)*, v, 194.
17 *Ibid.*, v, 203.
18 'Vospominaniya gr. A. A. Tolstoi,' *Perepiska L. N. Tolstogo s gr. A. A. Tolstoi* ('Recollections of Countess A. A. Tolstoy,' *Correspondence of L. N. Tolstoy with Countess A. A. Tolstoy*), *op. cit.*, p. 11.
19 *Dnevnik (Diary)* (August 16, 1857), xlvii, 152.
20 *Perepiska L. N. Tolstogo s gr. A. A. Tolstoi* [*Correspondence of L. N. Tolstoy with Countess A. A. Tolstoy*], *op. cit.*, pp. 98–99.
21 *Dnevnik (Diary)* (May 13, 1858), quoted in N. N. Gusev, *Letopis zhizni i tvorchestva L. N. Tolstogo (Chronicle of the Life and Works of L. N. Tolstoy)*, Moscow-Leningrad, 1936, p. 111.
22 'Vospominaniya E. I. Sytinoi,' *Literaturnoye nasledstvo* ('Recollections of E. I. Sytin,' *Literary Heritage*), No. 37–38, Moscow, 1939, ii, 404.
23 N. N. Gusev, *Zhizn L. N. Tolstogo (Life of L. N. Tolstoy)*, *op. cit.*, i, 302.
24 *Perepiska L. N. Tolstogo s gr. A. A. Tolstoi (Correspondence of L. N. Tolstoy with Countess A. A. Tolstoy)*, *op. cit.*, p. 119.
25 *Ibid.*, pp. 131–132.
26 *Dnevnik (Diary)* (July 6, 1855), xlvii, 50.
27 *Ibid.* (September 17, 1855), xlvii, 60.
28 *Ibid.* (November 23, 1856), xlvii, 101.
29 *Rech v obshchestve lyubitelei rossiskoi slovestnosti (Speech at the Society of Lovers of Russian Literature)*, v, 271–272.
30 *Zapisnyie knizhki (Notebooks)* (May 25, 1857), xlvii, 208–209.
31 *Ibid.* (April 13, 1857), xlvii, 204.
32 *Ibid.* (May 24, 1857), xlvii, 208.

Chapter 4  Educator

1 *Dnevnik (Diary)* (July 23, 1857), xlvii, 146.
2 'O zadachakh pedagogii' ('On Problems of Pedagogy'), viii, 383.
3 A. A. Fet, *Moi vospominaniya (My Recollections)*, Moscow, 1890, i, 350–351.
4 Julius Froebel, *Ein Lebenslauf: Aufzeichnungen, Erinnerungen und Bekenntnisse*, Stuttgart, 1891, ii, 74–75.
5 *O narodnom obrazovanii (On National Education)*, viii, 25.
6 *Zapisnyie knizhki (Notebooks)* (March 16, 1861), xlvii, 332.
7 *Yasno-Polyanskaya Shkola za noyabr i dekabr mesyatsy (Yasno-Polyana School for November and December)*, viii, 30–31.
8 *Ibid.*, viii, 70.

9 *Ibid.*, viii, 114.

10 *Ibid.*, viii, 115.

11 P. I. Biryukov, *Biografiya L. N. Tolstogo (Biography of L. N. Tolstoy), op. cit.*, i, 211.

12 V. S. Morozov, *Vospominaniya o L. N. Tolstom (Recollections of L. N. Tolstoy)*, Moscow, 1917, p. 136.

Chapter 5   *War and Peace*

1 A. A. Fet, *Moi vospominaniya (My Recollections), op. cit.*, i, 378.

2 I. S. Turgenev, *Sobranie sochineni v dvenadtsati tomakh (Collected Works in Twelve Volumes), op. cit.*, xii, 354.

3 E. M. Forster, *Aspects of the Novel*, London and New York, 1927, p. 242.

4 Some critics have argued that at the beginning of *War and Peace* Tolstoy set out to write a 'family novel.' R. F. Christian, in his illuminating study, *Tolstoy's 'War and Peace,'* London, 1962, makes a good case for the historical influence of the War of 1812 on the initial planning of the novel. Somewhat the contrary position is taken by Kathryn Feuer in her perceptive article: 'The Book that Became *War and Peace,' The Reporter*, New York, May 14, 1959, pp. 33–36.

5 *Perepiska L. N. Tolstogo s gr. A. A. Tolstoi (Correspondence of L. N. Tolstoy with Countess A. A. Tolstoy), op. cit.*, p. 192.

6 *Dnevnik (Diary)* (March 19, 1865), quoted in *Literaturnoye nasledstvo (Literary Heritage), op. cit.*, No. 37–38, ii, 90.

7 *Ibid.* (September 16, 1864), *Literaturnoye nasledstvo (Literary Heritage), op. cit.*, ii, 105.

8 *Voina i Mir (War and Peace)*, xiii, 73.

9 *Literaturny post (Literary Post)*, No. 10, 1928, pp. 64–65.

10 Isaiah Berlin, *The Hedgehog and the Fox: An Essay on Tolstoy's View of History*, New York, 1953, p. 39.

11 N. N. Gusev, *Zhizn L. N. Tolstogo (Life of L. N. Tolstoy), op. cit.*, ii, 79.

12 R. F. Christian, *Tolstoy, A Critical Introduction, op. cit.*, p. 116.

13 This long study has been translated into English: *Essays in Russian Literature*, selected, edited, translated, and with an Introduction by Spencer E. Roberts, Athens, Ohio, 1968, pp. 225–356.

14 N. N. Strakhov, 'Statyi o *Voine i Mire,' Zarya* ('Articles on *War and Peace,'* Dawn), 1869–1870.

15 S. A. Tolstaya, 'Avtobiografiya,' *Nachala* ('Autobiography,' *Beginnings*) 1926, p. 1.

Chapter 6   *Anna Karenina*

1 A. A. Fet, *Moi vospominaniya (My Recollections), op. cit.*, ii, 199.

2 *Ibid.*, ii, 226.

3 *Dnevniki Sofyi Andreyevny Tolstoi (Diaries of Sofya Andreyevna Tolstaya),* *1860–1891*, ed. S. L. Tolstoi, Leningrad, 1928, p. 32.
4 Matthew Arnold, 'Count Leo Tolstoy,' *Fortnightly Review*, xlviii, London, 1887, pp. 783–799.
5 George Lukács, *Studies in European Realism,* translated by Edith Bone, London, 1950, p. 157.
6 Quoted in Kathryn Feuer's article, 'The Book that Became *War and Peace,*' *op. cit.*

Chapter 7    Spiritual Crisis and Religious Faith

1 *Dnevnik (Dairy)* (October 28, 1879), quoted in P. I. Biryukov, *Biografiya L. N. Tolstogo (Biography of L. N. Tolstoy)*, *op. cit.*, ii, 158.
2 Aylmer Maude, *The Life of Tolstoy*, Oxford, London, 1930, ii, 32.
3 N. N. Gusev, *Letopis zhizni i tvorchestva L. N. Tolstogo (Chronicle of the Life and Works of L. N. Tolstoy)*, *op. cit.*, p. 302.
4 'The Dead Church' in *What I Believe*, chapter xi.
5 *Pisma (Letters)* (December 20, 1882–January 20, 1883), lxiii, 112–124.
6 *Dnevnik (Diary)*, liv, note, p. 459.
7 *Ibid.*, note, p. 463.
8 'A Reply to the Synod's Edict of Excommunication,' *On Life and Essays on Religion*, Maude Edition, xii, 223–225.

Chapter 8    *What Then Must We Do?*

1 *Pisma (Letters)* (March 8–15, 1881), lxiii, 45–52.
2 S. A. Tolstaya, 'Moya zhizn' (My Life), p. 668 (unpublished manuscript in the Lenin Public Library; see *Pisma (Letters)*, lxiii, 55).
3 *K. P. Pobedonostsev i yego korrespondentsy (K. P. Pobedonostsev and His Correspondents)*, Moscow, 1923, i, 47–48.
4 *Dnevnik (Diary)* (October 5, 1881), quoted in P. I. Biryukov, *Biografiya L. N. Tolstogo (Biography of L. N. Tolstoy)*, *op. cit.*, ii, 189.
5 *Pisma (Letters)* (June 6–7, 1885), lxxxv, 223–224.
6 *Ibid.* (December 15–19, 1885), lxxxxiii, 539–548.
7 *What Then Must We Do?*, Maude Edition, xiv, 357–358.
8 *Ibid.*, 384.
9 *Ibid.*, 390.
10 P. I. Biryukov, *Biografiya L. N. Tolstogo (Biography of L. N. Tolstoy)*, *op. cit.*, iii, 181–182.
11 N. N. Apostolov, *Zhivoi Tolstoi (The Living Tolstoy)*, *op. cit.*, pp. 329–330.
12 N. N. Gusev, *Letopis zhizni i tvorchestva L. N. Tolstogo (Chronicle of the Life and Works of L. N. Tolstoy)*, *op. cit.*, p. 467.
13 S. A. Tolstaya, *Pisma k L. N. Tolstomu (Letters to L. N. Tolstoy), 1862–1910*, ed. A. I. Tolstaya and P. S. Popov, Moscow-Leningrad, 1936, p. 535.

14 P. I. Biryukov, *Biografiya L. N. Tolstogo (Biography of L. N. Tolstoy)*, *op. cit.*, iii, 171.

15 Vera Velichkina, *V golodny god s Lvom Tolstym (In the Famine Year with Leo Tolstoy)*, Moscow, 1928, p. 116.

16 P. I. Biryukov, *Biografiya L. N. Tolstogo (Biography of L. N. Tolstoy)*, *op. cit.*, iii, 192–193.

## Chapter 9    Back to Art

1 A. K. Chertkova, 'Vospominaniya o Tolstom,' *Trudy tolstovskogo muzeya. L. N. Tolstoi ('Recollections of Tolstoy,' Works of the Tolstoy Museum. L. N. Tolstoy)*, Moscow, 1929, pp. 151–159.

2 *Tolstoi i Turgenev: Perepiska (Tolstoy and Turgenev: Correspondence)*, ed. M. O. Gershenzon, Moscow, 1916, p. 114.

3 *Pisma (Letters)* (June 6–7, 1885), lxxxv, 223–224.

4 Quoted by Aylmer Maude in 'Preface. Tolstoy as a Dramatist,' *Plays*, Maude Edition, xvii, p. xxv.

5 'Iz perepiski L. N. Tolstogo,' *Vestnik Evropy*, No. 3, 1915, p. 19.

6 *Iz razgovorova L. N. Tolstogo* ('From the Conversation of L. N. Tolstoy,' *Herald of Europe*), quoted by N. N. Gusev, *Zhizn L. N. Tolstogo (Life of L. N. Tolstoy)*, *op. cit.*, ii, 5.

7 *Pisma (Letters)* (November 6, 1888), lxxxvi, 181–182.

8 A. P. Chekhov, *Polnoe sobranie sochinenii i pisem (Complete Collected Works and Letters)*, Moscow, 1949, xii, 15–16.

9 'Vospominaniya gr. A. A. Tolstoi,' *Perepiska L. N. Tolstogo s gr. A. A. Tolstoi ('Recollections of Countess A. A. Tolstoy,' Correspondence of L. N. Tolstoy with Countess A. A. Tolstoy)*, *op. cit.*, pp. 35–36.

10 *Dnevnik (Diary)* (January 3, 1890), quoted in P. I. Biryukov, *Biografiya L. N. Tolstogo (Biography of L. N. Tolstoy)*, *op. cit.*, iii, 122.

11 *Ibid.*

12 *Pisma (Letters)* (April 15, 1891), lxxxvii, 88.

13 Aylmer Maude, *The Life of Tolstoy*, *op. cit.*, ii, 180.

14 *Dnevniki Sofyi Andreyevny Tolstoi (Diaries of Sofya Andreyevna Tolstaya)*, *op. cit.*, pp. 147, 158.

## Chapter 10    *The Kingdom of God Is Within You*

1 *Dnevnik (Diary)* (July 14, 1891), quoted in V. Zhdanov, *Lyubov v zhizni Lva Tolstogo (Love in the Life of Leo Tolstoy)*, Moscow, 1928, II, 105.

2 *Perepiska L. N. Tolstogo s N. N. Strakhovym (Correspondence of L. N. Tolstoy with N. N. Strakhov)*, ed. B. I. Modzalevski, St Petersburg, 1924, p. 265.

3 *The Kingdom of God and Peace Essays*, Maude Edition, xx, 109.

4 *Ibid.*, 135.

5 *Ibid.*, 181–182.

6 *Ibid.*, 196–197.

7 *Ibid.*, 245.

8 *Ibid.*, 235.

9 'Advice to a Draftee,' *Atlantic,* Boston, February, 1968, p. 57.

10 *The Kingdom of God and Peace Essays,* Maude Edition, xx, 330.

11 *Ibid.*, 444.

12 Cf. 'Predisloviye k angliskoi biografii Garrisona' ('Foreword to the English Biography of Garrison'), xxxvi, 97–98.

13 For a recital of some of the more ludicrous conflicts, see the excellent article of William B. Edgerton, 'The Artist Turned Prophet: Leo Tolstoy After 1880,' *American Contributions to the Sixth International Congress of Slavists,* vol. II, Literary Contributions, The Hague, 1968.

14 A. S. Butkevich, 'Vospominaniya,' *Letopisi. L. N. Tolstoi* ('Recollections,' Chronicle. L. N. Tolstoy), ii, 342.

15 *The Kingdom of God and Peace Essays,* Maude Edition, xx, p. 489.

16 *Ibid.*, 247.

17 *The Law of Love and the Law of Violence,* translated from the French by Mary Koutouzow Tolstoy, New York, 1948, p. 9. The first corrected and complete Russian edition was not published until 1956. Slight alterations in the quotations here have been made on the basis of the Russian edition.

18 *Ibid.*, p. 24.


Chapter 11  *What Is Art?*

1 V. Zhdanov, *Lyubov v zhizni Lva Tolstogo (Love in the Life of Leo Tolstoy),* Moscow, 1928, ii, 134.

2 *Dnevnik (Diary)* (March 12, 1895), quoted in V. Zhdanov, *Lyubov z zhizni Lva Tolstogo (Love in the Life of Leo Tolstoy),* ii, 136.

3 *Pisma (Letters)* (May 5, 1895), quoted in V. Zhdanov, *Lyubov i zhizni Lva Tolstogo (Love in the Life of Leo Tolstoy),* ii, 141.

4 *Dnevnik (Diary)* (October 13, 1895), see S. A. Tolstaya, *Pisma k L. N. Tolstomu (Letters to L. N. Tolstoy), op. cit.,* note, p. 618.

5 *Pisma L. N. Tolstogo (Letters of L. N. Tolstoy), op. cit.,* i, 246–250.

6 *Dnevnik S. I. Taneyeva. Istoriya russkoi muzyki v issledovaniyakh i materialakh (Diary of S. I. Taneyev. History of Russian Music in Studies and Materials),* ed. K. N. Kuznetsov, Moscow, 1924, i, 196.

7 Cf. *L. N. Tolstoi. O literature. Stati, pisma, dnevniki (L. N. Tolstoy. On Literature. Articles, Letters, Diaries),* Moscow, 1955.

8 Cf. 'Predislovie k *Krestyanskim Rasskazam* S. T. Semyonova,' *L. N. Tolstoi. O literature. Stati, pisma, dnevniki* ('Foreword to Peasant Stories of S. T. Semyonov,' *L. N. Tolstoy. On Literature. Articles, Letters, Diaries),* p. 292.

9 *L. N. Tolstoi v vospominaniyakh sovremennikov (L. N. Tolstoy in the Recollections of Contemporaries),* Moscow, 1955, p. 232.

# Notes

10 Quoted in *L. N. Tolstoi. O literature. Stati, pisma, dnevniki (L. N. Tolstoy. On Literature. Articles, Letters, Diaries)*, *op. cit.*, Preface, p. xxi.
11 All this material has been published in *Literaturnoye nasledstvo (Literary Heritage)*, *op. cit.*, No. 37–38.
12 *What Is Art? and Essays on Art*, Maude Edition, xviii, 123.
13 *Ibid.*, xviii, 186.
14 *Ibid.*, xviii, 189.
15 *Ibid.*, xviii, 286.
16 *Ibid.*, xviii, 246, footnote.
17 See R. F. Christian, *Tolstoy. A Critical Introduction*, *op. cit.*, p. 248.
18 *What Is Art? and Essays on Art*, Maude Edition, xviii, 150.
19 G. Wilson Knight, *Shakespeare and Tolstoy*, London, 1934, quoted in *Recollections and Essays*, Maude Edition, Preface, xxi, p. xxx.

## Chapter 12    *Resurrection*

1 An entirely uncensored text of *Resurrection*, along with all the drafts, was first published in 1936 in the Soviet edition of Tolstoy's Complete Works (vols xxxii–xxxiii). It is estimated that 497 deletions and changes had been made by tsarist censors.
2 *Dnevnik (Diary)* (December 18, 1899), liv, 13.
3 P. I. Biryukov, *Biografiya L. N. Tolstogo (Biography of L. N. Tolstoy)*, *op. cit.*, iii, 317.
4 *Voskreseniye (Resurrection)*, xxxii, 445.
5 *Dnevnik (Diary)* (June 22, 1900), liv, 27
6 *The Death of Ivan Ilych and Other Stories*, Maude Edition, xv, Preface, p. ix.
7 Cf. 'Tolstoy's *Master and Man* – Symbolic Narrative,' *Slavic and East European Journal*, iii, Indiana, 1963.
8 *Dnevnik (Diary)* (December, 1904), lv, 104.
9 *The Cause of It All*, a slight dramatic vignette on peasant life, which Tolstoy wrote in 1910 for an amateur performance in the home of a disciple, did not seem to require treatment here.
10 *London Mercury*, May, 1921, quoted by Aylmer Maude in *Plays*, Maude Edition, Preface, xviii, p. xxviii.

## Chapter 13    Government – War – Revolution – Land Question – Death

1 N. N. Apostolov, *Zhivoi Tolstoi (The Living Tolstoy)*, *op. cit.*, p. 312.
2 'Perepiska Tolstogo s V. S. Solovyovym,' *Literaturnoye nasledstvo* ('Correspondence of Tolstoy with V. S. Solovyov,' *Literary Heritage*), *op. cit.*, No. 37–38, ii, 270.
3 P. I. Biryukov, *Biografiya L. N. Tolstogo (Biography of L. N. Tolstoy)*, *op. cit.*, iv, 81.

4 *Dnevnik (Diary)*, lv, note, 442.
5 *Ibid.*, lv, note, 468.
6 *Ibid.* (December 31, 1904), lv, 111.
7 M. Chistyakova, 'Tolstoi i evropeiskie kongressy mira,' *Literaturnoye nasledstvo* ('Tolstoy and the European Peace Congress,' *Literary Heritage*), *op. cit.*, No. 37–38, ii, 603.
8 A. B. Goldenveizer, *Vblizi Tolstogo (Companion of Tolstoy)*, *op. cit.*, i, 118.
9 N. Serebrov (A. Tikhonov), 'Yasnaya Polyana,' *Novy mir* ('Yasnaya Polyana,' *New World*), No. 6, Moscow, 1940, p. 205.
10 *Ibid.*, p. 211.
11 *Dnevnik Lva Nikolayevicha Tolstogo (Diary of Leo Nikolayevich Tolstoy), 1895–1899*, ed. V. G. Chertkov, Moscow, 1916, p. 133.
12 *Ibid.*, p. 154.
13 *The Kingdom of God and Peace Essays*, Maude Edition, xx, 235.
14 *Zapisnaya knizhka (Notebook)* (September 1905), lv, 316.
15 *Dnevnik (Diary)* (July 31, 1905), lv, 153.
16 A. B. Goldenveizer, *Vblizi Tolstogo (Companion of Tolstoy)*, *op. cit.*, i, 155.
17 D. P. Makovitski, *Yasnopolyanskiye zapiski (Yasnopolyana Notes)*, Moscow, 1922, i, 90.
18 *Lenin o Tolstom (Lenin on Tolstoy)*, Moscow-Leningrad, 1928, p. 24.
19 *O znachenii russkoi revolyutsii (On the Significance of the Russian Revolution)*, xxxvi, 360.
20 'Perepiska Tolstogo s S. I. Muntyanovym,' *Literaturnoye nasledstvo* ('Correspondence of Tolstoy with S. I. Muntyanov,' *Literary Heritage*), *op. cit.*, No. 37–38, ii, 354–355.
21 *I Cannot Be Silent*, Maude Edition, xxi, 404–411.
22 *Dnevnik (Diary)*, lvi, note, p. 504.
23 *Dnevniki Sofyi Andreyevny Tolstoi (Diaries of Sofya Andreyevna Tolstaya), 1910*, ed. S. L. Tolstoi, Moscow, 1936, note, p. 369.
24 *Ibid.*, note, p. 367.

Chapter 14    International Recognition

1 T. Motyleva, *O mirovom znachenii L. N. Tolstogo (On the World Significance of L. N. Tolstoy)*, Moscow, 1957.
2 Cf. William B. Edgerton, 'The Penetration of Nineteenth-Century Russian Literature into the Other Slavic Countries,' *American Contributions to the Fifth International Congress of Slavists*, The Hague, 1964, pp. 60–61.
3 Quoted in Gilbert Phelps, *The Russian Novel in English Fiction*, London, 1956, p. 38.
4 William B. Edgerton, 'The Penetration of Nineteenth-Century Russian Literature into the Other Slavic Countries,' *op. cit.*, p. 64.
5 Quoted in Gilbert Phelps, *The Russian Novel in English Fiction*, *op. cit.*, p. 39.

6 T. W. H., 'The Russian School of Writers,' *Harper's Bazaar*, xx, No. 38 (September 17, 1887), quoted by William B. Edgerton, *op. cit.*, pp. 64–65.

7 Quoted in Gilbert Phelps, *The Russian Novel in English Fiction*, *op. cit.*, pp. 139–140. I am indebted to Mr Phelps's research on Tolstoy's acceptance in England.

8 *Ibid.*, pp. 138–155.

9 A partial answer to this need is an unpublished dissertation: J. Allen Smith, 'Tolstoy's Fiction in England and America,' University of Illinois, 1939.

10 'Lyof N. Tolstoy,' *North American Review*, clxxxviii, New York, 1908, pp. 842–859.

11 See the unpublished dissertation of Clare B. Goldfarb: 'Journey to Altruria: William D. Howells' Use of Tolstoy,' Indiana University, June 1964.

12 Thaïs S. Lindstrom, *Tolstoï en France (1886–1910)*, Paris, 1952.

13 *Ibid.*, p. 152.

14 A. P. Chckhov, *Polnoe sobranie sochinenii i pisem (Complete Collected Works and Letters)*, *op. cit.*, xviii, 312–313 (letter to M. O. Menshikov, January 28, 1900).

15 *Pismo k Kitaitsu (Letter to a Chinese)*, xxxvi, 292.

16 M. E. Gandhi, *An Autobiography, or the Story of My Experiments with Truth*, Ahmedabad, India, 1948, p. 172.

17 *Dnevnik (Diary)* (November 18, 1907), lvi, 77.

18 *Ibid.* (November 14, 1903), liv, 193.

19 Quoted in P. I. Biryukov, *Biografiya L. N. Tolstogo (Biography of L. N. Tolstoy)*, *op. cit.*, iii, 238.

# Selected Bibliography

Difficulties involved in selecting from the immense bibiliography on Tolstoy are outlined in 'Bibliographical Survey': Ernest J. Simmons, *Leo Tolstoy*, Boston, 1946, pp. 815–836. The most recent work on the subject is confined to a listing of more than 5,000 titles published only in Russia since the 1917 Revolution: N. G. Shelyapina *et al.*, *Bibliografiya literatury o Tolstom (Bibliography of Literature on Tolstoy)*, *1917–1958*, Moscow, 1960. A much more selective effort, and covering only Tolstoy's lifetime, is: E. N. Zhilina, *L. N. Tolstoi, 1828–1910*, Leningrad, 1960. The titles listed below under several headings include some, but by no means all, of the sources mentioned in the notes. The intention is simply to provide a small selection of what seem to be indispensable works concerning Tolstoy.

*Editions:* the definitive Russian edition of Tolstoy's works is *Polnoye sobraniye sochinenii (Complete Collected Works)*, 90 vols, ed. V. G. Chertkov *et al.*, Moscow, 1928–1958 (45 volumes are devoted to artistic, non-literary works), and drafts of them; 45 to letters, diaries, and notebooks); a more recent smaller edition: *Sobraniye sochineni (Collected Works)*, 20 vols, Moscow, 1960–1965 (16 vols of works, 2 of letters, and 2 of diaries); of the several editions in English translation, which exlude letters and diaries, the two most considerable are: *The Complete Works of Count Tolstoy*, translated from the original Russian and edited by Leo Wiener, 24 vols, Boston, 1904–1905 (the fullest in English but by no means complete, and the translation is often inadequate); *Tolstoy Centenary Edition*, translated and Louise and Aylmer Maude, 21 vols, London, 1929–1937 (contains nearly all the important works and is the best English translation).

Besides these editions, there have been numerous publications of separate works and collections of stories in Russia and in translation in many countries. Among the most notable recent such endeavours in England and America have been translations of the major novels and stories published by Penguin Classics and four volumes of the shorter fiction by Modern Library.

*Letters:* no effort has been made to publish abroad, in translation, extensive selections of Tolstoy's letters culled from the more than 8,000 of them in the definitive Soviet edition of his writings. A few earlier specialized Russian collections have appeared in French and German, and two in English: *The*

*Letters of Tolstoy and His Cousin, Countess Alexandra Tolstoy 1857–1903*, translated by Leo Islavin, New York and London, 1929 (incomplete and a rather poor translation); *Tolstoy's Love Letters to Valerya Arseneva, 1856–1857*, translated by S. S. Koteliansky and Virginia Woolf, Richmond, 1923; a few letters may be found in: *Tolstoy. Literary Fragments, Letters, and Reminiscences*, ed. by René Fülöp-Miller and translated by Paul England, New York, 1931 (published in the UK as *New Light on Tolstoy*, 1931); and it should be mentioned that numerous quotations from Tolstoy's letters may be found in English biographic works on him.

*Diaries*: the importance of Tolstoy's extensive diaries and notebooks as uninhibited primary source material about his life, writings, and his opinions on a large variety of subjects was early recognized. Though fully accessible for some time in the definitive Soviet edition of his works, not a great deal of this material has appeared in foreign translation. In English there are: *The Diaries of Leo Tolstoy, 1847–1852*, translated by C. J. Hogarth and A. Sirnis, New York, 1918; *The Private Diary of Leo Tolstoy, 1853–1857*, translated by Louise and Aylmer Maude, New York, 1927; *The Journal of Leo Tolstoy, 1895–1899*, translated by Rose Strunsky, New York, 1917; *Leo Tolstoy. Last Diaries, 1910*, translated by Lydia Weston-Kesich, edited and with an introduction by Leon Stilman, New York, 1960.

*Memoirs, Diaries and Letters About Tolstoy*: under this heading there is rich material. Members of the family and close friends kept diaries and wrote reminiscences about Tolstoy. Nearly all these works are in Russian, and below appears a small selection of those which seem to be most substantial and authoritative. Whenever translated into English, this fact is noted.

Apostolov, N. N., *Zhivoi Tolstoi (The Living Tolstoy)*, Moscow, 1928.

Boyer, Paul, *Chez Tolstoï: Entretiens à Jasnaïa Poliana*, Paris, 1950.

Bulgakov, Valentin, *L. N. Tolstoi v postednii god yego*, Moscow, 1960. (*The Last Year of Leo Tolstoy*, translated from the Russian by Ann Dunnigan, introduction by George Steiner, New York and London, 1971.)

*Dnevniki Sofyi Andreyevny Tolstoi, 1860–1897*, 2 vols, ed. S. L. Tolstoi, Leningrad, 1928–1929 (*The Diary of Tolstoy's Wife, 1860–1891*, and *The Countess Tolstoy's Later Diary, 1891–1897*, translated by Alexander Werth, London, 1929).

*Dnevniki Sofyi Andreyevny Tolstoi (Diaries of Sofya Andreyevna Tolstaya), 1897–1909*, ed. S. L. Tolstoi, Moscow, 1932.

Goldenveizer, A. B., *Vblizi Tolstogo*, 2 vols, Moscow, 1922–1923 (a small part of these two volumes has been translated by S. S. Koteliansky and Virginia Woolf: *Talks with Tolstoy*, Richmond, 1923).

Gorki, M., *Vosponinaniya o L. N. Tolstom*, Petrograd, 1919 (M. Gorky, *Remi-*

niscences of Tolstoy, Chekhov, and Andreyev, translated by K. Mansfield, S. S. Koteliansky, and L. Woolf, London, 1934).

Kuzminskaya, T. A., *Moya zhizn doma i v Yasnoi Polyane,* 3 vols, Moscow, 1926–1928 *(Tolstoy As I Knew Him,* translated by Nora Sigerist, *et al.,* New York, 1948).

Sukhotin-Tolstoy, T. L., *The Tolstoy Home,* London, 1950.

Tolstoi, I. L., *Moi vospominaniya,* Moscow, 1913 *(Reminiscences of Tolstoy,* by his son Count Ilya Tolstoy, translated by George Calderon, New York, 1914).

Tolstoi, L. L., *Pravda o moyom ottse,* Leningrad, 1924 (Count Léon L. Tolstoi, *The Truth About My Father,* New York, 1924).

*L. N. Tolstoi v vospominaniyakh sovremennikov (L. N. Tolstoy in the Recollections of Contemporaries),* 2 vols, Moscow, 1960.

Tolstoy, S. L., *Tolstoy Remembered by His Son Sergei Tolstoy,* translated by Moura Budberg, New York, 1962.

*Biographies:* The fascination of Tolstoy's life and personality, as well as the mass of primary and secondary sources available for their study, have attracted many biographers. Listed here, with a few exceptions, are full-length studies of his life by writers who have had access to this wealth of material or who knew him personally.

Biryukov, Pavel, *Biografiya L. N. Tolstogo (Biography of L. N. Tolstoy),* 3rd ed., 4 vols, Moscow, 1923.

Gusev, N. N., *Lev Nikolayevich Tolstoi. Materialy k biografii s 1828 po 1855 god (Leo Nikolayevich Tolstoy, Materials towards a Biography from 1828 to 1855),* Moscow, 1957; *Leo Nikolayevich Tolstoi. Materialy k biografii s 1855 po 1869 god,* Moscow, 1957; *Lev Nikolayevich Tolstoi. Materialy k biografii s 1870 po 1881 god,* Moscow, 1963; *Lev Nikolayevich Tolstoi. Materialy k biografii s 1881 po 1885 god,* Moscow, 1970.

Gusev, N. N., *Letopis zhizni i tvorchestva Lva Nikolayevicha Tolstogo (Chronicle of the Life and Works of Leo Nikolayevich Tolstoy), 1828–1890,* Moscow, 1958; *Letopis zhizni i tvorchestva Lva Nikolayevicha Tolstogo, 1891–1910,* Moscow, 1960.

Maude, Aylmer, *The Life of Tolstoy,* 2 vols, London, 1929–1930.

Rolland, Romain, *La Vie de Tolstoi,* Paris, 1911 *(The Life of Tolstoy,* translated by Bernard Miall, New York and London, 1911).

Shklovsky, Viktor, *Lev Tolstoi,* Moscow, 1963.

Simmons, Ernest J., *Leo Tolstoy,* Boston, 1946 (paperback edition, 2 vols, New York, 1960).

Tolstoy, Alexandra, *Tolstoy. A Life of My Father,* New York, 1953, London, 1954.

Troyat, Henri, *Tolstoy,* translated from the French by Nancy Amphoux, New York, 1967.

*Literary Criticism and Interpretation of Tolstoy's Life and Thought:* here again, it has been necessary to offer a very restricted listing of works that fall under this heading.

Archambault, Reginald D., ed., *Tolstoy on Education*, Chicago, 1967.

Ardens, N. N., *Tvorcheskii put L. N. Tolstogo (Creative Path of L. N. Tolstoy)*, Moscow, 1965.

Bayley, John, *Tolstoy and the Novel*, London, 1966.

Berlin, Isaiah, *The Hedgehog and the Fox,* New York and London, 1953.

Bilinkis, Y. A., *O tvorchestve L. N. Tolstogo (L. N. Tolstoy's Creative Power)*, Moscow, 1959.

Bursov, B. I., *Lev Tolstoi. Ideinye iskaniya i tvorcheskii metod (Leo Tolstoy. Ideational Searchings and Creative Method), 1847–1862,* Moscow, 1960.

Christian, R. F., *Tolstoy's 'War and Peace': A Study,* London, 1962.

Christian, R. F., *Tolstoy, A Critical Introduction,* Cambridge, 1969.

Craufurd, A. H., *The Religion and Ethics of Tolstoy,* London, 1912.

Eykhenbaum, B. M., *Molodoi Tolstoi (The Young Tolstoy),* Petrograd, 1922.

Eykhenbaum, B. M., *Lev Tolstoi, kniga pervaya, 50-e gody (Leo Tolstoy, I, the 1850's),* Leningrad, 1928; *Lev Tolstoi, kniga vtoraya, 60-e gody (Leo Tolstoy, II, the 1860's),* Moscow, 1931; *Lev Tolstoi, semidesyatye gody (Leo Tolstoy, the 1870's),* Leningrad, 1960.

Fausset, H. I., *Tolstoy, the Inner Drama,* London, 1927.

Gibian, George, *Tolstoy and Shakespeare,* The Hague, 1957.

Gourfinkel, N., *Tolstoï sans tolstoïsme,* Paris, 1946.

Gudzy, N. K., *Kak rabotal L. Tolstoi (How L. Tolstoy Worked),* Moscow, 1936.

Gudzy, N. K., *Lev Tolstoi,* Moscow, 1960.

Khrapchenko, M. B., *Lev Tolstoi kak Khudozhnik (Leo Tolstoy as an Artist),* Moscow, 1963.

Kupreyanova, E. N., *Estetika L. N. Tolstogo (The Esthetics of L. N. Tolstoy),* Moscow–Leningrad, 1966.

Kvitko, D. Y., *A Philosophic Study of Tolstoy,* New York, 1927.

Lavrin, Janko, *Tolstoy: An Approach,* London, 1944.

Lenin, V. I., *Stati o Tolstom (Articles on Tolstoy),* Moscow, 1960.

Leontiev, Konstantin, *O romanakh gr. L. N. Tolstogo. Analiz, stil i veyaniya (The Novels of Count L. N. Tolstoy. Analysis, Style, and Ideas),* Moscow, 1911.

*Literaturnoye nasledstvo (Literary Heritage),* 35–36, 37–38, Moscow, 1939; 69, 2 vols, Moscow, 1961; 75, 2 vols, Moscow, 1965.

Markovitch, Milan, *Jean-Jaques Rousseau et Tolstoï,* Paris, 1928.

Markovitch, Milan, *Tolstoi et Gandhi,* Paris, 1928.

Maude, Aylmer, *Tolstoy and His Problems,* 2nd ed., London, 1902, New York, 1911.

Merezhkovsky, Dmitri, *Tolstoy as Man and Artist,* New York, 1902.

Mittal, S., *Tolstoy: Social and Political Ideals,* Meerut, India, 1966.

Motyleva, T. L., *O mirovom znachenii L. N. Tolstogo (On the World Significance of L. N. Tolstoy),* Moscow, 1956.

Myshkovskaya, L. M., *Masterstvo L. N. Tolstogo (L. N. Tolstoy's Mastery)*, Moscow, 1958.

Noyes, George R., *Tolstoy*, New York, 1918, London, 1919.

Prugavin, A. S., *O Lev Tolstom i tolstovtsakh (Leo Tolstoy and Tolstoyans)*, Moscow, 1911.

Saburov, A. A., *'Voina i mir' Tolstogo. Problematika i poetika ('Tolstoy's 'War and Peace'. The Problematics and the Poetics)*, Moscow, 1959.

Shklovsky, Viktor, *Material i stil v romane Lva Tolstolgo 'Voina i mir' (Material and Style in Tolstoy's Novel 'War and Peace')*, Moscow, 1928.

Simmons, Ernest, J., *Introduction to Tolstoy's Writings*, Chicago, 1968.

Spence, G. W, *Tolstoy the Ascetic*, London, 1967.

Steiner, George, *Tolstoy or Dostoevsky, an Essay in the Old Criticism*, New York, 1959.

Tolstoy, Alexandra, *The Tragedy of Tolstoy*, New Haven and London, 1933.

Turner, Charles, *Count Tolstoi as Novelist and Thinker*, London, 1888.

Yarovslavski, E., *L. N. Tolstoi i Tolstovsy (Tolstoy and the Tolstoyists)*, Moscow, 1938.

Zaidenshnur, E. E., *'Voina i mir' L. N. Tolstogo. Sozdanie velikoi knigi (L. N. Tolstoy's 'War and Peace'. The Creation of a Masterpiece)*, Moscow, 1966.

Zhdanov, V., *Lyubov v zhizni Lva Tolstogo (Love in the Life of Leo Tolstoy)*, 2 vols, Moscow, 1928.

# Index

# Index

# Index

Tkachev, P. N., 8
Tolstoy, Count (grandfather), 17, 23
Tolstoy, Countess (grandmother), 21
Tolstoy, Alexandra, Countess Osten-Saken (aunt), 21, 23
Tolstoy, Countess Alexandra (cousin, called 'Granny'), 44, 47–8, 50, 83, 141
Tolstoy, Alexandra (daughter), 129, 221
Tolstoy, Dmitri (brother), 18, 22, 24
Tolstoy, Ilya (son), 140
Tolstoy, Leo (son), 140
Tolstoy, Count Leo Nikolayevich: birth, 1, 17; character, 5, 17; childhood, 17–20, 30, 34; education, 19–26, 28; youth, 23–9, 153, 200; at Yasnaya Polyana, 17–20, 23, 25–8, 37, 39, 40, 45–6, 49–50, 56–72, 74, 77, 79, 85, 94–5, 127–9, 131, 143, 148, 150, 153, 156, 157–8, 175–6, 206, 216, 218–21; in Moscow, 20–2, 28–9, 49–50, 126–7, 129, 130–3; at Kazan, 23–6, 200; as landowner, 6, 27, 43, 45–6, 49, 160; in the Caucasus, 29–39, 53, 198; army life, 32, 36, 39–42, 47; in the Crimea, 40–2, 44, 53; in St Petersburg, 43–5, 49, 206; travels, 6, 47–9, 57–60; as educator, 9, 56–78, 94, 146; marriage, 7, 71, 79; children, 79, 93, 94, 126, 129, 150, 157, 160–1, 202, 220; theory of history, 7, 86–9, 117, 233; spiritual crisis, 8, 10, 103–4, 107, 145, 193, 202; religious faith, 5, 11, 12–13, 22, 30, 38–9, 43, 50–1, 103–30, 135,138, 145, 151, 153, 154, 158, 160, 161–4, 166–74, 175–6, 177, 185, 191, 193, 195–6, 202, 206, 210, 213, 215, 217, 219, 220, 224, 234; views on sex, 24, 33, 50, 93, 96–8, 114, 136–7, 153–8, 192; political views, 6–16, 206–18; social views, 14, 132–9, 141, 143, 160, 164, 170, 194, 210–13, 216, 226, 236–7; relief work, 11, 130–2, 139–44; opposition to violence, 11, 15, 41–2, 105–7, 109, 111, 113–15, 120, 124–5, 161–74, 195, 208–13, 217–18, 234–6; excommunication, 14, 119–20, 206; death, 221

# Index